Sieges of the '45

Siege Warfare during the Jacobite Rebellion of 1745-1746

Jonathan D. Oates

Helion & Company

Dedicated to Arran Johnston

Helion & Company Limited
Unit 8 Amherst Business Centre
Budbrooke Road
Warwick
CV34 5WE
England
Tel. 01926 499619
Email: info@helion.co.uk
Website: www.helion.co.uk
Twitter: @helionbooks
blog.helion.co.uk/

Published by Helion & Company 2021
Designed and typeset by Mach 3 Solutions Ltd (www.mach3solutions.co.uk)
Cover designed by Paul Hewitt, Battlefield Design (www.battlefield-design.co.uk)

Cover: The South-West Prospect of the City of Carlisle, hand-coloured engraving by and after Samuel and Nathaniel Buck. (Anne S.K. Brown Collection)

ISBN 978-1-913336-55-4

British Library Cataloguing-in-Publication Data.
A catalogue record for this book is available from the British Library.

Contents

Introduction

It has been argued that the Jacobite campaign of 1745 has been written about far too often (even, with tongue in cheek, that a law be passed that no more histories of Mary Queen of Scots or the Jacobites should ever be written), yet books continue to pour from the presses and some of these are very good indeed, showing fresh facts and perspectives of a tale whose outline is well known, or focussing on new angles.[1] Many are histories of the campaign and many focus on one battle, usually Culloden, or all of the battles, or on the key personalities involved. It may, therefore, be rightly asked what need is there for yet another book on the '45. The answer is this: despite variable coverage in the general histories (one recent history allots but a sentence to one of the actions in this book),[2] all of which refer to them as part of a larger narrative, siege warfare in this campaign has largely been side-lined and never properly studied in its own right. That said, some sieges have been covered in some detail – both those of Carlisle and that of Blair Castle, the latter focussing on the relief efforts – and there has been a chapter on siege warfare in this era as part of a wider study.[3] Yet there is no overall detailed account. As Christopher Duffy noted decades ago, 'the historians are obsessed with marches and field actions, and pass on very rapidly from the about-turn at Derby to the combats at Falkirk and Culloden'.[4]

Siege warfare was the most common part of European warfare in the early- to mid-eighteenth century, as it had been in the seventeenth. With the rise of artillery as a major tool in the armoury of war in the sixteenth century, new fortifications had been constructed; in France these had been under the oversight of the foremost military engineer of the era, Sebastien

1 Most notably, Christopher Duffy, *Fight for a Throne: the Jacobite '45 reconsidered* (Solihull: Helion, 2015).

2 Jacqueline Riding, *Jacobites: A New History of the '45 Rebellion* (London: Bloomsbury, 2016).

3 Christopher Duffy, *The Best of Enemies: Germans against Jacobites, 1746* (London: Bitter Books, 2013); D. Hepburn and C. Richardson, 'Documents relating to the transportation of cannon from Whitehaven to Carlisle during the Jacobite Rising of 1745', *Transactions of the Cumberland and Westmorland Antiquarian and Archaeological Society,* series 2, Vol.LXXXIV (1984), pp.141-166; Jonathan Oates, 'The Last siege on English Soil: Carlisle, 1745', *Transactions of the Cumberland and Westmorland Antiquarian and Archaeological Society,* Vol.III (2003), pp.169-184.

4 Christopher Duffy, *The Fortress on the Age of Vauban and Frederick the Great, 1660-1789* (London: Routledge and Kegan Paul, 1985), p.174.

le Prestre de Vauban. Gone were the lofty towers and walls of the Middle Ages, now so vulnerable to the new guns. Instead, fortifications were sited at strategic border points and were built to maximise defensive fire and make it as difficult for the attackers to approach them as possible. Walls were low and thick, there were concentric defensive rings, with bastions for gun platforms. However, Britain, being an island, invested in relatively few such new defences. Some had been built in England under Henry VIII and Elizabeth in the sixteenth century, but the poorer kingdom of Scotland did not build any of these new fortifications, relying on its ancient castles whilst strengthening and rebuilding some of its city walls.

Siege certainly predominated over battle, yet it is the latter that most works focus on. During the War of the Spanish Succession (1701-1714), the Duke of Marlborough fought four major battles yet conducted 30 sieges (in all of which he was successful). In the War of the Quadruple Alliance (1718-1720), the French undertook four sieges in Spain but fought no battles; in the same war, there was only one major battle in Sicily, but several sieges. The same could be said about Marshal de Saxe's campaign in the Low Countries in 1745; one battle at Fontenoy and numerous sieges, including Tournai and Ostend. In fact, where battles did occur, it was often in relation to siege warfare; Fontenoy was fought in the attempt to relieve Tournai and there was a battle at Laffelt two years later as the French threatened Maestricht and Bergen op Zoom, the latter falling to them later that year. In 1748 Maestricht was added to this bag, in a year without battles. States spent considerable sums in the seventeenth and eighteenth centuries in the construction of forts or the strengthening of existing defences of towns and cities. In England, siege warfare had been commonplace during the civil wars of the 1640s as walled towns, castles, and fortified manor houses often held out against lengthy sieges, but apart from at Oxford and London there were few new fortifications and these were never put to the test.

In the late seventeenth and early eighteenth century the British state paid intermittent attention to the need for security in Scotland. This was because of the very real threat of another Jacobite attempt to retake the thrones lost in 1688 by James II. From 1690 new fortresses were built and existing royal castles were strengthened, with garrisons being provided from the Scottish, later British, Army to man these. Although there were no sieges in the campaigns of 1715-1716 and 1719 (though Eilean Donan Castle was under naval bombardment for a day), numerous sieges took place both in Scotland and on the borders in 1745-1746, with hugely differing outcomes. Some sieges did, or had the potential, to have decisive impacts on the campaign itself; in 1745 had Carlisle not been taken by the Jacobites, the whole invasion of England would have taken a different course; had Edinburgh Castle fallen earlier that year the Jacobite position in Scotland would have been far stronger. In the following year, the siege of Stirling led to the Battle of Falkirk, the siege of Blair Castle ensured control of a crucial strategic district, and the siege of Fort William helped weaken and demoralise the Jacobite army before it unknowingly moved to disaster at Culloden.

This book aims to provide detailed accounts of the siege warfare in Scotland and the borders during the Jacobite campaigns of 1745-1746. They were more numerous than battles; Ruthven Barracks (twice), Edinburgh and its Castle, Carlisle (twice), Stirling and its Castle, Forts George, Augustus and William, and Blair Castle; ten in all, as against the three major battles of Prestonpans, Falkirk and Culloden. Each chapter will consider the origins and design of the fortress, the opposing strengths of the forces involved, the course of the siege, its conclusion, casualties and the wider impact of the siege. Some of the besieged fortresses were taken by the besiegers, but just as many held out.

The sources used for this book are as follows; the Cumberland Papers and to a far lesser degree, the Stuart Papers, both from the Royal Archives; State Papers Domestic and Scotland, War Office and Admiralty papers from the National Archives; Campbell archives from the National Library of Scotland; and archives from the National Records of Scotland and the borough archives of Carlisle, Stirling and Edinburgh. Printed contemporary sources, including papers of enquiries and trials, Jacobite memoirs and correspondence of government supporters and soldiers are also used. Source material for the chapters is very variable; there is far more for both Edinburgh and Carlisle than there are for the sieges of the Highland forts, and shorter episodes, such as that of Ruthven Barracks, generate less paper than those of lengthier ones, such as that of Fort William.

As well as the sources already mentioned, there are a couple of works which deal with the sieges as central, though neither is all encompassing. There is a Historic Scotland book which deal with fortresses in Scotland from 1650 onwards, but it spends most of its time dealing with the building and strengthening of the fortresses, with only about a page on the actual sieges themselves.[5] An almost-forgotten article focusses on the sieges of the three Highland forts and Ruthven Barracks in 1745-1746, though material from the National Archives is the main manuscript source and the author mounts a powerful defence of Captain Scott and the Duke of Cumberland.[6]

The 1745 Jacobite campaign is a well-known subject of films, TV series,and books, both fiction and non-fiction. Fortifications appear in the 1971 *Kidnapped* film (Stirling Castle standing in for Edinburgh Castle) and in the first and third series of *Outlander* (though the depiction of Fort William is laughably wrong), being used as prisons in all these depictions, as well as a fort being taken by assault by Rob Roy MacGregor of Disney's *Rob Roy* film (another fantasy of the film makers). Rather more realistically, part of *Chasing the Deer* (1995) is supposedly set in Ruthven Barracks, though it is a barracks never shown to be threatened by the Jacobites and is also guarded by militia not regulars as in reality. This film also portrays the Duke of Cumberland leading the British army as it marches out of Fort George, decades before this fort was ever built.

Sieges usually only plays a fleeting part in these narratives, but in this book they will be centre stage as episodes in their own right. This necessitates giving just enough information about the battles, marches, and personalities

5 C. Tabraham and G. Grove, *Fortress Scotland and the Jacobites* (London: Batsford, 1995).

6 C.L. Kingford, 'The Highland Forts in 1745', *English Historical Review*, Vol.XXVII (1922), pp.361-397.

to enable a reader who is not familiar with these events to follow the siege warfare in context.

The outcome of sieges were determined by a variety of factors. Firstly, the strength of the physical defences and the number of guns relative to those of the attackers. Then there is the quality, numbers and morale of the garrison. Thirdly there is the level of supplies, both in ammunition and in food. Fourthly there is the determination and ability of the garrison commander. Fifthly there is the ability and strength of the besiegers, and finally there is the question of the prospect of an effectual relief.

Siege warfare was ruled by formal etiquette, that was expected to be followed by both sides. First, a besieger would send forth a messenger under a flag of truce, to ask the besieged to surrender, with the expectancy that they would not. Then the besiegers would position their artillery under cover and begin to pound away at the defences, at the same time erecting their own defences to deter a sally by the defenders and block any relief attempt. The defenders could interrupt this barrage by counter-battery fire with their own guns and might also send out sally parties to wreck the besieging guns. If the besieging guns did make a breach in the defences that could then be stormed by the attacking infantry, another deputation would be sent to the defenders to request that they now surrender or risk being attacked and if the latter course was chosen, warning that the consequences for the garrison and the civilian population, if any, would be dire. If a breach was not made, then the besiegers might try and starve the garrison into surrender, but this long-term strategy risked the besiegers being caught between two fires if a relief force was able to arrive.

Thus we will begin with the story of the building of the fortresses and their justification, before moving to the opening siege – if it may be termed such – the attempted taking of the thinly-held Ruthven Barracks at the beginning of September 1745; and though this will not follow a strictly chronological approach, the second attempt to take it, in the following year, will also be discussed here. Then there is the case of Edinburgh, and its Castle in particular, in the following months. With the Jacobite invasion of England in November, we have the two sieges of Carlisle; that of the Jacobite army and in the next month the only siege undertaken by the British Army. With the campaigning in Scotland once again, sieges come thick and fast; Stirling was under siege and the biggest battle of the campaign fought because of it. The Jacobite retreat to the Highlands resulted in a flurry of sieges in February and March, with the three Highland Forts coming under attack, as well as Blair Castle, the last castle to be under siege in Britain.

Thus, the Jacobite army can be seen to have been the one on the tactical offensive in all cases but one. Given that its strength was in the rush to melee in open battle, this would suggest that it was in a relatively weak position against fortresses. Fortifications favoured the defenders as defensive firepower could be maximised. Yet in 1745, unlike the case in the previous Risings, the Jacobites were, from October 1745, reinforced with artillery and gunners from France, who were to play a notable part in the sieges of 1746. This was far from being an irregular army pitted against regular troops behind defences, but a force that had the means to crack open fortifications, as shall be seen. Even so, some of the defences and defenders were formidable indeed.

1

Problems and Solutions?

We need to analyse why fortresses were under siege in Britain in 1745-1746. Part of the answer lies in the challenge posed against the status quo in Church and State, and the other is the efforts of their defenders to defeat that danger. In order to discover why there was such a struggle, we need to examine events in the century preceding 1745.

Two major challenges had beset British politics in the seventeenth century. One was the relationship between Crown and Parliament; the other was that between the differing forms of Christianity and their relationship with the state. There had been civil wars fought over these issues in the mid-century, leading to a monarch executed and the establishment of a republic, as well as the abolition of episcopacy. This solution had been short lived and the monarchy and the bishops were restored in 1660, to much rejoicing. Yet the crisis continued in the following decades and was heightened, at least in most of England and Scotland, after 1685 when a Catholic monarch, James II and VII (1633-1701), succeeded to the throne. It was not just his religion that was at odds with nearly all his Protestant subjects; it was the policies he pursued and the authoritarian methods he employed to further them. Unlike his late brother, James was determined to enable Catholicism to prosper and that meant straining what was politically possible. It meant the repeal of the anti-Catholic legislation and neither country's Parliament agreed to that.

James aroused opposition, but, as he was in the possession of a large standing army which he had built up, his position seemed unassailable. Few wanted a return to civil war. However, following an invasion led by his Protestant son-in-law, William of Orange (1650-1702), stadtholder of the Dutch Republic, and a distinct lack of support from most of his subjects in mainland Britain, James retired to France at the end of 1688. William became King William III, ruling with his wife, James' eldest daughter, Mary II (1662-1694), from 1689-1694 and then alone after her death in the latter year. This solved one issue, that of an overbearing Catholic monarch, but created new ones. The principal issue was that James continued to believe that he was the rightful monarch and had the support of many in Britain, especially in Catholic Ireland, but also among Catholics and Episcopalians elsewhere in the Kingdoms, and among those who saw William's seizure of power as illegal.

Thus, the political movement called Jacobitism was born. Supporters were known as Jacobites, after the Latin for James; Jacobus. They called for a return to the throne of James II and VII, and after his death, his son James Francis Stuart (1688-1766), known to them as James III and VIII. The exiled Stuarts established an alternative court on the continent, first at St Germain, near Paris, and later at Rome. There, with the help of other European states with a grudge against Britain, they sought to regain the thrones lost in 1688.

Their supporters were not entirely motivated by a sense of dynastic legitimacy. There were religious, nationalistic and political grievances at work, too. Catholics had been second class subjects in Britain since the sixteenth century; unable to take up posts in government at all levels, to become MPs or sit in the House of Lords, become army or naval officers, or to attend university. Non-attendance at an Anglican Church was a finable offence and holding mass was illegal. With a Catholic monarch these grievances could be dealt with. Outside Ireland, Catholics in Britain were relatively few, but some Protestants were also offended by the new religious status quo made necessary by the revolution. In Scotland the revolution had led to the imposition of a Presbyterian form of Protestant Church and the previous Episcopalian settlement was swept away. In England, some Anglicans were disturbed by having to break their oaths of allegiances to James II and to swear loyalty to a new monarch. They refused to do so, became disenfranchised and were termed Non-Jurors. With the Toleration Act of 1689 and the easing of burdens on nonconformist Protestants, some Anglicans saw the Church of England's religious monopoly being challenged.

As time went by, new grievances emerged. In 1707 the countries of England and Scotland were merged into one country; Great Britain. This had been a controversial move with many in Scotland who saw that they had much to lose by this. It was no surprise that the largest gathering in favour of the exiled Stuarts took place in 1715, when nationalistic grievances were at their height, not 1745. Finally, after 1714 and the arrival of a new royal dynasty from the German electorate of Hanover on the British throne, those politicians who were at best lukewarm about the new King, known as Tories, found themselves out of their accustomed positions of power both at Westminster and often in the provinces, too.

All these discontents led to a number of armed attempts to restore the Stuarts. The first took place in Ireland, and to a lesser extent in Scotland, in 1689-1691, with a number of battles taking place in both countries. In both cases, though, the Jacobite forces were eventually defeated. There was an invasion attempt by a French force in 1708 which failed. The most significant threat took place in 1715, with major insurrections in both Scotland and England. Again, these were defeated; there was another attempt in 1719, aided by the Spanish, but once more extinguished in a relatively short time. Apart from Ireland in 1689-1691 and England in 1715, the internal military threat came primarily from Scotland, and the Highlands in particular, though plotting in England continued.

Through the Highland clans, non-clan feudal levies of Highland magnates and Lowlanders, formidable numbers of armed men could be raised to fight for the Stuart cause, dwarfing any armed support the Stuarts could expect in the far more populous, but less militaristic, England. Despite Disarming Acts following 1715, the majority did not surrender their weapons and little effort was made to make them do so. There were many in Scotland, such as the most powerful clan of all, the Campbells, who opposed the Jacobite cause, but the military potential in the Highlands remained. Apart from Scotland, the exiled Stuarts also looked to foreign powers with a grievance against Britain and her monarch; intermittently France, Spain, and Sweden, to assist with military and/or financial aid.

One estimate of the Highland's military potential, drawn up after 1715, was as follows.

> Anti-government, 29,100 men
> Pro-government, 14,300 men
> Neutrals, 1,000 men.[1]

The Jacobites had been defeated in battle in 1715 and 1719, but this did not put a stop to Stuart hopes. It was true that as James Stuart aged, he became less inclined for activity, but his eldest son, Charles Edward Stuart (1720-1788) was eager to play his part in restoring the dynasty and knew that there were many in Britain who were sympathetic to his cause, especially if he could bring foreign aid with him. An article in a newspaper in 1723 argued, about the Highlands and Islands of Scotland:

> [T]hese people will never fail to join with Foreign popish powers, to advance the interest they have espoused; so they always have been, and infallibly will be instruments and tools in the hands of those who have a design to enslave or embroil the British nation…notwithstanding the pains taken by the government to disarm them, they are still well armed, by supplies from abroad, sent them on purpose to put them in case to encourage and support foreign invasions, which it is not possible to prevent by any naval power, because of the wildness of their country, and the many convenient harbours and landing places that are on their coasts.[2]

There were other issues in the 1720s which gave the government cause for concern. The financial crash and scandal following the South Sea Bubble in 1720 led to worries that the Jacobites might exploit the situation to bring down the discredited government, and, indeed, in its wake there was the Atterbury Plot. It was detected and Bishop Francis Atterbury of Rochester was exiled, but it did indicate that the Jacobites were far from cowed. Various concerns were also held as regard the intentions of the Continental powers and troops and naval forces were called out to deter such. Although there were no risings in the 1720s and 1730s, Jacobitism was far from dead and remained an active concern of British governments in these decades.

Jacobitism in England as well as Scotland was feared, but it was the latter kingdom where significant armed forces opposed to the regime could be

1 Robert Patten, *History of the Rebellion* (London: J. Baker and T. Warner, 1745), pp.191-199.
2 Jeremy Black, *Culloden and the '45* (Stroud: Sutton, 1997), p.36.

raised, as they had been before. There were several steps taken to secure Scotland. One of them was to have a system of fortifications in place. Such a policy had been implemented after the Cromwellian conquest of the country in the 1650s. Purpose built forts were constructed at Inverlochy, at Perth, at Leith, and at Inverness, each housing a garrison of soldiers who made regular patrols of the countryside and in doing so also brought about a degree of law and order. However, with the return of the monarchy in 1660, the forts were abandoned and the troops mostly disbanded. Royal authority was upheld from the four royal castles in the Lowlands; Edinburgh, Stirling, Dumbarton, and Blackness (on the Firth of Forth, west of Edinburgh).

The Jacobite threat did not immediately result in much siege warfare; Edinburgh Castle was held for James II from March to June 1689, but was too strong to be taken except possibly by a bloody assault, so was starved to submission, likewise Ruthven Castle quickly fell to the Jacobites in 1689 due to inadequate supplies, and Blair Castle, held by the Jacobites, surrendered without a fight when William III's Scottish troops marched towards it in the September of 1689. In September 1715 there was an unsuccessful attempt at a coup de main against Edinburgh Castle, but in this the Jacobites were unsuccessful. In 1719 Jacobite-held Eilean Donan Castle was to bear a brunt of a day of seaborne bombardment and subsequently surrendered to naval forces.

Commander in chief in Scotland of the Crown's forces in 1689-1690 was Major General Hugh Mackay (1640-1692), a Highlander. In 1689 he was convinced of the need for a fort in the Western Highlands, following the Cromwellian example, in order to curb the potential of the clans there from supporting the Jacobite cause. What was needed was a permanent garrison, as in Cromwell's day, 'at Inverlochy which may very speedily be executed if the lords of the council give present orders', though this would be no small undertaking. Mackay reasoned that to build a fort there would need supplies of biscuit, cheese and butter from Glasgow for 4,000 men for six weeks, two frigates to convoy these as well as horses and 1,500 pioneers from Ross, Inveraray, Murray, and Nairnshire with spades, pick axes and shovels, as well as wrights to cut and prepare the palisades for the fortress.[3]

On 12 July, Mackay was disconsolate at the thought that his plan for placing a garrison at Inverlochy could not be put into operation that year 'because the rains begin soon in the Highlands'. He believed that 'to subdue the rebels, to which there must needs a Fort be built'. There was also a lack of materials needed for construction. Mackay proposed the scheme to the council for the men, horses and meal necessary for the expedition. The government was slow in formulating a response and eventually offered too few men, too late. It also tied Mackay to Edinburgh for two weeks, whilst the Jacobite field army secured Atholl and Badenoch.[4]

The first prong of Mackay's strategy in 1690 was to have a garrisoned fort in the West Highlands, an issue which he had raised in the previous year. He

3 National Records of Scotland (NRS), GD406/1/3608, Mackay to Hamilton, c.25 July 1689.

4 Hugh Mackay, *Memoirs of the War carried out in Scotland and Ireland 1689-1691* (Edinburgh: Bannantyne Club, 1833), pp.227, 230.

later wrote 'the only formidable rebels then in the kingdom might be subdued by placing a garrison in Inverlochy'. This meant ships, boats, spades, shovels, and pickaxes, and frigates to convoy them there. Yet delays occurred, due to the overriding precedence claimed by William's expedition to Ireland and to the Scottish government lacking money. It was not until March that such necessaries could be supplied. Mackay met members of the privy council and gave them an account of what he had requested to the court.[5]

Feeling that the privy council would be unreceptive to his plan, he suggested to them that troops be transported along the coast to prevent any of the Islanders from reinforcing the Jacobites on the mainland. Paying for it was difficult; the Lords of the Treasury supplying £600, but this was inadequate given 'so great was the disorder and poverty of the government'. Glasgow was zealous for the cause and made up the shortfall in funding.[6] Fort William was thus established. It had three 6-pounders, six 3-pounders with 130 balls, and a dozen culverins, with 20 balls each. There were also 800 grenades.[7] However, instead of 1,200 men in the garrison as planned, only 900 were allocated, which was further reduced by desertions. The palisade was weak. On 21 July, Colonel John Hill, the garrison commander, wrote of the Jacobites, 'they stir not yet but come not in'.[8]

Fortifications were not merely for defence, but were envisaged as springboards for offensive action. In 1692, companies of Argyll's Regiment were stationed at Fort William. The Jacobites had been given a deadline of 31 December 1691 to submit to civil authority or face the consequences. Some did so but by no means all, and the Scottish government felt that an example should be made. The result was that on 13 February, two companies from Fort William, after having been billeted with the MacDonalds of Glencoe, received the order to massacre the clan with the result that 38 were killed. Tragic though this was, it had the desired result and the recalcitrant clans made their peace (temporarily) with the government.

The defences at Fort William were improved as time went by, with stone walls replacing the wooden ones. The garrison there remained after the end of the campaign in 1692, but little else was done with Scotland's defences as the danger was apparently over. Although the invasion of 1708 never landed either James Stuart nor any French troops, it did signal the need to strengthen Scotland's defences. In July, Captain John Drury of the Board of Ordnance made recommendations for strengthening the defences of Fort William, Edinburgh and Stirling Castles. Three new gun batteries were built to cover the south and west approaches to Edinburgh Castle – Drury's Battery, Butts Battery and an upper battery, though his ambitious plans for additional outer defences were abandoned. At Stirling a thick frontal wall with bastions was built, allowing artillery cross fire to decimate any attackers. Stone buildings replaced the wooden ones at Fort William, with a more secure powder

5 Mackay, *Memoirs*, pp.103-104.
6 Mackay, *Memoirs*, p.104.
7 NRS, E96/33/7, Inventory of arms and stores, 1689-1691.
8 NRS, GD26/9/274/2, Hill to Unknown, 21 July 1690.

Stirling Castle wall, 2017. (Author's Photo)

magazine, designed, as with those at Stirling, to withstand a direct hit by enemy artillery.[9]

These defences were never put to the test in 1715, but, after the end of the campaign of that year, it was decided that four barracks be built in the Highlands, to support existing garrisons and to be sited at major crossroads. These were at Bernera; Inversnaid, near Ben Lomond; Kiliwhimen on the shores of Loch Ness; and Ruthven in Badenoch, on the site of the old castle there. None had any part to play in the short-lived Jacobite campaign of 1719 when far fewer Jacobites rose, to be quickly defeated, even with a modicum of military aid from Spain.

Simon Fraser (1667-1747), 11th Lord Lovat, sent a memorandum to George I by 1724 about the unsettled state of the Highlands. On 3 July 1724 Major General George Wade (1673-1748), who had already built up his credentials in dealing with the Jacobites in England, was tasked with making a tour of the Scottish Highlands to 'report how far Lovat's memorandum was founded on fact…and to suggest to the King such other remedies as may conduce to the quiet of His Majesty's faithful subjects and the good settlement in that part of the kingdom'.[10] At the end of the year, on 10 December 1724, Wade made his report to the King. He declared that there were 22,000 armed fighting men in the Highlands and of these, 12,000 had sided with the Jacobite cause in 1715. He cast doubt on the effectiveness of the Disarming

9 Tabraham and Grove, *Fortress Scotland*, pp.48-50.
10 Tabraham and Grove, *Fortress Scotland*, p.69.

Act of 1716 and asserted that the bulk of the clansmen were armed, were loyal to their chiefs, and were a threat to both loyal Scotsmen and formed a potential for armed insurrection in the future. Furthermore, they were often able to use the mountainous terrain to great effect compared to the regular troops.[11] Wade stated that what was needed were proper garrisons in new barracks and fortresses. He argued, 'if the number of troops they are built to contain, was constantly quartered on them (where there is now in some but 30 men) …they might be of some use in preventing the insurrections of the Highlanders'.[12] Wade's main recommendation was the formation of Highland companies to police the Highlands which became the regiment known as the Black Watch.

George Wade by and published by John Faber Jr, after Johan van Diest, mezzotint, published 1736 (circa 1731). (Anne S.K. Brown Collection)

Wade's recommendations concerning fortresses were as follows:

> That a Redoubte or Barrack be erected at Inverness, as well for preventing the Highlanders descending in the Low Country in time of rebellion, as for the better quartering His majesty's troops, and keeping them in a Body sufficient to prevent or subdue rebellion.
>
> That in order to render the Barrack of Kiliwhimen of more use than I conceive it to be at present (from its being situate at too great a distance from Lake Ness) a Redoubte be built at the west end adjoining to it, which with the said Barrack may be able to contain a battalion of Foot and a communication made for their mutual support, the space of Ground between Inverness and the other being less than 500 yards. This appears to be more necessary from the situation of the place, which is the most centrical point of the Highlands, a considerable pass, equally distant from Fort William and Inverness, and where a body of 1000 men may be drawn together from these Garrisons in 24 hours to suppress any insurrections of the Highlands.
>
> That a small vessel with oars and sails be built on the Lake Ness, sufficient to carry a Party of 60 or 80 soldiers and provisions for the garrison, what will be a Means to keep the Garrison, which will be a Means to keep the communication open between that place and Inverness and be a safe and ready way of sending Parties to the Country, bordering on the said Lake, which is navigable for the largest vessels. It is 24 miles or more in length, and a mile or more in breadth, the country being mountainous on both sides.
>
> That the governors or such as His Majesty is pleased to appoint to command at Fort William, Inverness or Kiliwhimen till the Peace of the Highlands is better established, be required to reside at their respective station, and to give an account

11 James Allardyce (ed.), *Historical Papers relating to the Jacobite Period, 1699-1750* (Edinburgh: New Spalding Club, 1895), Vol.I, pp.131-139.

12 Allardyce (ed.), *Historical Papers*, Vol.I, p.138.

> of what passes in that country to the commander in chief of the forces in Scotland, and to such other whom His Majesty is pleased to appoint.[13]

He further added:

> That Inspection be made into the present condition of the Garrisons and castles in North Britain, and necessary Repairs made, to secure them from the danger of a sudden Surprize, and more especially the Castle of Edinburgh, which remains exposed to the same Attempt as was made on it in the year 1715, their being nothing effectually done to it since that time for the security of that important place, on which depends not only the safety of the city but of all that part of the kingdom.[14]

In order to accomplish all this, money would be needed to build a vessel for traversing Loch Ness, for repairing the fortifications at Fort William and at Edinburgh Castle, for building the new barracks at Inverness and Kiliwhimen so each could hold a battalion of infantry, and for mending the roads between the garrisons and forts. It would cost £10,000 for each of the two years that the building would take.[15]

Two years later, Wade returned to Scotland to review progress and was not pleased: 'In regard to the Fortifications in Scotland, I humbly presume to represent to your Majesty, that till the last year, nothing had been effectually done to secure them from the danger of a surprise, to which they have been exposed for many years past'. In particular, Edinburgh Castle, 'a place of the greatest importance to the safety of that part of your Majesty's Dominions' had so ruinous parapets that once the castle gates were locked, soldiers were able to leave it and re-enter it with the greatest of ease. As an experiment, Wade had four soldiers together with their weapons attempt to scale the cliff face and over the castle walls. It took them five minutes. However, although he reported that the north wall of Dumbarton Castle had collapsed, it had been repaired.[16]

The fort at Inverness was being built at half the musket range from the bridge to command the route from the north to the southern Highlands. It would take another two years to complete and would hold 300 men. According to Wade it will 'in all probability will never be attacked by Artillery'. The fortress near Loch Ness had not been begun yet but work was expected to commence in a year's time. It was to hold a battalion of infantry. Wade also envisaged a tower of stone being built at each end of the Loch, each to hold 21 men. There would be a harbour at each end and £100 for three sailors at Inverness as well as repairs to the boat. There would also be a stable for 30 horses at Ruthven Barracks. All in all, when these measures were carried out, they would be able 'to curb the insolence of such of the inhabitants, who, depending on the strength of their inaccessible Mountains shall presume to rebell against their Sovereign'.[17]

---

13 Allardyce (ed.), *Historical Papers*, Vol.I, pp.140-141.
14 Allardyce (ed.), *Historical Papers*, Vol.I, pp.141-142.
15 Allardyce (ed.), *Historical Papers*, Vol.I, p.149.
16 Allardyce (ed.), *Historical Papers*, Vol.I, p.162.
17 Allardyce (ed.), *Historical Papers*, Vol.I, pp.163-164.

Progress on the barracks was slow and it was not until 1724 that all were completed, under the supervision of Captain John Romer. Unlike the forts and castles, these barracks were not designed to withstand a formal siege with artillery, but to house troops and to withstand an attack by lightly-armed Highlanders. They were to accommodate troops in barracks surrounded by walls and varied in size, with Kiliwhimen capable of holding six companies whilst Ruthven and Inversnaid were to hold but two. At the same time, the number of artillery pieces at Edinburgh Castle and Fort William was drastically cut back; respectively from 50 to 40 and from 68 to 30, whilst Stirling Castle lost but two guns.[18]

These barracks were criticised by Captain Edward Burt who had travelled in the Highlands: 'Barracks were made at a very great expense'. Firstly, there were insufficient troops in them, 'if the number of troops they are built to contain, were constantly quartered in them...they might be of some use to prevent the insurrection of the Highlanders'. Even if that was the case, 'The regular troops were never used to make such marches, with their arms and accoutrements; were not able to pursue the Highlanders'. He was also critical of their siting, 'two of the four are not built in a proper situation as they might have been'.[19]

Thomas Pelham-Holles (1693-1768), Duke of Newcastle and Secretary of State, seemed pleased with Wade's scheme, believing that the forts would 'be of the greatest use for restraining the Highlanders'.[20] Wade was confident, too, 'the Pretender's interest in the clans is so low that I think he can now hope for no effectual assistance from that quarter'.[21] On 20 August 1725 the King ordered the construction of the forts at Inverness and Kiliwhimen.[22]

Work began at Inverness in 1727 and the fort there became known as Fort George, after the monarch. At Kiliwhimen, where work began in 1729, the fort was named after the King's second surviving son, William Augustus (1721-1765), Duke of Cumberland, so was called Fort Augustus. It was not completed until 1742, such was its scale. There were also improvements made to the existing barracks, forts and castles at this time. Edinburgh Castle had zigzagged artillery outworks built to improve its western defences.[23] Wade also had 250 miles of roads and bridges built to connect the new network of forts.

However, for all this time and expense spent on them, the forts had their limitations. Chiefly, as Captain Burt had pointed out in the 1720s, there were never enough troops in each to be able to do more than maintain a police role. Dealing with a major insurrection required far more men than the small numbers of infantry that these forts held. Those men that did form the garrisons tended to be elderly veterans unfit for active service but suited to the more sedentary role as garrison troops. The full scale of the plans drawn up by Wade never came to pass; the barracks in the towns and cities were

---

18 Tabraham and Grove, *Fortress Scotland*, pp.61-64, 56.

19 Edward Burt, *Letters from a Gentleman in the north of Scotland to his friend in London* (London: R. Fenner,1818), pp.223, 278.

20 The National Archives (TNA), State Papers (SP), 54/15, 61, Newcastle to Wade, 5 August 1725.

21 TNA, SP54/17, 47, Wade to Newcastle, 9 August 1726.

22 TNA, SP54/15, 70, Wade to Newcastle, 20 August 1725.

23 Tabraham and Grove, *Fortress Scotland*, pp.76-86.

Aberfeldy Bridge, 2017. (Author's Photo)

never built and there does not seem to have ever been the regular inspections that he desired. Yet given that there was external peace from 1720-1739, it was an achievement that any military expenditure was undertaken when the political priority was to keep spending, and thus taxation, at the lowest levels possible. In 1745-1746 these structures and their garrisons were to be put to a rigorous test and the results were distinctly mixed, especially as their enemies were not only Highlanders but regular troops with heavy artillery.

There were concerns on the eve and onset of the campaign as to the state of Scotland's defences. John Hay (1692-1762), fourth Marquis of Tweeddale, Secretary of State for Scotland, wrote to Sir John Cope (1690-1760), the new commander in chief there, on 6 March 1744, in the aftermath of an invasion scare in England, 'It was well known here that none of the castles in Scotland were in any good condition of Defence, but His Majesty did not think it necessary to be at any great charge in the Repair and it was not imagined any attempt would be made to besiege them at this time.'[24] Such complacency in face of apparent and real dangers in wartime did not bode well. Seventeen months later, with news that Charles Edward Stuart had arrived in Scotland, Cope was told that 'he should despatch proper orders for the security of the forts and barracks in the Highlands' and this led to the first blood being spilt as two newly raised companies were prevented from arriving at Fort William.[25]

24 TNA, SP55/13, 88-89, Tweeddale to Cope, 6 March 1744.
25 TNA, SP54/25, 42, Tweeddale to Harrington, 2 August 1745.

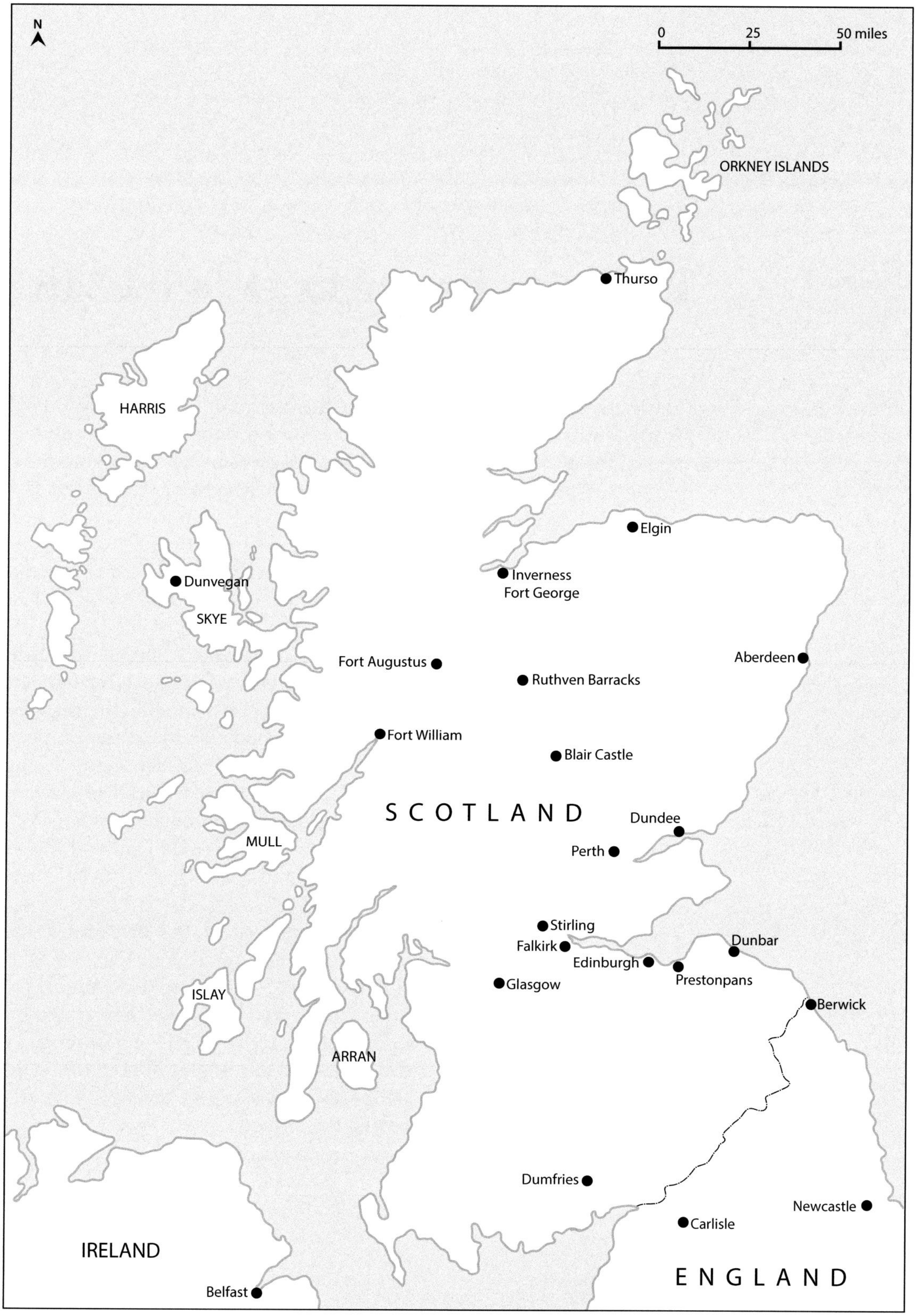

Forts, Castles, and Key Locations in Scotland and Northern England.

2

Ruthven Barracks, 1745-1746

Charles Edward Stuart arrived on the Scottish mainland on 25 July 1745 in an attempt to regain the British thrones for his father. He was confident of support from the Highlands, with powerful clans being opposed to the clan Campbell, which was supportive of the current government of George II. The Camerons, the MacDonalds and the Stewarts of Appin were among the first to rally to Charles' cause.

Defending Scotland for George II were troops under the command of Lieutenant General Sir John Cope, an experienced soldier who had been on active service on the Continent in 1743. He had at his disposal four battalions of infantry and two regiments of dragoons. Among the former were Guise's Regiment, which had recently served in the West Indies and had taken serious casualties there. Recruiting in Scotland (the number of Scots in the British Army was far greater a proportion than their proportion of the population of the British Isles) brought the regiment up to strength, but meant that the majority of the men were inexperienced in warfare. It was men from this regiment who formed the bulk of the garrisons of the fortresses in Scotland; three companies were at Fort William and the same at Fort Augustus; two were at Fort George and one each at Ruthven Barracks and at Bernera Barracks.[1]

There was concern among those stationed at the barracks as these were close to the onset of the Jacobite campaign. Captain Edward Wilson at Bernera Barracks felt particularly exposed and wrote on 9 August to his superior at Fort Augustus, Major Hugh Wentworth, 'if they attempt this barrack, we cannot hold out long, but shall give them all the powder and ball we have'. The men stood to arms for the next two nights, but lacking artillery, were unconfident that they could beat off any serious attack. Yet he need not have worried; the Jacobites bypassed the fort.[2]

Cope was more concerned with Fort William, which was deep in Jacobite country, and strove to reinforce its garrison, sending two raw companies of St. Clair's battalion to their relief. However, at the pass of Highbridge, a

1 C.L. Kingsford, 'The Highland Forts in the Forty Five', *English Historical Review*, XXXVII (1922), pp.361-362.

2 Kingsford, 'The Highland Forts', p.362.

Glenfinnan Memorial. (Author's postcard)

mere six miles from their destination, on 15 August, they were attacked and after a running battle, were forced to surrender. First blood of the campaign had gone to the Jacobite army.[3] Four days later, the Jacobite standard was unfurled at Glenfinnan and the Highland forts were overlooked: indicative of their weaknesses, for after all, as noted in the previous chapter, their purpose was not to withstand siege but to prevent another Jacobite insurrection and this they had signally failed to do. The Jacobites' initial target was not the static positions but Cope's field army, which avoided a Highland battle but thereby left the Lowlands relatively open.

The first attempt to take a fortified place during the campaign of 1745 is not mentioned in all accounts of it. This is partly because it occurred before some of the major participants, such as Lord George Murray, had joined the Jacobite army and partly because it was of a relatively minor nature. However, it gave Ruthven Barracks the distinction of being the only place in Scotland to have been besieged twice in the same campaign and the only place to have been defended and attacked by the same forces on both occasions, though with different outcomes.

Ruthven Barracks had been held by a company of Grant's infantry in 1689, but had fallen to a superior Jacobite force, albeit one lacking artillery, in that year, partly because of a lack of supplies and partly as there was no prospect of any relief. The old barracks had then been destroyed. They were rebuilt in 1719 as part of the programme of fortress building at that time. The fort was on a hill to the south of the village of Kingussie and was well connected by Wade's roads to Inverness.

3 Kingsford, 'The Highland Forts', p.363.

Ruthven Barracks. (Postcard of Paul Lang)

In late August of 1745 Ruthven was garrisoned by a mere handful of men, most having been taken by Cope on his march northwards through the Highlands towards Inverness, as Cope himself recalled, 'We reached Ruthven the 27th and passed the Spey that night; I took from thence a company of Guise's, leaving only a sergeant and twelve men and some Invalids in the Barrack'.[4] The fort was described thus:

> [T]wo buldings on a sugre loaf, joined together by a very high rampart with a parepet, wch formed a Square & flanked at every corner; there were stables detached from the barricks, & surrounded by a wall brest-high & the ramp inaccessible in a manner.[5]

The decision to try to take the barracks was the responsibility of the clan chiefs, the Camerons and the MacDonalds, on 28 August. This was for two reasons. First, in order to 'have the country free', meaning free of any British soldiers who might endanger their homesteads and secondly, 'upon account of oatmeal yt might be found there'. Charles was spoken to about this and he sent out for intelligence about the barracks. When he heard about its defences, in the light of his men lacking artillery and it not being easy to craft scaling

4 George Wade, *A Report of the Proceedings and Opinions of the Board of General Officers, on Their Examination of the Conduct, Proceedings and Behaviour of Lieutenant General Sir John Cope* (Dublin: George Faulkner, 1749), p.31.

5 Alastair and Henrietta Tayler (eds.), *1745 and After* (London: Thomas Nelson and Sons, 1938), p.65.

ladders, he 'judged it more proper to let it alone as a place of no consequence and unequall to the lives of those who might fall in the attempt'.[6]

This advice went unheeded and the chiefs successfully pleaded with Charles to allow them to make the attempt. On 29 August a detachment from the Jacobite army marched to Ruthven, led by Colonel Cameron, the chief's brother, with Colonel John William O'Sullivan (1700-1759), the army's quartermaster and an experienced officer. The number of troops with them has been variously stated; John Murray of Broughton (1720-1778), Charles' secretary, refers to them as being 100 Camerons.[7] Sergeant Terrance Molloy, left in command at Ruthven, refers to the Jacobites as being 300 strong, with only 150 actually attacking the fort. [8]

Fort William and Fort Augustus had already been bypassed by the Jacobite army; besieging them would take time, and, given the Jacobites had no artillery, the odds of success were minimal. Ruthven was weakly held and so perhaps seemed a tempting target, but it was a distraction from the Jacobites' prime aim to gather forces and march into the Scottish Lowlands.

Despite the weak strength of the garrison – only a sergeant and 16 men according to O'Sullivan (Molloy stated he had only a dozen men, as stated above) and lacking any artillery – O'Sullivan was reluctant to obey the order to take the place, 'but represented the difficulty he foresaw he'd find in the execution of it, & yt there were no Barricks, without being surrounded by walls & flancked'. At least that is what he wrote in his memoirs, with the benefit of hindsight. Veteran Jacobite Gordon of Glenbucket, who lived locally, was adamant that it was ripe for taking 'it was an open house only'. O'Sullivan 'clad himself in highland cloaths & went to reconnoitre'.[9]

O'Sullivan reported his findings back to Gordon; namely that the barracks were not 'an open house'. Furthermore, he judged it 'unatackeable wth highlanders, & without Cannon'. Gordon remained adamant, and stressed that the amount of arms and oatmeal stored there made it a valuable prize. O'Sullivan then asked him whether there were any convenient scaling ladders and Gordon assured him that there would be. Gordon asked the Camerons if they were willing to attempt such an operation, which they agreed to. Yet when they looked for scaling ladders, only one could be found.[10]

The plan then was to arrive at night time, take possession of the stables near to the barracks, put some combustible material near to the back door or sally port, whilst the garrison was occupied with musketry. Once this had been planned, a Cameron who had deserted from one of the Independent Companies, having served as a corporal, had a suggestion to make. This was that he and another 10-12 deserters, all still in their uniforms, could arrive at the fort and pretend that they were reinforcements from Cope's main force. Many of these men were probably those Scots formerly from among the two

---

6 Robert Bell (ed.), 'Memorials of John Murray of Broughton, 1740-1747, *Scottish History Society*, 1st series, (Edinburgh, 1897), p.184.

7 Bell (ed.), 'Memorials', p.184.

8 TNA, SP54/25, 106D, Molloy to Cope, 30 August 1745.

9 Tayler and Tayler (eds), *1745*, p.65.

10 Tayler and Tayler (eds), *1745*, p.65.

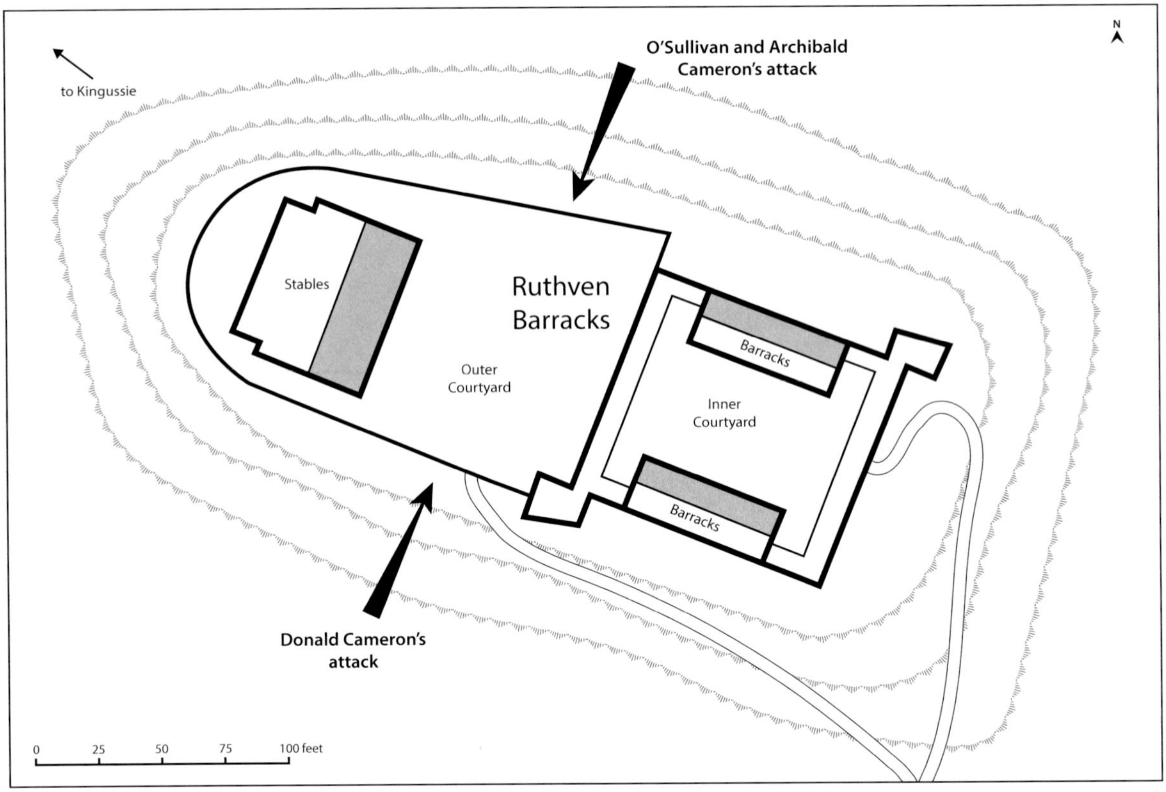

Plan of Ruthven Barracks.

companies of St Clair's Regiment taken en route to Fort William, as, of those men, all but 15 of the rank and file joined the Jacobites. They could then enter the fort without further question and take the fort from within.[11]

It was thought that this scheme was superior to the one first proposed, and it was immediately ordered to be put into operation. The men were told to put themselves at a particular place on the road and then to receive their orders from O'Sullivan. He was sent with another detachment towards Ruthven in case the deserters were not be admitted into the barracks. However, the corporal and his men, after waiting for several hours without any orders, marched off to join the main Jacobite army at Dalwhinnie, arriving there in the early hours of the next day.[12]

O'Sullivan, Dr Archibald Cameron (1707-1753) and one Gordon, who claimed he knew the place, arrived near the barracks that night as planned. As arranged, they got to the stables and secured combustibles enough to be set on fire at the barracks door.[13] According to Molloy, however, and not mentioned in either Jacobite account of the confrontation, there was some preliminary dialogue as the Jacobites:

> [S]ent Proposals to me to surrender this Redoubt, upon Condition that I should have Liberty to carry off Bag and Baggage. My answer was that I was too old

11 Bell (ed.), 'Memorials', pp.184-185.
12 Bell (ed.), 'Memorials', p.185.
13 Bell (ed.), 'Memorials', p.185.

> a Soldier to surrender a garrison of such strength without Bloody Noses. They threatened hanging me and my Men for Refusal. I told them I would take my Chance.[14]

The attack took place at about midnight on 29 August and carried on into the early hours of the next day. It was to be two-pronged. Donald Cameron and 30 men would scale the wall at one side and at another, O'Sullivan and Archibald Cameron would attack. Another 30 men were stationed in Kingussie as a reserve, though Molloy claimed that there were above 150 attackers in all. O'Sullivan and Cameron and their men got into the stables 'without opposition, but not without difficulty'.[15]

The fire barrel was prepared there and a man took it to the sally port door in order to destroy the door, where the barrel was set alight. It was then that an insurmountable difficulty presented itself. That was that 'there were three steps to mount to this door, wch hindred the fire of maskeing its effect'. Seeing that there were, apparently, no men on the rampart above, it seemed safe to send two men out of cover and over to the barrel to raise it up in order to set the flames against the door. At that point the defenders opened fire and killed one of the men who had been sent on this task and the other withdrew. The defenders also poured water over the sally gate in order to make it harder to set alight. The attack with the scaling ladder was also a failure, as it was not possible to bring it to the walls.[16]

All this took a long time and it was 3:30 a.m. that the Jacobites ceased their attacks. Two hours later, they sent Molloy a message that two of their leaders wanted to talk to him. He agreed to this and talked with them from the parapets. They offered to allow him to conditionally surrender, but he refused. They then asked him if they could retrieve their dead, and he allowed this. The Jacobites left at eight that morning, O'Sullivan 'very sorry to have attempted it'.[17]

On being told the news of this setback, Charles, who had spent the evening in writing letters to potential supporters in the north of Scotland, 'was not att all disappointed att the miscarriage having been against the attempt from the beginning as a thing unlikely to succeed, but expressed his concern for the loss of the brave fellows, who he said deserved a better fate'.[18]

Casualties had been relatively light. Molloy stated that there were two Jacobite dead and three wounded and O'Sullivan concurred with this. Molloy 'lost one Man shot through the Head by foolishly holding his Head too high over the Parapet, contrary to orders'.[19] This unfortunate action was attributed to the man attempting 'to spy their motions'. A later report stated that there were 14 Jacobite killed and wounded, another to having 'killed several of

14 TNA, SP54/25, 106D, Molloy to Cope, 30 August 1745.
15 Tayler and Tayler (eds), *1745*, p.66; TNA, SP54/25, 106D, Molloy to Cope, 30 August 1745.
16 TNA, SP54/25, 106D, Molloy to Cope, 30 August 1745.
17 TNA, SP54/25, 106D, Molloy to Cope, 30 August 1745.
18 Bell (ed.), 'Memorials', p.185.
19 TNA, SP54/25, 106D, Molloy to Cope, 30 August 1745; Tayler and Tayler (eds), *1745*, p.66.

them'. Cameron later said that he had nine holes in his outside coat but was otherwise unscathed.[20]

As for the defenders, Molloy expected that the Jacobites would make another attack on the night of the 30th, perhaps with artillery, and he resolved to resist, 'I shall give them the warmest Reception my weak Party can afford. I shall hold out as long as possible'. That same day one Mrs McPherson, 'the Barrack-Wife and a merchant of the Town', advised Molloy to write an account of what had happened to Cope. He did so, and also told his commander that the Jacobites' main body was camped at Dalwhinnie and that they had Cluny MacPherson held prisoner. Cope passed the letter onto Tweeddale and on 12 September the latter promoted Molloy to lieutenant, a relative rarity for a man from the ranks.[21]

In the scheme of the campaign, this was a minor triumph for the British Army and a minor setback for the Jacobites. James Maxwell, a Jacobite officer, wrote, dismissingly, 'The place was of little consequence, and not worth while to retard the march of the army'.[22] However, it showed the importance of having the right equipment to undertake a siege and also the advantage to the defenders of being high in morale, or at least having a leader who was stubborn in the defence. However, should one or both of these variables be different, a different outcome could and would occur, as was to be proved in the following year. The events at Ruthven also showed that Wade's scheme on the forts being able to prevent insurrection was unfounded, though it could also be argued that such forts needed to be properly garrisoned to achieve this role and that they were not. It was generally a little-noticed event, but it did feature, approvingly, in a letter of Horace Walpole (1717-1797), son of a former chief minister, to his friend, Horace Mann, 'It is certain that a sergeant of Cope's, with twelve men, put to flight two hundred; on killing only six or seven'.[23]

Ruthven Barracks then passed into insignificance for the next few months as the centre of the campaign moved southwards. This was not to last. On 10 February 1746, with the Jacobite army on the retreat from Stirling (see Chapter 5), Gordon of Glenbucket with 300 men arrived at Kingussie village. He clearly had not forgotten his previous desire to take the barracks. Yet, unlike the case in 1745, one account puts the decision to attack Ruthven on Charles' shoulders, 'Charles saw the trouble it might give and therefore determined to set about besieging it'. This was because 'though in itself of small importance, would have made it possible, if left unoccupied in the rear, for the enemy to cross the river and advance at will'.[24] John Daniel, an Englishman in the Jacobite army, though, thought otherwise, referring to the barracks as 'a great eye sore to them, having been built to keep them in order',

20 John Marchant, *History of the Present Rebellion* (London: R. Walker, 1746), pp.370-371.

21 TNA, SP54/25, 106D, Molloy to Cope, 30 August 1745.

22 James Maxwell, *Narrative of the Expedition in Scotland of Prince Charles Edward Stuart* (Edinburgh: T. Constable, 1841), p.31.

23 W.S. Lewis (ed.), *Correspondence of Horace Walpole* (New Haven: Yale University, 1955), Vol.19, p.105.

24 Bruce Seton (ed.), 'Commentary on the Expedition to Scotland made by Prince Charles Edward Stuart', *Scottish History Society* 3rd series, Vol.IX, Miscellany, IV (Edinburgh, 1926), p.107.

suggesting that the desire to capture the place had more to do with morale and psychological factors.[25]

Gordon requested that Molloy surrender in return for favourable terms. As before, Molloy refused and claimed he would defend the place as well as he could, though he had not been reinforced since the previous year. It was now eight o'clock in the morning. Seven hours later, Jacobite artillery (calibre unknown, but almost certainly 4-pounders or smaller, the heavy siege guns being left at Stirling) was seen in the village and the guns fired three cannon balls against the barracks. Seeing that the garrison did not fly a white flag of truce, Colonel James Grant sent a message to Molloy:

> These are by his Royal Highness' Order. I send you this to desire you will surrender without loss of Time to give up the Barrack, and so render yourselves Prisoners at discretion, or these are to certify you are to expect no Mercy.
>
> Gordon.[26]

The ensuing contest was not conducted with firepower but with pen and ink. Molloy was in a far more difficult situation now than he had been in the previous year, because the attackers had guns, light in calibre to be sure, and of little use against castles or fortresses, but effective against his thin walls.

Molloy was a realist who saw no point in wasting lives uselessly leading to a result he full well knew, and so gave the following reply:

> Sir,
>
> I don't see but that I am in a Condition to make a good Defence in my Garrison. Still I know I cannot stand a long and regular siege, especially against Cannon, yet I am resolved, to the last extremity, in every Respect to sustain the Character of a Gentleman, and to answer the Expectation and Confidence of my Royal Master, with Regard to what he has committed to my Trust.
>
> To be brief, I will not surrender until your Prince's Approach to this Place, and then upon the following Conditions only.
>
> 1st, That my Men and I be humanely treated, as I am well inform'd of the Revenge and Threats denounced against us by the Clans who attacked this garrison last August 2dly, That we shall not be rifled or pillaged, and that your Prince grant me my parole of Honour, and set my Men at Liberty, as he has done other Prisoners hitherto, considering the Difference between Prisoners of this Kind, and those taken in the Field of Battle. General Gordon, an experienced humane Officer, can't deny this reasonable Entreatment, and upon Performance therof, I will deliver the Keys of the Garrison to your Prince, upon giving a Guarantee to fulfil the above Conditions.
>
> Further, I permit General Gordon to send his Horses and Grooms to my stables this Night, without Arms, all I require for my Honour and Security on this Head, is, that Col. Grant may be permitted to stay as Hostage in my House until the Prince's Arrival.

---

25 Walter Blaikie (ed.), 'Origins of the Forty Five', *Scottish History Society*, 2nd series, Vol.2 (Edinburgh, 1916), p.204.

26 Marchant, *History*, p.371.

This was sent at six that evening.[27]

Gordon replied, clearly after some thought, four hours later:

> Sir,
>
> I Receiv'd your Proposals, which I think too high to propose your giving the Keys to none but the Prince, I think my having his Commands to attack your Barrack is sufficient, upon your surrendering, to receive the Keys from, and if you rightly consider and ponder the Thing, you shall find it to your Advantage.
>
> I have again troubled Col Grant to shew you, that I understand you are afraid of Maltreatment, and risking your Honour in giving up the Keys immediately to me. To avoid all Scruples of this Kind, and to shew you that I am Resolved to treat you with all humanity and civil Usage, if you give up your Arms to me this Night, and suffer 20 or 30 Men I shall answer, you shall live peaceably in the Barrack until the Prince come, from whose Lenity you may expect all good Treatment.
>
> These shall be the last Conditions you'll have from me, and shall be very sorry of you force me to do what you may repent of and will not be agreeable to me. For any Thing more I refer to Colonel Grant.

This was sent at ten that night.[28]

Molloy did not need long to answer, for his reply came at eleven o'clock.

> Sir,
>
> I receiv'd yours concerning my delivering up my Arms this Night, and receiving Men into my Garrison. I cannot comply to it. To-morrow Morning at Ten O'clock, if you make the demand, and give a guarantee to fulfil your Letter, and let me Continue in Possession of my Room and Kitchen, and Provisions, with the like Liberty for my Men, until your Prince comes, I shall then comply to render you my Arms, and receive 16 Men only, for whose Conduct towards me and my men you'll be answerable.[29]

The Jacobites agreed to this negotiated settlement and gave the defenders the terms they had demanded. At noon on the following day, Molloy with his dozen men, three of whom were disabled, were first escorted to Blair and may have remained in the vicinity until Charles himself arrived at Ruthven, which he did on 21 February. They arrived in Perth on 27 February. Meanwhile, the Jacobites, considering the fort useless for themselves, though 'most serviceable for the enemy' burnt the barracks and marched northwards.[30]

A few days after the brief siege, Lord Loudoun, commander of the loyalist Scots at Inverness, commented on the impact of the fort's fall, 'which put it out of our power to assemble People that were to come at a distance, and those that were near were so terrified, that they would not stir, when they found the danger so near them'.[31]

---

27 Marchant, *History*, pp.371-72.
28 Marchant, *History*, pp.372-373.
29 Marchant, *History*, p.373.
30 Seton (ed.), 'Commentary', p.107.
31 TNA, SP54/29, 10b, Loudoun to Stair, 2 March 1746.

Unlike other commanders of forts, castles or cities which surrendered to the Jacobites, there was no Board of Enquiry or Court Martial held into the surrender of Ruthven Barracks. Clearly Molloy had done well to hold off the Jacobites in August 1745 but was deemed unable to do the same when they arrived with artillery in the following February, through which the Jacobites secured a minor triumph.

There was nothing inevitable about the repulse of the Jacobites at the barracks in 1745. The other small government outpost at Inversnaid was taken, with its garrison, a few days later, as reported by James Smollett.[32] Apparently it was surprised by the MacGregors, to the number of 24 (12 according to one account), at midday and 89 soldiers were taken prisoner. The clansmen also captured a number of soldiers engaged on road building nearby.[33] A newspaper claimed, however, that the garrison had already left this 'little fortress' as being 'untenable' and gone to Dumbarton Castle, taking all the military supplies from there, 'so that the Highlanders had nothing left to them but bare walls'.[34]

These two little sieges were relatively minor in the grand scheme of the campaign. The next siege we shall examine was quite the reverse and led to major developments and consequences for both sides.

32 TNA, SP54/26, 2b, Smollett to Craigie, 1 September 1745.
33 TNA, SP54/26, 3a, Craigie to ?, 3 September 1745; Burt, *Letters from a Gentleman*, Vol.II, p.352.
34 *Caledonian Mercury*, 3 Sept. 1745.

3

Edinburgh: City and Castle, 1745

Despite the minor setback at Ruthven in August 1745, the Jacobite army gathered strength and progressed southwards, staying at Blair Atholl and appointing two lieutenant generals; Lord George Murray (1694-1760) who had already served in three campaigns, albeit always at a very junior level, and the youthful James Drummond, Duke of Perth (1713-1746). Their numbers had swollen to 2,000 Highlanders, but they had very little cavalry and only one cannon. Many were poorly armed. Equally important, their funds were low, but they were unopposed in their march southwards, to Perth.

As the capital of Scotland, even after it had lost its Parliament in 1707 and Privy Council in 1708, Edinburgh was still an important place. It was Scotland's largest city and the country's ecclesiastical, legal, and financial centre, as well as being hugely symbolic, both politically and emotionally. It possessed one of Scotland's major castles. For both sides it was an important strategic possession. In 1689 events in Edinburgh had played a crucial part in the revolution as Scotland's Parliament decided to accept William and Mary and reject the status quo as offered by James II and VII, and in 1715 there had been two attempts to take the place for the Jacobites, both failing.

In early September 1745, with the newly-raised Jacobite forces at Perth, only 40 miles away, and Cope's army in the Highlands to their north, the Scottish capital was exposed. Although initially those in the city were ignorant of the marches in the Highlands, on 31 August, an express arrived from the north, with an account of what was happening. Until then, the Jacobite insurrection had been treated as a matter of only a little interest as it was taking place far away, as if it were a country dance or a mere riot.[1]

Edinburgh was not a fortified city and had not stood a siege in centuries. Its defensive walls, with six main gates, dated from the early sixteenth century and before. The wall was of unequal height, varying from 10-12 to 18-20 feet high on three sides, with the castle to the city's west and North Loch to the

1 John Home, *History of the Rebellion* (London: T. Cadell jun. and W. Davies, 1802), p.65.

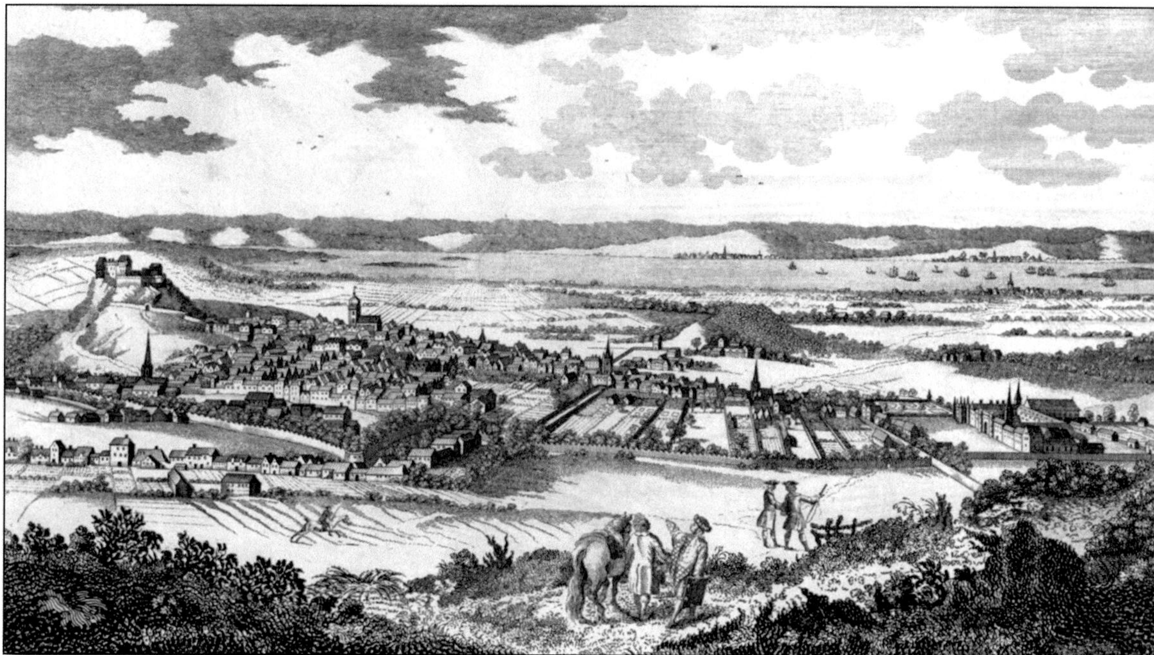

1760 perspective view of Edinburgh, showing the castle to the left and the Palace of Holyrood to the right. (New York Public Library)

north. There were some bastions with embrasures for artillery along the city walls, but no cannon had been mounted here. Apparently:

> [F]or a considerable part of the circuit, it was no better than a garden wall, or park wall of unusual height. In several places it had been built upon, so that dwelling houses made part of the wall, and some of these houses were commanded by higher houses, opposite them, and without the city: of such houses there was one continued now from the Cowgate Port [on the east side of the city] to the Netherbow Port [on the north side of the city].[2]

When the Jacobite army was at Perth, they had to decide where to march next. To the north was Cope's army and 'the bad consequences of the Enemy being entire, and in possession of the north…it not only prevented his friends in these parts from joining him, but made those of the south much cooler than probably they would have been'.[3] They could thus march north and intercept Cope on his way to Aberdeen. Charles considered the possibility, but Cope could have found a strong defensive position and this would have left the two dragoon regiments in the Lowlands free to harass the Jacobite rear. The Jacobite army could thus have become exhausted, lose time and then fail in their enterprise.[4]

Then there was the other alternative, of marching south, 'to waite for the Enemy there, and of what consequence it would be to render himself Master of the Capital, before it was possible for the Enemy to come to its relief'. This

2 Home, *History*, p.66.
3 Bell (ed.), 'Memorials', p.189.
4 Bell (ed.), 'Memorials', pp.190-191.

course of action was decided upon. Therefore, orders were given to march to Dunblane on the 11 September. The army halted there on that day.[5]

A memorandum dated 9 September pointed to cogent reasons why the Jacobite army should march southward:

> That most people about Edinburgh were dispirited by Sir John Cope's escaping to Inverness without a total defeat, that its of great use in all such courses to keep up the spirits of the people by new steps of success therefore if the well wishers in and about Edinburgh are surprised that the prince and his army don't push onto the neighbourhood of Edinburgh where there no forces to oppose him so quickly, to be masters of Edinburgh and the heart of Scotland.

Maxwell wrote likewise, 'Nothing could give so great reputation to his arms, as making himself master of the capital. Besides that advantage he would certainly get money there, and perhaps arms, both of which he would soon stand in need of'.[6]

Gardiner's Dragoons, stationed near Stirling, were dismissed, 'who behoved to fly or to be taken in spite of the castle unless they went into it where there is no forage for their horses'. On 12 September the Jacobite army was at Stirling; not only did Gardiner's troopers flee on their advance, but the castle's garrison was then unable to oppose them and the city opened its gates to the Jacobite army without demur.[7]

According to David Wemyss, Lord Elcho (1722-1787), a Jacobite staff officer, Charles' army consisted of 2,000 infantry, 'the half Completely armed, the others with pitch forks, Scythes, a sword or pistol, or some only with a Staf or Stick'. There was also a small troop of cavalry, 36 strong, and one cannon.[8] Patrick Crichton, a hostile observer, concurred, noting that the Jacobites had 'rusty rapiers, matchlocks and fyerlocks'. He added:

> I observed theyr arms, they were guns of different syses, and some of innormowows length, some with bitts twed up lick, some tyed with pick thread, some without locks and some matchlocks, some had swords over their shoulders instead of guns, one or two had pitchforks and some bits of scythes upon poles with a check, some old Lochaber axes.

As to the men, there were 'a great many old men and boys'.[9]

Edinburgh's defenders were eventually as follows, excluding the two regiments of dragoons, Hamilton's and Gardiner's.

In the city were:

5 Bell (ed.), 'Memorials', pp.191-192.

6 Maxwell, *Narrative*, p.32.

7 Royal Archives (RA), Cumberland Papers (CP), 5/272, Anon., Memorial to Prince Charles, 9 September 1745.

8 Elcho, Lord (ed. Ewan Charteris), *A Short Account of the Affairs of Scotland, 1744-1746* (Edinburgh: John Donald, 1907), p.253.

9 A. Francis Stewart (ed.), *Woodhouselee MS: A narrative of events in Edinburgh and district during the Jacobite occupation, September to October 1745* (Edinburgh: W.R. Chambers, 1908), pp.20, 26-27

- The Trained Bands, 16 companies numbering 50-100 men each, 1,000 in total, musket armed, led by Robert Tennent, a merchant, and officered by the city's merchants and craftsmen, such as John Dalgleish, a watchmaker and Alexander Hepburn, a merchant. Never in arms except for the King's birthday, since 1689. One observer noted, they were 'rather elderly men, but Pretty well disciplined; indeed the only real Force the Provost was master of'.[10] They were also described as being 'men who would have gladly have taken arms against His Majesty had they been sure the event would have turned out well for them'.[11]
- The City Guard, a single company of three squads led by Alexander Maitland, Thomas Dalziel and Walter Hamilton, uniformed, armed with muskets and bayonets, permanently in being, paid for by the city and under the Provost's control, 114 men, 'old trained soldiers'.
- The Edinburgh Regiment, of six companies totalling 300-600 men. A contemporary noted, 'I had a very contemptible Idea of their Courage… their Appearance reminded very much that of Falstaff's Tatterdemallion Company'.[12]
- Six Volunteer Companies, 500 men
- Robert Dickson's 150 volunteers from Musselburgh
- Seceders of Gill's Meeting House, 400 men
- Excise men, 60 men
- Dalkeith Volunteers, 200 men
- Haddington Volunteers, 200 men
- Musselburgh Volunteers, 200 men

  Total: 2,124-2,424

In the Castle, Lieutenant General Joshua Guest (1660-1747) was in command as deputy governor. He had enlisted in the ranks in 1685, receiving a commission in 1704 as a cornet; brigadier in 1735 and lieutenant general in 1745. He had been a cavalryman all this while, seeing service in Scotland in 1715-1716 and in 1725. He had only recently been installed as lieutenant governor of the castle. His second in command was the almost equally elderly Major General George Preston (1659-1748), a Scot who had served in the Nine Years War and the War of Spanish Succession and had served at Edinburgh Castle since 1715.[13] Cope had left Guest with two companies of Lascelles' Regiment, meant to be 70 men in each but both incomplete.[14]

Table 1 lists what should have been the strength of the castle garrison, but there is no known contemporary assessment as to actual numbers there.

---

10 Anon., *A True Account of the Defence and Conduct of Alastair Stewart* (London: unknown publisher, 1748), pp.7-8.

11 NRS, RH4/213, Duncan's Journal, 1750.

12 Anon., *A True Account*, p.8.

13 *Oxford Dictionary of National Biography* (Oxford: Oxford University Press, 2004), Vol.24, pp.177-178, Vol.45, p.256.

14 Anon., *Trial*, Part 2, p.105.

Table 1 Establishment Strength and Pay, Edinburgh Castle Garrison

Rank	Number	Daily pay (per man)
Governor (absent)	1	16s
Deputy Governor	1	10s
Major	1	5s
Lieutenant	2	4s
Ensign	1	3s
Sergeant	4	1s 6d
Corporal	4	1s
Drummer	2	1s
Private	100	8d
Chaplain	1	2s 6d
Surgeon	1	2s 6d
Master Gunner (absent)	1	2s
Gunner	3	1s
Gunsmith	1	1s 6d

Source: TNA, War Office (WO), 24/246, Papers Concerning Establishments, 1745-1746

It was alleged on 13 September, though without any confirmatory evidence, by Horace Walpole, that 'the Deputy Governor of Edinburgh Castle has threatened the magistrates to beat their town about their ears, if they admit the rebels'.[15]

As early as 23 August, Edinburgh's first citizen, Provost Alastair Stewart, MP, (1697-1780), read his fellow councillors a letter from Tweeddale, written in London 10 days previously, urging them to 'exert your care and vigilance on this occasion, and make use of such precautions as you shall judge necessary for preserving the publick peace within the bounds of your jurisdiction' as regards the city.[16] Stewart had told Tweeddale that the city had 'never been better affected'. It was internal enemies that were to be dealt with, to suppress any Jacobite meetings, not an external army at this stage, that latter being the job of Cope's army.

The council voted to increase the City's Trained Bands by 30 men, the Treasurer to provide the money for their 'clothing and necessaries'. The officers of the Trained Bands were to make lists of their men and report these to the council. They were to ensure that each man was ready if it came to a crisis. Meanwhile, the city constables were to check for any strangers within their jurisdictions. Innkeepers were to do likewise.[17]

Crichton noted the diverse loyalties of Edinburgh at this time. Generally, he believed 'Edinburgh had a good dale of zeale and spirit'. This agreed with official pronouncements: so far so good. Yet he went on to state 'the Lord Provost was justly suspected of corresponding with the rebells' and 'it was said of the trained band captains, 12 of 15 were Jacobite and the

15 Home, *History*, p.67; RA, CP5/163, Account of Prestonpans, 1745; Lewis (ed.), *Correspondence*, Vol.19, p.107.

16 TNA, SP54/26, 17, Minutes, 23 August–13 September 1745.

17 Edinburgh City Archives (ECA), Town Council Minutes, 1744-1745, SL1/1/65, p.276-278.

commandant a Jacobite, the town was full of friends of Prince Charles'.[18] A later source argued the reverse, 'the greatest part of the Inhabitants of the town have so eminently distinguished themselves on behalf of the present happy establishment'.[19]

On 27 August, just before the startling news of the Jacobite advance arrived, a meeting of the city council was summoned to decide what to do. It was resolved to put the city into a defensive state, to repair the walls and to raise a regiment of volunteer infantry, paid for by voluntary subscriptions. They also recommended that a standing committee of the council be formed, supplemented by other citizens, to consult Scotland's foremost lawyer, the Lord Justice Clerk, Andrew Fletcher (1692-1766), and other lawyers, what other steps they could legally take to oppose the Jacobite army.[20]

The committee met with the lawyers and the latter stated that the King's warrant would be needed to raise such a regiment. This was in accordance to a law passed in the first Parliament of Charles II, stating that the power of raising forces was the monarch's alone and that if his subjects did so without such, they were committing high treason (such legal concerns also worried magnates in the north of England in September and October when it came to the suggestion of raising volunteers). Therefore, an application to raise such men was prepared and sent to Robert Craigie (1685-1760), the Lord Advocate, and on to London. Thus, the council and committee were awaiting an answer when the unwelcome news arrived that the Jacobites were on the verge of the Lowlands.[21]

Some critics of Stewart believed he was scornful of the suggestion to raise a volunteer regiment. Apparently 'at first received the proposal with a laugh'. Later he 'seemed to laugh at the proposal, believing that money could not be got to pay them'. He also observed that without the King's Sign manual it would be treason to form a volunteer regiment.[22] Meanwhile, the constables supplied lists of the strangers within their jurisdictions.[23]

Stewart wrote to Tweeddale to assure him of the city's loyalty and the latter replied on 31 August, 'you assure me that the town of Edinburgh was never better affected nor more peaceable than at present and that nothing shall be neglected on your part to preserve people in their Duty to their King and Country'.[24] This impression of the city's loyalty was reflected in a letter from Tweeddale a week later, 'the zeal expressed by the inhabitants of the city of Edinburgh of their own Defence'. However, the castle's absentee governor, Lord Mark Kerr (1676-1752), was to travel there as there were concerns about the health and age of the elderly deputy governor, Lieutenant General Guest.[25]

---

18 Stewart, *Woodhouselee MS*, pp.14-15.

19 NRS, GD1/1440/5/31, Statement in defence of the loyalty of the city of Edinburgh, circa May 1746.

20 Home, *History*, pp.67-68.

21 Home, *History*, p.68.

22 Anon., *Trial*, Part 2, pp.61-62.

23 TNA, SP54/26, 17, Minutes, 23 August–13 September 1745.

24 TNA, SP55/13, 250, Tweeddale to Stewart, 31 August 1745.

25 TNA, SP55/13, 257, Tweeddale to Unknown, 7 September 1745.

On 2 September a deputation which included Colin MacLaurin (1698-1746), professor of mathematics, with suggestions for measures to be taken for the city to be put in 'as good a state of defence as possible with all expedition', was made. A similar request had been made a week previously but that 'had not met with due encouragement' and the petitioners' zeal had then been met with ridicule and jest. MacLaurin and his fellows suggested that moulds be made for the production of bullets, that the fluence from the North Loch be shut up and secured so as to make a moat, and that all Jacobite suspects in the city be relieved of their weapons. The Provost agreed to the first two measures but not the third. The petitioners were confident that a firm defence should succeed given 'the unskillfulness the Highlanders had always shown in attacking stone walls, their want of artillery and being ill armed'.[26]

On the 3 September, news reached Edinburgh that the Jacobite army was at Perth. On the following day, Captain Rogers, an aide to Cope, reached the city with an order to Guest to send transport ships to Aberdeen from Leith to transport Cope's forces from there to Edinburgh. This came as welcome news, that the city had not been entirely abandoned to its fate.[27]

Meanwhile MacLaurin and his fellows made further suggestions; that the parapet of the city walls be cleared, that stairs there be made and that cannon be mounted near the gates and on the flanks. However, when Stewart and his fellow councillors viewed the city defences they were pessimistic about their worth in keeping the Jacobite army out. Apparently, Stewart 'could not see but if 2,000 had a mind to get into the town they must succeed'. However, he did ask MacLaurin to make a plan of the walls.[28] MacLaurin 'seem'd to have no doubt that he could make the walls defensible against a sudden attack, but complained of want of service'.[29]

On that same day, 6 September, a petition was sent to the council signed by about 100 citizens, requesting that they be authorised to associate as volunteers for the city's defence. They also wanted to be able to name their own officers and for Guest to provide them with the necessary arms from the castle's magazine.[30]

Provost Stewart ordered an extraordinary meeting of the council for the 7 September. Beforehand, he consulted with Robert Craigie and the city solicitor whether it was lawful for the council to grant the petitioners' request. Despite being the same men who had previously stated that the King's warrant was necessary to raise men to form the Edinburgh Regiment, they now gave it as their opinion that it was legal for the raising of a similar force.[31] The city also penned a loyal address to the King, stating, 'We beg

26 B.A. Hedman (ed.), 'Colin MacLaurin's Journal of the Forty Five', *Scottish History Society* 5th series, Miscellany Vol.13 (Edinburgh, 2004), pp.317-318.

27 Home, *History*, p.68.

28 Hedman (ed.), 'Colin MacLaurin's Journal', pp.318-319.

29 James Kinsley (ed.), *Autobiography of Dr Alexander Carlyle: Anecdotes and Characters of the Times* (Oxford: Oxford University Press, 1973), p.59.

30 Home, *History*, p.69.

31 Home, *History*, p.69.

Plan of Edinburgh.

leave at this time to assure your Majesty, that we will stand by you, and your Royal Family, with our lives and fortunes'.[32]

MacLaurin submitted plans of the city's defences to the council on the evening of 7 September. They indicated where the vulnerable points were and how they could be remedied. The Provost asked for an estimate of the expenditure involved and claimed 'that could not be easily done and would require time'. MacLaurin noted that 'dispatch was necessary above all things'. The magistrates were ordered 'to employ persons with all possible speed to put the city in a posture of defence and particularly the walls'. However, despite Stewart's misgivings, work began on the following day. Even so, initially far too few workmen were employed; on 7 September there were only seven, the number doubling on the next day; later only 24 set to work when hundreds were needed, though finding so large a workforce at short notice could not have been easy even if money was forthcoming. The work they began on was to extend the parapets by use of scaffolding, but given few workers, this could only be done in some of the places where it was needed. On 9 September they worked on the embrasures and flanks.[33] Press warrants signed by the Deacon were used, but allegedly Stewart was unenthusiastic 'on account of the Expense, and the Lowness of the Town's Funds', though in 1715 repairing the defences had only cost between £200-300.[34]

On 9 September, Stewart announced that he had received a warrant dated from 4 September, from the King enabling the council to raise a regiment of 1,000 men for the city's defence.[35] The council nominated Stewart, as civic head, though he had no military experience, as the regiment's colonel; he and a committee of four others would oversee the regiment, which would be paid for out of public subscriptions, perhaps no easy a task, given that the insurrection had resulted in a 'stop [being] put to all sorts of trade and commerce'.[36] These monies could be received at the Goldsmiths' Hall at 11 and four o'clock each day. Allan Burns, formerly of the Earl of Rothes' Regiment, was to be their adjutant.[37] They were known as the Edinburgh Regiment, whose members would be paid.

Then there were the volunteer companies, composed of men who served at their own expense. Stewart asked the volunteers to prepare a list of 20-30 of their own number whom they thought should become officers. This was quickly accomplished and on 11 September six men were named as captains and each appointed two lieutenants for his own company. Two captains were former Provosts, one a former city baillie, another a former city dean, another a baronet and another a city councillor. [38] In one of the companies, titled the College Company, the men were 'about twenty students of the

32 ECA, Town Council Minutes, 1744-1745, SL1/1/65, p.303.

33 Hedman (ed.), 'Colin MacLaurin's Journal', p.319; ECA, Town Council Minutes, 1744-1745, SL1/1/65, p.304.

34 Anon., *Trial*, Part 2, p.55.

35 Home, *History*, pp.72-73.

36 NRS, GD1/1440/5/31, Statement in defence of the loyalty of the city of Edinburgh, circa May 1746.

37 ECA, Town Council Minutes, 1744-1745, SL1/1/65, pp.308-309, 312.

38 Home, *History* p.73.

University, and other young people; some of them further advanced in their different professions, class fellows, companions and friends'.[39] According to a contemporary historian, the ranks were also made up of 'five hundred of the chief inhabitants of the City, Lawyers, Writers, Physicians and even Divines'.[40]

John Hislop was the keeper of the city's arsenal. In 1745 it contained 1,250 muskets, mostly old but most could fire. There were another 200 muskets which were unusable. There were also 200 bayonets and 300 cartridge boxes, but little gunpowder. He also had 75 muskets with bayonets and cartridge boxes for the City Guard. On 15 September he provided 50-60 muskets to each of the 16 companies of the trained bands and another 39 for the City Guard. On the next day he doled out 500 cartridges to each company.[41]

The Volunteer regiment assembled in the College Yards on the following day. The privates chose which captain they were to serve under. That evening they were provided with 200 muskets, bayonets, and cartridge boxes by David Lyon, storekeeper of the castle; another 100 were provided two days later.[42] A number of ex-soldiers, corporals and sergeants, began to train them. This continued on the following day, 'learning the most necessary parts of the exercise of arms'. This continued on 14 September, too. It was on this day that one Richard Jack joined Captain James Nimmo's company and referred to 'receiving our lessons on the manual exercise of the firelock'. This was all the more urgent for news came to the city that the Jacobites had left Perth and had crossed the river Forth. However, by the evening of that day, not all the volunteers were armed, so more muskets were ordered from the castle, totalling 400 in the end. They were ordered to return to the College Yards at noon on the following morning.[43]

The Trained Bands also tried to recruit more men, as a sergeant, corporal and drummer marched through the city, beating up for recruits. Each man was to be given sixpence a day and provided with a hat if he did not possess one, into which a black cockade would be fixed. John Forrest, City Collector, was to oversee this activity.[44]

Stewart wanted the City Guard and volunteers to be trained in the use of hand grenades, and requested that Guest facilitate this. Guest claimed he had only 200 grenades in the castle's armoury and so he could not spare any. However, the store keeper there claimed there were actually 1,000 and that the Provost could have some of them if he made a formal request. Apparently he never did so and the city only had 23 in their possession. [45]

Military stores were also provided by the city's merchants. Robert Forrester sold 350 pounds of gunpowder for £16 3s 9d; John Watson three barrels of gunpowder for £7 18s 4d, James Scott, half a hundred weight of powder for £2 10s, James Martine two casks for £5 and Walter Scott three barrels for £7 4s 6d. Patrick Henderson provided 4,400 flints for £5 10s and John Goodman

---

39 Home, *History*, p.79.
40 Ray, *History*, p.29.
41 Anon., *Trial*, Part 2, pp.142-143.
42 ECA, Town Council Minutes, 1744-1745, SL1/1/65, p.313, 316.
43 Home, *History*, pp.74-75; RA, CP5/163, Account of Prestonpans, 1745.
44 ECA, Town Council Minutes, 1744-1745, SL1/1/65, p.310.
45 Hedman (ed.), 'Colin MacLaurin's Journal', p.320.

48 dozen cartridge boxes for £2 4s. Archibald Inglis, a pewterer, provided 254 pounds of lead for musket balls for £3 3s 6d. Finally, six ramrods for the artillery were provided for 6s.[46]

There was also the question as to the need for artillery on the city walls and the men to operate them. On about 12 September a meeting was held and it was realised that between 30 and 50 sailors 'who were most expert in managing of cannon' be requested. Lying off Edinburgh was a Royal Navy vessel, HMS *Ursula*, and a request was made to the captain to ask if he could spare any of his gunners. Stewart apparently did not like the idea and remarked, 'Sir, while I am Provost of Edinburgh, sailors shall not be admitted'. When he was pressed to elaborate, he replied, 'If they should be admitted here, it would be damn your blood Jack, fire away, and be damn'd, and so they would fire upon, and murder the inhabitants. And it is my Duty to protect the lives of the inhabitants as well as defend the city'. However, this was all academic. When the captain of the *Ursula* was approached, he declared that he had no men to spare.[47] The only gunner that could be brought in was one Macgill, commander of the custom house boat.[48]

By this time there had been additional work on the physical defences. A plan of the defences had been drawn up for Guest's benefit. There was also the suggestion made for the construction of a communicating wall to a tall house in Potterrow, but the council delayed making a decision on this matter for another six days. Work was also slowed by there being a city election and fewer still workers were in employment. On 11 September, cannon were taken from ships at Leith and placed on the city walls, perhaps 23 in all. A ditch was dug at Wallace Tower, but on the wrong side of the dyke. On 12 September MacLaurin noted 'The work went slowly'.[49]

To raise money, subscription papers were placed in the old Church on 9 September to make it easier for people to promise the necessary money for the volunteer force. There was great enthusiasm to subscribe. A letter was sent to Stewart from a number of former councillors, asking him to request 200 stands of arms from Guest.[50]

Meanwhile, on 14 September MacLaurin alleged that little work was taking place on the walls or on the scaffolding. However, all the cannon there were now primed and stores of cannon ball were ready for use. There were other encouraging signs. The Provost gave additional orders for work to be carried out on the gates and at last, 'There were more men employed this day than ever before and everybody seemed to exert themselves'. At six that evening the bombardiers and volunteers asked Stewart for permission to load the guns but 'he kept them waiting until eight' and then had another man sign the necessary orders. Eventually all the cannon were loaded.[51]

46 ECA, City Treasurer's accounts, 1742-1752, pp.204, 205, 220.
47 Anon., *Trial*, Part 2, pp.45-46, 56.
48 Anon., *Trial*, Part 2, p.193.
49 Hedman (ed.), 'Colin MacLaurin's Journal', p.320; James Ray, *A Compleat History of the Rebellion* (Bristol: S. Farley, 1754), p.29.
50 Home, *History*, pp.71-73.
51 Hedman (ed.), 'Colin MacLaurin's Journal', p.321.

On the same day, Jack was asked to view the condition of the walls and he made a most gloomy prognosis:

> [F]rom a certain infatuation, to give it no worse name, they were neglected to such a degree, that it was impossible for the town to stand out a few hours, tho within it there should be thrice the number of rebels. The principal defect was that the parapet of the embrasures was so low as not to cover any man of a middling size above the thighs, and none above two feet wide, so that the whole chest of a man was exposed as a mark to the enemy and before he possibly could have time to present his firelock, he would necessarily have been shot by the besiegers.[52]

He further noticed large holes in the south wall 'to make it uniformly impossible of defence'. Jack told MacLaurin and others of these defects and they asked him to tell Robert Baillie, a councillor, to press men to repair the walls and Baillie and Stewart gave Jack the city warrant to conscript workmen for the task. That night 50 cartloads of turf were thrown up to strengthen Potterrow Port and part of Bristo Port.[53]

The men and material used to make these repairs were provided, at a cost, by a number of contractors in the city. For 42 and a half man days spent in clearing the parapets, building up the gates at College Yard and fixing cannon, £2 19s was spent. Twenty-two and a half man days were spent repairing the gate at College Kirk for 18s 4d. Charles Mack provided lime and sand for the gates and windows of the city for 12s, and for sloping and clearing the city walls, together with 108 man days, £7 10s. James Herriot, a wright, providing the scaffolding near the walls for £16 and Colon Alison the new palisade at Bristo Port for £5 8s.[54]

At the same time there was a great degree of trepidation among the citizens, judging from a letter sent from Edinburgh on 14 September. The writer gave it as their opinion, 'We expect them with us, how far we are in a condition to repulse them I know not, and I believe we shall not be able to do it without military aid'. There was a belief that the Jacobites were treble the number they really possessed – between five and six thousand men – and so the two regiments of dragoons were inadequate for the city's defence. Treasure and plate had been removed to the castle for safety as 'all degrees of people are in the utmost consternation'. The letter concluded, 'I pray Almighty God to order all things for the publick good and the peace and tranquillity of these Realms'.[55]

On 15 September the city authorities concluded that 'they were ignorant of military matters, and convinced that the deponent understood more of them then they did'. The man in question was James Murray, Receiver General, and he was asked to organise the city defence. He assigned men to the walls, the gates, barricade gates and to organise patrols. When he viewed the results later that day he was unimpressed, 'he neither found the guards

52 RA, CP5/163, Account of Prestonpans, 1745.
53 RA, CP5/163, Account of Prestonpans, 1745.
54 ECA, City Treasurer's Accounts, 1742-1752, pp.213, 212, 218, 219.
55 TNA, SP36/68, f.17r, Unknown to Unknown, 14 September 1745.

nor sentries alert, but that they were huddled together, under the shelter of the walls'. By the day's end he had rectified matters.[56]

It was on the morning of 15 September that the volunteers gathered at the College Yards. Captain George Drummond of the College Company spent time talking with his fellow officers in the Guard Hall. He left and then addressed his company, telling them of the advance of the Jacobites beyond Stirling. He told them that it had been suggested to Guest that the Jacobites be resisted outside the city walls, the city's defenders joining with the two regiments of dragoons. Guest had previously objected to there being no infantry to act with the dragoons and to draw their fire. Drummond asked then if 250 men would be sufficient and if the Provost would allow 50 of the City Guard to accompany them, and Guest agreed that it would be.[57]

Drummond then asked the volunteers if they were willing to risk their lives for the defence of the city and their honour for their country; he was willing to lead them into battle. They threw up their hats and cheered in agreement. Some in the company were less than enthusiastic, having seen the city defences on the previous day and thought them inadequate and therefore unable to resist an attack. They therefore hoped that by advancing from behind the walls the dragoons would bear the brunt of any battle, rather than they.[58]

Drummond then went from company to company, telling them that the resolution to conquer or die was only appropriate to those who did not have families. Many, therefore, were concerned at the proposal to march from the city, but those unattached men, who made up the majority of his company, prevailed. Guest was then informed that the regiment was about to march out with the dragoons. Guest sent a messenger to Stewart to order 50 men of the City Guard to accompany them. Stewart had not been party to these decisions and so was surprised at the request, but Robert Baillie advised him to support it, so he ordered out 90 men of the Guard and as many of the Edinburgh Regiment as were fit for service. Guest had the dragoons march from Leith to Costorphine, to the west of the city.[59]

The volunteers loaded their muskets for the first time and the city fire bell was rung for them to assemble at Lawn Market. They saw the dragoons and cheered. However, this being Sunday and with people leaving the churches, many were concerned that their relatives and friends were about to risk their lives and implored that they desisted in such a dangerous enterprise. Mrs Pringle wrote, 'everybody was in Terror for their friends the volunteers imaging the town would resist'.[60] Other spectators 'were in tears and uttering loud lamentations'.[61] Argument and weeping failed to move the men who marched up the High Street, and to the Grass Market and arrived at the West Port. It was then seen that only Drummond's company was still intact;

56 Anon., *Trial*, Part 2, p.139.
57 Home, *History*, p.79.
58 Home, *History*, p.80.
59 Home, *History*, pp.80-81.
60 Henrietta Tayler (ed.), A *Jacobite Miscellany* (Oxford: Roxburghe Club, 1948), p.38.
61 Kinsley (ed.), *Autobiography*, p.60.

no other company had followed them.[62] Carlyle's 15-year-old brother was concerned that his older brother was in the volunteers and clergymen were also fearful.[63]

Learning this, they halted and one Lieutenant Lindsey was sent back to see what had prevented the others from joining them. Lindsey had previously suggested to Drummond that they separate the company between those willing to march out and those who were not but Drummond disagreed, as the bell calling them to arms would ring immediately. Lindsey discovered that such a division had been made among the other companies. Several officers told him they were willing to march out but that very few of their men were. Some men said that they were ready to go but had no officers to lead them. Lindsey and Sir George Preston, a captain, collected all the willing men and took them to Grass Market where they met Drummond's company. In all they numbered 183 men, including 42 from Drummond's company. There were another 180 men with them, from the City Guard and the Edinburgh Regiment.[64]

When they were at the Grass Market, a number of clergymen including Dr Wishart, the university's chancellor, implored the men to stay within the walls for the city's defence. Some rejected his counsel. When the clergy left, Drummond sent Lieutenant Ormiston with a message to Stewart, asking him if he agreed to their marching out, for if not, they would not proceed. He came back with the instruction not to do so, so the men marched back to the College Yards, but the City Guard and the Edinburgh Regiment were told to join the dragoons and obey Gardner's orders. Some of the volunteers, however, went eastwards to await Cope's army, now convinced that their captain and the Provost had no desire to make a defence.[65]

That day there arrived in the city numerous men from adjacent parts to assist in its defence. They met with a less than enthusiastic response from the Provost. Between two and three in the afternoon came Lewis Douglas and Dr Tait from Dalkeith with 47 men. Similarly, Sir Robert Dickson of Carberry arrived in the evening with 150 men from Inveresk and Musselburgh. Both asked Stewart for arms and he eventually promised delivery on the following day. They also asked for subsistence but were again disappointed. The Dalkeith men were given accommodation in the High School and were assigned to Cowgate, but no fuel was provided. When Stewart saw the Dalkeith men between one and two on the next morning, he did not even speak to them. Eventually Guest provided 50 muskets for the Dalkeith men, but Stewart merely told Dickson that his men should join the Trained Bands of Edinburgh. Dr Tait commented that Stewart, 'had used him roughly and was in a passion at him, for no other reason, as he said, but for bringing in his men'.[66]

62 Home, *History*, pp.81-82.
63 Kinsley (ed.), *Autobiography*, p.61.
64 Home, *History*, pp.82-83.
65 Home, *History*, pp.84-85.
66 Anon., *Trial*, Part 2, pp.75-76, 53-54, 56.

This attitude on Stewart's part is not surprising for on the previous day the Rev. Alexander Webster had offered to raise a company of servants and journeymen, paying each a guinea. Stewart did not give him the permission he needed, though Webster offered to raise £500 by subscription to meet all the costs.[67]

That night, the Trained Bands, the Edinburgh Regiment, and volunteers from Musselburgh and Dalkeith, numbering in total between 600 and 700 men, stood guard on the city gates. There were no disturbances.[68]

Meanwhile, a great deal more work was taking place on the defences. The work on Bristo Port which had commenced on the previous day, was completed, as it was on the adjacent bastion to the south. MacLaurin then had Jack view the north part of the wall. Jack thought that the wall near Trinity Hospital was 'the weakest part of the town', with its low parapets and the easily accessible college church and the hospital with its door and seven windows. Some of these windows were blocked up with dry stone and the building was guarded all night.[69]

The 16th was the day of decision. Work carried out on the walls continued, however. Jack had 100 workmen building up the parapets with turf and the gates with stone, making them four feet thick. Stone and lime were used to block up the remainder of the hospital windows. A trench was dug parallel to the southern wall. The northern wall, which was the weakest was in one day's time rendered the strongest. He was convinced that this would be impossible for the Jacobites to take without losing half of their men.[70]

Between 10 and 11 that morning two messages were sent to the city. One was to the Provost, the other was from one Andrew Alves, a writer from the Signet Office. The latter message was sent to the people and was disseminated at the city cross. According to Home, the slow Jacobite advance had 'giving them time for the terror of their approach to operate upon the minds of unwarlike citizens in a divided city'. The threat on paper seemed all the more severe 'and conveyed a confused idea of every thing that could happen in a town taken by storm'.[71]

The decisive event that day took place in the afternoon. Apparently, despite the abortive march of the volunteers and others of the previous day, the Edinburgh Regiment and the City Guard were to be sent to join the dragoon regiments now at Coltbridge, and

> [I]t was at that time expected by almost the whole inhabitants that a battle would have ensued, nor was it doubted but these dragoons, with the Edinburgh Regiment and Guard, would have given a very good account of the rebels, which in a great measure contributed to quiet the minds of the inhabitants.[72]

---

67 Anon., *Trial*, Part 2, p.97.
68 Home, *History*, p.86.
69 RA, CP5/163, Account of Prestonpans, 1745.
70 RA, CP5/163, Account of Prestonpans, 1745.
71 Home, *History*, pp.86-87.
72 NRS, GD1/1440/5/31, Statement in defence of the loyalty of the city of Edinburgh, circa May 1746.

Yet this was not to be, for 'The conduct of the dragoons was not at all expected'.[73] Gardiner's and Hamilton's Dragoons fled eastwards from the Jacobite advance in a panic (known as the Coltbridge Canter), and so the Jacobite army now lay about two or three miles to the west of Edinburgh, camping at the south west of the city, at Gray's Mills.[74] A loyalist observer had been unimpressed with the dragoons anyway, noting that Gardiner was unwell and 'his regiment was fatigued having had long marches for three days before. They looked very unlicke men who would stand to it. I saw General Hamilton's squadron they looked better, but alace they were Irishmen!'[75] Some argued 'it was not the duty of subjects to throw away any lives, when they paid the regular army to defend them, they could not be blamed for saving the blood of their fellow citizens'.[76]

Apparently some in the crowd asked Stewart 'would he continue his Design of defending the city and have them all murdered now the dragoons had fled', to which he replied, 'Would they now be guilty of Cowardice, in giving up the Town'.[77] This concern led to a petition signed by 48 citizens, being presented to the Provost, requesting that a meeting of the inhabitants to be called to consult with him as to the best course of action to be chosen. Initially Stewart resisted the call, but that afternoon, between three and four, with the approach of the Jacobite army and the flight of the two regiments of dragoons in full view of the inhabitants, matters were seen differently. Home wrote, 'Instantly the clamour rose, and crowds of people ran about the streets crying that it was madness to think of resistance'.[78] John Campbell, an Edinburgh banker, wrote in his diary, 'The town in a consternation all day'.[79]

At two there had been a meeting in the castle between the Lord Advocate, the Solicitor General, and Guest. They concluded that a request be made to Brigadier Thomas Fowke, in command of the dragoons, to ask for 100 dragoons to be sent into the city to aid its defence. Colonel Clayton, Fowke's aide, claimed the request must be in writing. The men sent could be from Gardiner's Dragoons because their horses had been exhausted from frequent recent marches and so their loss from Cope's army would not be significant. Guest signed an order for this, but insisted that Stewart also sign it, as the city was the Provost's jurisdiction, not his. Initially Stewart did so and the order was returned to the castle. By this time, the situation had changed, as we shall see.[80]

Stewart was met by some of the citizens after he had returned from West Port, where he had gone to give orders after the dragoons' departure. Fearful of a massacre, the citizens pleaded with him not to persist in wishing

73 NRS, GD1/1440/5/31 Statement in defence of the loyalty of the city of Edinburgh, circa May 1746.

74 Bell (ed.), 'Memorials', p.193.

75 Stewart, *Woodhouselee MS*, p.19.

76 NRS, RH4/213, Duncan's Journal, 1750.

77 Anon., *Trial*, Part 2, p.160.

78 Home, *History*, pp.87-88.

79 Henry Paton (ed.), 'Leaves from the Diary of John Campbell, an Edinburgh Banker in 1745', *Scottish History Society, Miscellany*, Vol.I (Edinburgh, 1895), p.537.

80 Anon., *Trial*, pp.107-109, 24.

to defend the city. He reprimanded them and then went to the Goldsmiths' Hall, where he met with the assembled magistrates and councillors.[81] Carlyle referred to an unknown horseman riding by announcing that the Jacobite army was 16,000 strong.[82]

There were also 'a good many of the inhabitants' there, too. The Lord Justice Clerk, the Advocate and the Solicitor's presence were also requested, but the former, on seeing the dragoons retreat, left the city and retired to his house at Bunstane, after burning some of his papers at his Edinburgh house. Their advice was sought, but none were present. Stewart addressed the officers of the volunteers and the Trained Bands. Apparently, he declared:

> That he hoped they would not now suffer Cowardice to poison their Councils, and that after obtaining His Majesty's Royal Sign Manual and doing so much with spirit, they would not now think of giving up the Defence of the City. That for his own part, he would go to the city walls, and the place of greatest Danger, and so long as he could find 10 men to stand by him, he would persevere in the act.[83]

Joseph Williamson was one of the officers and he stated that he would fight but that he thought that only 5-10 men from his company could be relied on. Stewart then asked George Drummond if he could be counted on, but he declined to answer. Captain John Murray was equivocal in his response, stating that those volunteers who wished to fight 'they might make a good defence' but if the decision was taken not to, then the arms should be sent to the castle so as to not fall into Jacobite hands. Other officers were less certain about whether their men were willing to fight, one claiming 'he did not find any Disposition in his men to fight' and another thought that of the 15 men remaining in his company, only five would stand by him in the event of a crisis. The other officers did not answer. Drummond later told Stewart, 'I do most heartily pity you, my Lord Provost. I cannot, nor can any man advise you; you must yourself decide it; and I am afraid you will get very little advice.'[84] Other citizens gave differing opinions and the whole was carried on with much acrimony on both sides.[85]

Walter Grossett, a customs officer, and zealous loyalist, later wrote that he went to the Goldsmiths' Hall 'to press for the defence of the city', to let Stewart know that more than 100 dragoons could be requested for the city's defence. Grossett had been sent from the now absent Lord Justice Clerk and Lord Advocate to seek the Provost's permission to request these troops. However, he prevaricated, 'he declined giving a direct answer upon being pressed thereto he declared he would do nothing unworthy of the station he was in…concluded with words that implied he was against defending the Town, urged the uncertainty of the troops under Sir John Cope's coming in

81 Home, *History*, pp.88-89.
82 Kinsley (ed.), *Autobiography*, p.64.
83 Anon., *Trial*, Part 2, p.161.
84 Anon, *Trial*, Part 1, pp.161-163, 118-119.
85 Home, *History*, pp.88-89.

time, to their relief & the hazard the lives & properties of the inhabitants would in that case be exposed to'.[86]

Grossett assured him that Cope's army had sailed from Aberdeen on 14/15 September and so should arrive very soon.[87] He said to Stewart 'if he should take a hearty resolution, and proper measures to defend the Town, but for 24 hours, not one moment should be lost in bringing the Troops to their effectual relief'. However, he 'could at no rate get ten persuaded to undertake the defence of the town, which they had agreed to give up'.[88]

More people came to the meeting so it was adjourned to a larger place, to that of the New Church aisle. There, the majority was for a capitulation, with those speaking against being howled down.[89] It was claimed that the meeting was predominantly made up of Jacobite sympathisers, 'very few of the well affected inhabitants' attended and 'several of the meeting were not well affected to the government'. Those supporting the motion to persist in the city's defence were 'treated with very scurrilous and opprobrious language', especially one Rev. George Logan.[90]

At this point a letter from Prince Charles was received, addressed to Stewart and the councillors. Stewart said he would not be witness to its reading so he and the councillors returned to the Goldsmiths' Hall. Many of the assembled citizens followed them, requesting that it be read in their presence. Others claimed that reading it would constitute treason.[91]

Meanwhile, the defenders began to disperse. Four companies of the volunteers delivered their arms to the castle at five without seeking Stewart's permission, after Stewart refused to give Captain John Murray an answer (the Trained Bands gave their arms to the council). They had come from the College Yards to the Lawn Market, following the retreat of the dragoons. When the captains had left them to attend the foresaid meeting at the Goldsmiths' Hall, the lieutenants were left in command. Two of them found Stewart and asked for their orders, and on returning to the men after having received none, they also told how the meeting was advocating capitulation. One volunteer suggested they should go to the meeting, armed, and tell those assembled their opinion. Two volunteers fought one another.[92] The volunteers from Haddington, Dalkeith and Inervesk then decided to march out of the city as it seemed that no defence was being planned.[93]

Eventually their captains returned and went into conversation with the lieutenants. They told Lindsey to go to Guest and let him know that they would return their arms to the castle, for it was pointless to have them if the city was to surrender. The volunteers did so as the sun was setting. Many were reluctant to do this and some were tearful. Carlyle wrote that they were 'not

86 RA, CP5/282, Account of the surrender of Edinburgh, 1745.
87 RA, CP5/282, Account of the surrender of Edinburgh, 1745.
88 TNA, SP54/26, 27, Grossett to Fletcher, 17 September 1745.
89 Home, *History*, pp.88-89.
90 Anon., *Trial*, Part 2, p.91.
91 Home, *History*, pp.89-90.
92 Home, *History*, pp.90-91.
93 RA, CP5/163, Account of Prestonpans, 1745.

a little ashamed and afflicted at our inglorious campaign'.[94] John Dalgleish, a captain in the Trained Bands, when been told to dismiss the men and lay down the arms, 'which he did not incline to do', so sent an ensign to have the order confirmed by the Provost. They were, but nothing was said about the disposal of the weapons; once he told the men the news they rushed off home and dropped their weapons.[95]

Instructions to disband were not uniformly passed onto all the Trained Bands. There were three companies still at their posts and in arms until just after three on the following morning. These were the men at the West Port and those at the Weigh House. At three they were told to disband and leave their weapons in the makeshift guard rooms, in order that they not be attacked by Jacobite troops for carrying arms.[96] Half an hour after sunset only two companies were still in arms. [97]

Meanwhile, at about six, further steps were taken to dismantle the defences. Ensign William Roberts was despatched from the castle along with Sergeant Joseph Read, Gunner Robert Griffiths and another 21 soldiers. They joined a number of blacksmiths' boys, with carts, horses and tools. They were sent by Guest to either spike the cannon on the city walls or to take them to the castle. However, first they had to seek out Stewart and ask his permission to do this, as he had authority in the city not Guest. The Provost was found but he was reluctant to make a decision. He suggested that they return to the castle and seek Guest's opinion instead. Guest ordered they return to the castle, the guns still in position and ready for use.[98]

Meanwhile, discussion was still taking place at the Goldsmiths' Hall as to whether Charles' letter should be read or no. No one would advise whether it should be and Stewart remarked, despairingly, 'Good God ! I am deserted by my arms and my assessors'. Eventually the letter was read and its contents were as follows:

> Being now in a condition to make our way into the capital of His Majesty's ancient kingdom of Scotland, we hereby summon you to receive us, as you are in duty bound to do: and in order to it, we hereby require you upon receipt of this, to summon the Town Council, and take proper measures for securing the peace and quiet of the city, which we are very desirous to protect. But if you suffer any of the usurper's troops to enter the town, or any of the cannon, arms or ammunition now in it (whether belonging to the public, or private persons) to be carried off, we shall take it as a breach of your duty, and a heinous offence against the King and us, and shall resent it accordingly. We promise to preserve all the rights and liberties of the city, and the particular property of every one of his Majesty's subjects. But if any opposition be made to us, we cannot answer for the consequences, being firmly resolved at any rate to enter the city; and in that case

94 Kinsley (ed.), *Autobiography*, p.65.
95 Anon., *Trial*, pp.91-92, Part 2, p.129.
96 Anon., *Trial*, Part 2, pp.122-27.
97 Anon., *Trial*, Part 2, p.16.
98 Anon., *Trial*, Part 2, pp.99-101.

> if any of the inhabitants are found in arms against us, they must not expected to be treated as prisoners of war.
>
> Charles PR.[99]

After this had been read, cries against any resistance became stronger than ever and it was resolved to send a deputation to the Jacobite camp to desire that time be given before any action, for the council to resolve how to answer the letter. At eight o' clock Bailie Gavin Hamilton, John Yetts, and David Inglis were sent to Charles' headquarters. [100]

At about eight o'clock on the 16 September, the Jacobite army sent a summons to the Provost and council of Edinburgh, requiring them to open their gates and receive their Prince.[101] Eventually, at ten o'clock, a deputation of four men from the city arrived, led by Bailie Hamilton, at the Mills. They arrived at Charles' quarters and he ordered Murray of Broughton, his secretary, to meet them and ask what their purpose was. They told him that they had been sent by the Provost to know what was wanted of them. Murray told them

> [T]hat his Master required no further than that they should open their gates to his army and deliver up the arms of the Town and garrison, with the ammunition and Military Stores than in the Town, in which case the liberties of the City should be preserved, and all necessary protection given them. [102]

Murray was told that they could not deliver the Edinburgh Volunteers' arms as they belonged to the garrison of the castle, not the city. On the other matters, they stated that they would need time to return to the city and consult with their colleagues. Murray reported the meeting to Charles and he allowed that they could have between two and three hours to return their final answer. No further time would be allowed, however, 'having good intelligence that they desired no more than to dallie of the time till they saw how far it was possible for them to be relived by Gll Cope'.[103]

By this time, with the changing circumstances, Guest thought he needed Stewart to put it in writing a second time that he wanted the dragoons in the city. When Stewart received this second request he felt unable to sign it and told the messenger that Guest must do as he thought best. Guest did nothing.[104]

Just after the deputation had left the city, however, news came that Cope's army was about to land at Dunbar and then march to Edinburgh. Grossett had left Edinburgh and had ridden to Musselburgh, four miles to the east of the city, where Fletcher and the Lords Advocate were, along with

99 Home, *History*, pp.92-93
100 Home, *History*, p.93.
101 Bell (ed.), 'Memorials', p.193.
102 Bell (ed.), 'Memorials' p.193-194.
103 Bell (ed.), 'Memorials', p.194.
104 Anon., *Trial*, Part 2, p.109.

Brigadier Fowke and the dragoon regiments. He learnt that Cope's arrival was imminent and so rode back to the city with this news.[105]

Grossett claimed that his news was greeted enthusiastically, he being 'huzza'd and the strongest acclamations of joy' greeting him. Yet the council and Stewart specifically initially told him that he was too late; that the deputation had already left the city. Grossett suggested that they be recalled and overtaken, which was agreed.[106] Messengers were sent to overtake the deputation and stop them from their task, but clearly were too late. Guest was approached for arms and the return of the dragoon regiments. Guest was positive about the first but did not think that the dragoons could be returned for they would be needed as part of Cope's army.[107]

Some of the Edinburgh Volunteer officers, on hearing Grossett's news, began to press for the city being defended. Drummond told Stewart 'no time was to be lost in speaking, it was time to act'. He suggested that the city's alarm bells be rang to summon the volunteers. Stewart was cautious, stating that they 'must be carefull of the blood of the inhabitants' as the deputation was in the Jacobite camp and so could be in danger as the bells would be heard there. Drummond argued that if the city was in a state of defence they would be offered better terms. According to Grossett, Stewart did not have the volunteers summoned by bells or other means. He would have to consult his colleagues first.[108]

The councillors suggested that the volunteers be reassembled, but most of them had already left the city after laying down their arms.[109] Stewart claimed the city was indefensible and refused to risk the inhabitants' lives. Grossett claimed he would personally defend the weakest point in the defences with 50 men as he was certain the Jacobites were too weak to attack, 'who had neither cannon nor armes'. He claimed that of the Jacobite army of 2,000 men, only half had muskets.[110]

When the deputation from the Jacobite camp returned, they had with them another letter:

> His Royal Highness the Prince Regents thinks his Manifesto, and the King his father's declaration already published, a sufficient capitulation for all His Majesty's subjects, to accept with joy. His present demands are to be received into the city, as the son and representative of the King is father, and obeyed as such by them when there. His Royal Highness supposes, that since the receipt of his letter to the Provost, no arms or ammunition have been suffered to be carried off or concealed, and will expect a particular account of all things of that nature. Lastly, he expects a positive answer, before two o'clock in the morning, otherwise he will think himself obliged to take measures conform.

105 RA, CP5/282, Account of the surrender of Edinburgh, 1745.
106 RA, CP5/282, Account of the surrender of Edinburgh, 1745.
107 Home, *History*, pp.93-94.
108 RA, CP5/282, Account of the surrender of Edinburgh, 1745.
109 Home, *History*, pp.93-94.
110 RA, CP5/282, Account of the surrender of Edinburgh, 1745.

It was signed by Murray by Charles' command.[111]

Stewart then claimed that he would rather die than receive Charles 'son of the Pretender' as Prince Regent. There was much more deliberation and eventually it was decided to send a second deputation to the Jacobites, begging to have a deadline of nine on the next morning, so they could consult the citizens who were now mostly asleep in their beds. The deputies, Robert Baillie, Provost Coutts and two others were to go and were also asked what was meant by their having to 'receive' Charles as Prince Regent. They set out from the city at two in the morning.[112] According to Grossett, Stewart concluded, 'the King's servants and troops having deserted them & it being the opinion of all the officers he had spoke with that the town could not be defended'.[113]

The men left and another deputation arrived, this time made up of six councillors, including Alderman Coutts. They received a similar reply as the first:

> His Royal Highness has already given all the assurances he can that he intends to exert nothing of the city in general, of anything in particular, but what his character of Regent entitles him to. This he expects, and renews his summons to the magistrates to receive him as such.[114]

Charles, once again, refused to see them.[115] Convinced that the city was merely playing for time, Charles decided that he should use more direct methods. He summoned Cameron of Lochiel to put his men in readiness to march at a minute's notice. The force numbered between 800 and 900 and included men of the MacDonalds of Glengarry, Clanranald, and Keppoch. O'Sullivan was put in command. Murray of Broughton went with them as he knew the district around Edinburgh. The men were given strict instructions that once in the city, they were not to get drunk, to pay for anything they took and to behave well towards all the inhabitants. They were promised two shillings each once they had taken the city.[116]

They marched on the road by Merkistown and Hope Park and managed to avoid being seen by the castle's garrison, although they were so near to the latter that they could hear them call their rounds. They reached Netherbow Port without having met anyone on their way. That part of the city wall that they could see, was mounted with cannon, but they could not see anyone there.[117]

Cameron had one of his men 'in a great coat and hunting cape' to go to the gate and demand admittance. Once this had been accomplished, the rest would rush the gate. However, the Highlander was refused entrance. It was

111 Home, *History*, p.95.
112 Home, *History*, pp.95-96.
113 RA, CP5/282, Account of the surrender of Edinburgh, 1745.
114 Henry Paton (ed.), 'Lyon in Mourning', Vol.I, *Scottish History Society*, 1st series (Edinburgh, 1895) p.250.
115 Elcho, *Short Account*, p.256.
116 Bell (ed.), 'Memorials', p.194; Elcho, *Short Account*, p.256.
117 Bell (ed.), 'Memorials', p.194.

now daylight and so Murray suggested that they withdraw to St Leonard's Hill, so they could avoid being fired upon by the castle's guns. They could then wait for further orders from Charles, for although they could force their way into Edinburgh, yet their general orders were to avoid violence as much as possible. Once they had decided on this course, Murray went to their rear and was about to guide them away.[118]

Chance then played a part in proceedings. The city's second deputation was travelling back by coach and went to the Netherbow Port via the High Street. This gave the Highlanders their chance.[119] The gate had been guarded by two companies of men of the Trained Bands led by Sir George Preston and James Nimmo until the previous afternoon. They had then left and went to the Lawn Market as the force was being disbanded. Thomas Dalyell, a captain in the City Guard, sent some of his men to replace them. However, they got drunk and so another six men led by Sergeant Henderson replaced them. In overall charge of the gate was James Tait, a goldsmith, but he had been there all night on the two previous nights there, so had deputised his servant, James Gillespie, to support his deputy, and to be in charge on the night of 16/17 September.[120]

According to Murray, the arrival of the coach 'obliged the Guard to open the Port [made up of two gates], upon which Lochiel took the advantage and rushed in, the guard immediately dispersing'.[121] Another version of events is that when the carriage arrived, Alexander Corsar was the man who initially dealt with it and there was discussion over permission to enter. Gillespie was then involved and Corsar explained 'then the port was opened and the coach drove out, and was not past the deponent two yards when the Highlanders rushed in, and Lochiel grasped the deponent by the arm'. Gillespie stated, after he shut the first gate 'as he was shutting the other, the Highlanders rushed in upon him, and be at him back, and they possessed themselves of the Port, and entered the Town'.[122]

The guards were probably low in morale, for they were 'so harassed with the extraordinary Duty all the preceding week...they were hardly fit to do any Duty far less to oppose an Army'.[123] Apart from this entry into the city, there was another, made by 323 Jacobites, as related thus, 'your uncle Glencarnach, Ardshiel and your father [MacGregor] put their shoulders to the gate [the East Port] and opened it – there was neither Bolt nor Bar on it...we seized the Guard House and a few of the soldiers'.[124]

It was then about five in the morning of 17 September. The Jacobites posted guards on all the gates and relieved any of the remaining defenders of their arms. By the time the inhabitants awoke, they found the city was in the hands of the Jacobites. When Charles made his triumphal entry he was met with great acclamations from the citizens. Edinburgh was his.

---

118 Bell (ed.), 'Memorials', p.195.

119 Elcho, *Short Account*, p.257.

120 Anon., *Trial*, Part 2, pp.146-152.

121 Bell (ed.), 'Memorials', p.195.

122 Anon., *Trial*, pp.150-152.

123 Anon., *Trial*, Part 1, p.128.

124 NRS, GD1/53/85/1, MacGregor to Unknown, c.1745.

Could the city have been more forcefully defended? John Murray discussed the matter in his memoirs and he was definitely of the opinion that it could not have been so. This was for two main reasons; the incapability of the defenders and the weakness of the defences. In detail, of the former, he wrote:

> [A] body of men, three times the number who were then in the Citty, would have been insufficient to defend it…first, they was composed of a parcel of raw undisciplined fellows, numbers of whom had never seen nor heard a gun fired. Secondly, they had no officers to head them who were better versed in military matters then themselves, and consequently could not have been brought to the several attacks that would have been made, and thirdly, the gentlemen volunteers themselves, from who most was expected, were infinitely inferior in courage to their Enemy.[125]

He also said that had it come to an assault, then gunpowder could have been placed next to a wall on the south side near a house, from which Jacobite musketeers would have swept the defenders from the walls. The resulting explosion would have 'made a breech for a dozen to enter a-breast'. There was also a vulnerable point on the north side, whilst diversionary attacks were taking place near the Physic Gardens and the Hospital. Had the garrison resisted these, it would have 'occasioned a great deal of bloodshed'. He concluded, 'Thus in less than half a days time would the Town have been reduced, with the whole garrison made prisoners without terms, and a number of lives lost to no purpose under heaven, but to please some hotheaded ignorant fools'.[126]

After the whole campaign was over, a document emphasising the city's loyalty to the winning side, argued in Edinburgh's defence:

> [I]t will be allowed by every unprejudiced person, that in the unlucky circumstances they were at that time reduced to, their making a defence must have exposed the whole suburbs to the fury of the rebels, and would have been attended with consequences very fattall to the city itself, w'out doing any real service to the government, for w'out the proper and of the military, w'out the implements and skilful persons to manage them, its easily to be imagine what a small resistance it was in the power of some burghers to have made, in a place allowed by all military folk to be untenable, so that the town must inevitably soon have fallen to an enraged enemy, and the suburbs been ransomed and perhaps burnt.[127]

Jack disagreed with these assessments, writing that 'Had we got two or three days more respite, the whole south part of the Town would in the same manner have been repaired…it was capable of holding for fifteen days against thrice

125 Bell (ed.), 'Memorials', p.196.
126 Bell (ed.), 'Memorials', pp.196-197.
127 NRS, GD1/1440/5/31, Statement in defence of the loyalty of the city of Edinburgh, circa May 1746.

the number of rebels, tho well armes, but without cannon'. He concluded, 'in short we were most miserably betrayed'.[128] Crichton thought so, too, 'All these, with the two regiments of dragoons might have resisted and probable defeated four thousands or a few more ill armed and ill accoutred fatigued Highlanders, but this wanted a chief magistrate'.[129]

Carlyle was also of this opinion:

> It was very true that a half armed regiment of new Rais'd men with 400 volunteers of the City, and 200 from other places, might not be thought sufficient for the Defence of the City had it been seriously Besieg'd; yet considering that the Highlanders, were not more than 1800, and the half of them only arm'd, that they were averse to approaching walls and afraid of cannon, I am persuaded that had not the dragoons prov'd firm, and resolute…it was more than two to one that the rebels, had never approach'd the city.[130]

Some, from afar, believed that the city fell due to those within. Miss Saville, a wealthy Londoner, in her diary related how the city demonstrated their zeal and then went onto open their gates, 'O dredfull treachery'.[131] Andrew Stone, secretary of the Duke of Newcastle, wrote on 24 September, 'Tis composed they returned to Edenburgh, where they will, 'tis feared, soon be able to reduce the Castle, and consequently the Masters of all the Arms and Wealth of that Country'. [132] The fall of Edinburgh led to the Battle of Prestonpans on 21 September, another case of a siege precipitating a battle, where the would-be relieving army under Cope was decisively defeated and removed from the equation as a fighting force. However, the Jacobite army was not undisputed master of Scotland, nor even of Edinburgh.

The city might have fallen, but the castle was another matter. It had stood a siege of three months in 1689, only surrendering when provisions and ammunition were running low, and despite a small garrison, there had been no attempt to take it by storm, such was the strength of the artillery there. They had showed their mettle already by three cannon firing on Charles, Elcho, and Perth shortly after their entry into the city, forcing them to see a healthier spot.[133] The Jacobite army had no such heavy guns, even after destroying Cope's army at Prestonpans on 21 September, for he only had 1 1/2-pounder guns and mortars. After that battle, Crichton noted, 'The castle had given them some disturbance by some bombs thrown into their camp made them keep their distance'.[134]

A contemporary historian described the castle thus:

128 RA, CP 5/163, Account of Prestonpans, 1745.
129 Stewart, *Woodhouselee Ms*, p.14.
130 Kinsley (ed.), *Autobiography*, p.59.
131 A.Saville (ed.), 'Secret Comment: The Diaries of Gertrude Saville, 1722-1757', *Thoroton Society*, Vol.42 (1997), pp.259-260.
132 T.J. McCann (ed.), 'The Correspondence of the Dukes of Newcastle and Richmond, 1724-1750' (Lewes: Sussex Record Society, 1983), p.183.
133 Stewart, *Woodhouselee MS*, p.24.
134 Stewart, *Woodhouselee MS*, p.39.

Edinburgh Castle from the west. (Postcard of Paul Lang)

> It stands on the summit of that hill, on the slope of which lies the City of Edinburgh, and is, properly speaking, only accessible on that side next the City, where there is a considerable space between the houses and the Castle, which on that side, is covered by a Half-Moon well supplied with cannon, beyond which, there is a deep ditch, and a Drawbridge. The Form of the castle is very irregular, following that of the steep, rough and craggy Rock, upon which it stands, and may as near as one can guess, occupy about three fourths of a mile. It is well walled all round, and properly flanked with bastions, yet still its principal security consists in it situation, since it is not easy to approach it, either in order to scaling, or in the usual way of breaking Ground before it, neither is it very practicable to take it by Sap, the Rock being so hard that it is very difficult, if not impossible to penetrate it.[135]

Lord George Murray declared that it was impregnable, 'I declared from the beginning, as my opinion, that it was impracticable to take it without cannon, engineers and regular troops, but others thought it would be obliged to surrender for want of provisions, but General Guest was too knowing an officer to have neglected so material a thing, and I was sure we were not to stay long enough to bring them to any straits'.[136] As we shall see, in this Murray was wrong.

Scottish magnates were concerned about the castle's security because of its contents. Robert Craigie wrote on 23 September, 'a great part of the Specie

135 Marchant, *History*, p.115n.

136 Robert Forbes, *Jacobite Memoirs of the Rebellion of 1745* (Edinburgh: Robert and William Chambers), pp.43-45.

of the Nation is lodged in the castle as well as the arms and ammunition and plate and jewels to a great value'.[137] Fletcher wrote likewise, 'There is a great treasure in the castle of Edinburgh, for besides great quantities of artillery, ammunition and small arms, the whole publick and private money of ye country is in the castle, with a great quantity of plate.[138] Despite describing the castle as being 'impregnable' in a previous letter, Walpole seems to have altered his mind after hearing of the news of Prestonpans, 'and be set up with taking Edinburgh Castle, where there is to the value of a million, and which they would make a stronghold. It is scarcely victualled for a month, and must surely fall into their hands'.[139]

Provisions in the castle, unlike the case in 1689, were few. According to Craigie, there was 'but a month's provisions' and Fletcher thought that there was not much above two weeks' worth. Fletcher wrote that all 'idle mouths' should be sent away from the castle and additional provisions be brought inside.[140] George II was surprised that there was 'so small a quantity of provisions, notwithstanding the notice he must have had' had been laid in store.[141] It was thus essential that they be maintained. Tweeddale wrote to Lord Mark Kerr (the castle's absentee governor) on 25 September to inform Guest that he must 'declare to the magistrates and inhabitants of the town that if they do not furnish him with such provisions as shall be necessary for the Garrison, he will distress and annoy them by all means in his power, particularly by destroying the reservoir'.[142] Five days later, Guest was given a similar message, in case his supplies were in danger, 'he should threaten the town; and in the extremity, put his threats into execution; but in such a manner as to oblige the town: effectually to comply with his demands, and if possible, without executing these orders in their full extent'.[143]

The Jacobite army kept guard in the Weigh House ('very improperly placed' according to Lord George Murray) and the Grass Market. On the evening of 25 September, there was cannon fire and small arms fire against these sentries. Some houses in the West Port were damaged, but these were in the minority. Murray took his own men, from the Atholl Brigade, who were then taking their turn there, to a place under cover on the north side of a street nearby.[144]

Supplies for the castle were forthcoming, as a contemporary noted, 'the inhabitants supplied all manner of fresh provisions at the risk of their lives… The rebels having proclaimed an order that whoever should be apprehended supplying ye garrison should be immediately carried to execution'.[145] Such

137 TNA, SP54/26, 35, Craigie to Tweeddale, 23 September 1745.

138 Francis Douglas, *History of the Rebellion* (Aberdeen: F, Douglas and W. Murray, 1755), p.36.

139 Lewis (ed.), *Correspondence*, Vol.19, p.117.

140 Douglas, *History*, pp.25-26.

141 British Library (BL), Additional Manuscripts (Add.Mss.), 33004, f.93v, Minutes of committee meeting, 30 September 1745.

142 TNA, SP54/25, 37b, Tweeddale to Kerr, 25 September 1745.

143 BL.Add. Mss., 33004, f.93v, Minutes of committee meeting, 30 September 1745.

144 Forbes, *Jacobite Memoirs*, p.45.

145 NRS, GD1/440/5/31, Statement in defence of the loyalty of the city of Edinburgh, circa May 1746.

Edinburgh Castle from the east. (New York Public Library)

were the suspicions against him that 'there arose a surmise that Lord George [Murray] compounded with the governor of Edinburgh Castle and furnished the garrison privately with provisions and other necessaries, which was not very likely'.[146]

At first there seemed to be no danger to the castle, as Guest wrote:

> [T]hey suffer everything to com in and go out unmolested…they threaten to storm the place with scaling ladders, but as I have 400 good men and wee never go to bed; I hope I shall be able to prevent any surprise which I think nothing else will hurt me…no care shall be wanting in my doing my Duty as long as life remains in me.[147]

On 29 September the Jacobite guards were now authorised to not let anyone pass to or from the castle. Guest wrote to Stewart, telling him that unless communication between city and castle were resumed, there would be additional cannonfire from the castle. A message was sent to Guest and this earned 24 hours' respite. [148] Yet 'The Prince is resolute and would have all fall before him'.[149] The council argued that they were happy to see the castle supplied with food but that they were 'obstructed by a superior force which

146 NRS, GD1/53/81/2, Alec McNab to Unknown, 1745.
147 National Library of Scotland (NLS), MS 3036, f77r, Guest to Unknown, 29 September 1745.
148 Douglas, *History*, p.31.
149 Stewart, *Woodhouselee MS*, p.52.

they were unable altogether to withstand' and that Guest's threat 'justly put the whole inhabitants under the utmost terror and consternation'. When they met Guest, he showed them his orders 'which were positive, and told them he must obey them'.[150]

The council did not underestimate the views of the citizenry. John Campbell wrote, 'The consternation the town is in, the castle having threatened to fire if the Highland Guard of the Weigh House was not removed'. Wealthy citizens removed their families and effects from the city.[151] On the morning of 30 September, the council sent a deputation to Charles and showed him Guest's letter. He said that the council had no authority to do as Guest insisted and that he might with equal reason summon him to quit Edinburgh. He was sorry that the city might suffer any damage and promised reprisals against the estates of those in the castle who were authorising artillery fire. There followed negotiation and a temporary cessation of hostilities.[152]

Charles reacted strongly:

> I am equally surprised and concerned at the barbarity of the orders that have been signified to you from the castle, and which those who commanded in it, if they had received from the Elector of Hanover… in the meantime I shall make full Reprisals on the estates of those who are now in the castle.[153]

In detail, he threatened to destroy Preston's house, Valleyfield in Fife, if the guns did not fall silent, but Preston answered that if he did, he would have HMS *Fox* destroy Wemyss Castle, home to Lord Elcho, 'an odd sort of reprisal'.[154] Charles' resolution initially held: 'The Prince has sworn death to any come or goe from it, and placaded his orders publickly'.[155]

Yet on 1 October, firing broke out again, this time by Jacobite forces near the castle. They also dug a trench across the street. The castle garrison replied with both cannon and musket fire. Houses were damaged and some Jacobite troops were injured, and three were killed, disrupting the work on the trench. A servant maid was also a casualty and an innkeeper was killed. Some of the garrison may also have been wounded. On 2 October, Charles decreed that there should be an embargo of goods and people to and from the castle during his residence in the city. Anyone attempting to break this would risk death. The castle's guns now fired far more often, whenever any Jacobite troops were seen in the streets. This also resulted in the deaths and injuries to several of the city residents.[156]

In order to blockade the castle more effectively, on 3 October, guards, provided from the Cameron clan, were placed at the West Kirk and at Livingstone's yards. That day a member of the castle garrison, one Watson, sallied out, set fire to a Jacobite guard house and shot one Jacobite dead.

150 NLS, MS 70712, ff.67, 84, Memorial of Edinburgh citizens, 29 September 1745.
151 Paton (ed.), 'Leaves', p.541.
152 Douglas, *History*, pp.31-32.
153 NLS, MS 70712, f.107, Memorial of Prince Charles, 30 September 1745.
154 Elcho, *Short Affair*, p.292.
155 Stewart, *Woodhouselee MS*, p.56.
156 Douglas, *History*, p.32; Marchant, *History*, pp.117-118.

He returned safely, using a rope to re-enter the castle, having also taken a few guns from the besiegers. Once back, 'he was received with loud huzzas for his valour'. A party followed his example, sallying out killing some of the besiegers, and took several Jacobite soldiers prisoner and others fled. A house was set alight.[157] Jacobites called the castle 'that damned angry bitch'.[158] According to Murray, this setback for the Jacobites took place because O'Sullivan had put them near the West Kirk which isolated them from their colleagues who would take two hours to get around the outside of the castle. Murray did not know of O'Sullivan's decision until after the prisoners were taken. He brought additional troops into the city, from MacDonald of Keppoch's Regiment, to support them.[159]

On the next day, notices were sent for inhabitants of St James' Court and places nearby were to evacuate them in case any cannon balls were fired in their direction. Shortly afterwards there was a fierce bombardment. Houses in Castlehill, where Jacobite troops were believed to be, were damaged. That night another party sallied out, setting fire to two houses, both of which had been abandoned. They also threw up a trench across castle hill and fired grapeshot across the streets. Two civilians were killed and other wounded. Some of the deserted houses were pillaged by those who had sallied out from the garrison.[160] On the Cornmarket was seen 'a tradesman in blew frock coat had been just shot lying his brains dashed out and in his own blood'. This 'was a melancholy shean this street all ships shut up everybody scared off the streats'. It would seem that the garrison were able to bring provisions and barrels of ale from the city to the castle whilst beating back the blockaders.[161]

There was continued fire on 5 October and this 'distressed the inhabitants exceedingly'; allegedly 20 Jacobite soldiers were killed, although Elcho states it was only five or six. The Flesh Market was now a dangerous place to be. Other houses were damaged and some inhabitants left. Some had their possessions taken to safety. Apparently, 20 black cattle, bread, ale and water were procured by the townspeople. Murray of Broughton described the effect of the bombardment thus:

> The Cittizens, unaccustomed to such devastations made the most hideous complaints against the garrison, and used Such moving entreaties with the Chevalier, that not withstanding the just reason he had to be provoked, was nevertheless so much Struck with their unheard of sufferings that, to Show them the Superior Regard he had for their interest and well fare, determined the next day to comply with their request.

Therefore, he issued a proclamation that he regretted the loss of life and damage, caused by the garrison, allegedly against the rules of war. A truce was granted. After this the citizens could walk the streets in safety, though Jacobite

157 Douglas, *History*, pp.33-34; Paton (ed.), 'Leaves', pp.547-548.
158 Tayler (ed.), *Jacobite Miscellany*, p.40.
159 Forbes, *Jacobite Memoirs*, pp.45-46.
160 Douglas, *History*, p.33; Paton, 'Leaves', p.549.
161 Stewart, *Woodhouselee* MS, pp.58-59.

troops had to remain in cover where possible. Nor was anyone molested taking provisions to the castle. Although effective, the Jacobites complained of Guest's tactics, as Duncan noted 'The conduct of the commander of the castle whether responsible or not was exaggerated by all the Enemys of the Government to the highest degree and represented as barbarous'.[162]

As in 1715, there was apparently a Jacobite plan to take the castle by a coup de main, and a soldier was taken in the castle with rope and a letter of instruction on his person. Thereafter 'none but Men of Character were posted within the drawbridge'. There was another sally by the garrison which took a 3-pounder cannon and 15 barrels of powder.[163] Guest was reportedly alert to such fears and as Duncan noted:

> The honest old gentleman, tho' worn out with years and wounds and great fatigue in his younger days, gave orders with great care and saw them executed. For he was often at midnight seen round the castle in a chair to view all the posts and see that sentries were on their Duty faithfully.[164]

Fletcher wrote on 11 October, 'General Guest has behaved well in baffling the attempt of the rebels on the castle of Edinburgh'.[165] Walpole was also approving of the castle's stance, contradicting an earlier comment of his, 'they have no hopes of taking the castle, for old Preston, the deputy-governor, and General Guest, have obliged them to supply the Castle constantly with fresh provisions, on pain of having the town fired with red-hot bullets'.[166] The castle had held and an uneasy truce existing between the Jacobite army and the garrisoned castle as neither could budge the other, nor tried. The stalemate did not last forever, for at the onset of the following month, the Jacobite army marched southwards into England, hoping for significant support from France and England, as well as military victory and a second Stuart restoration. Two regiments of dragoons and two regiments of infantry under Lieutenant General Roger Handasyde (1684-1763) reoccupied the city on 14 November and its brief period as Jacobite capital was gone forever.

Another man who distinguished himself during the siege was Ensign William Robertson, who was described glowingly by Guest on 22 November, in a letter to Tweeddale, the young man acting as:

> [A]djutant during the present unnatural rebellion, his courage and conduct, his unwearied labours day and night in defence of the castle and brave successful sallies against the rebels, attracted the eyes of all the garrison, have been acknowledged in a publick manner by the inhabitants of the city and justly gained him our particular esteem.

162 NRS, RH4/213, Duncan's Journal, 1750.
163 Douglas, *History*, pp.34-35; Bell (ed.), 'Memorials', p.220.
164 NRS, RH4/213, Duncan's Journal, 1750.
165 TNA, SP54/26, 61B, Fletcher to Unknown, 11 October 1745.
166 Lewis (ed.), *Correspondence*, Vol.19, p.126.

Bust of General Joshua Guest in Westminster Abbey. (Copyright: Dean and Chapter of Westminster Abbey)

Guest hoped that Tweeddale would mention the young man's name to the King in order to secure him a promotion.[167]

The legacy of the siege was not yet over for one man, however. Stewart was believed by some to have been responsible for the city's fall. Carlyle wrote:

> [T]here was not a Whig in the town who did not suspect that [Stewart] favoured the Pretender's cause; as however cautiously he acted in his capacity as chief magistrate, there were not a few suspected that his backwardness and coldness in the measure of arming the people, was part of a plan to admit the Pretender to the City…if that part of the town council who were Whigs had found good ground to have put Stewart under arrest, the city would have held out.[168]

The government thought so, too. Indeed, Stewart was arrested in December 1745 and held in the Tower of London until January 1747. He was put on trial that year after having been bailed for £25,000. The charge was one of 'Neglect of Duty and Misbehaviours of Persons employed in Offices and Places of publick Trust, and all Violations of the Trust and Duty of such Offices are Cares of a High Nature'. He was deemed 'grossly faulty and negligent' and there were a dozen charges against him, ranging from quibbling over the legal niceties of forming a volunteer regiment, to acting slowly on improving the city defences, refusing to have the cannon loaded and not ordering men from the Royal Navy ship to man the guns. However, his defence was able to fend off these charges with the result that Stewart was acquitted and found not guilty on 2 November 1747.[169]

167 NLS, MS 7073, f.38r, Guest to Tweeddale, 22 November 1745.
168 Kinsley (ed.), *Autobiography*, pp.122-123.
169 Anon., *Trial*, Part 1, pp.11-21.

4

Carlisle: City and Castle, 1745

Despite controversy over whether the Jacobite army should march into England by the north-east route, or even march into England at all, the decision was taken otherwise, in order to avoid fighting Field Marshal George Wade's army at Newcastle. The only resistance to an invasion by the north-west route was the border town and castle of Carlisle, just to the south of the River Esk. In 1715 the Jacobite army had bypassed it completely. It would not do so in 1745.

This was the one place in England which stood siege in the campaign and furthermore it was uniquely besieged by both sides in successive months. As with Hull, Chester and Berwick, Carlisle was one of the garrisoned walled towns and cities of the north of England which still retained much of its medieval defences. It also possessed a castle, adjoining the north of the city, which had been built at the end of the eleventh century and altered much in the twelfth. It had withstood a siege by the Scots in the thirteenth century but had fallen to a long siege by the Parliamentary forces in 1644-1645. In 1715 it had been bypassed by the Jacobite army marching from the Borders into Cumberland, and thus, in 1745, had seen no military action for exactly a century. Unlike some fortified places in England, it had not been significantly altered in the light of what was later termed the military revolution where fortifications were amended to resist artillery. The castle was occupied by a small garrison, but both governor (Lieutenant General Sir John Folliot) and lieutenant governor (Lord Howard) were absentee. In this it was no different to the majority of royal fortresses in the British Isles.

On the north side of Carlisle was the River Eden and on the west side the River Caldew. There were three main entrances to the small city. To the north was Scotch Gate, leading to a stone bridge over the Eden. To the south were suburbs and the southern gate was the English Gate. There were also suburbs to the west and the entrance there was the Irish Gate.[1] At the end of the previous century, traveller Celia Fiennes had written 'the walls of the town and the battlements and towers are in very good repaire and looks well'.[2] Daniel Defoe, writing some decades later, put it likewise, 'the city is strong…

1 Ray, *History*, pp.81-82.

2 Christopher Morris (ed.), *The Journeys of Celia Fiennes* (London: Cresset Press, 1949), p.202.

part of the town rounds the sea, as the wall rounds the whole, is very firm and strong. But Carlisle is strong by situation, being almost surrounded with rivers'.[3] A contemporary historian declared that the town walls were six feet high and five feet broad, with a five foot ditch, which was hardly impressive as a defensive work.[4]

However, it seemed, in 1745, to some of the Jacobites, to be a difficult place to take. Maxwell wrote of it thus:

> In former times it was reckoned a place of great strength, and one of the keys of England. It's surrounded by a strong wall, flanked with towers, and on the north side of the town is a kind of citadel, seated upon a little eminence, which commands the town and country round. It's a triangular fortification, separated from the town by a good ditch and rampart…It's a large building, and as strong as the thickness of stone walls can make it.[5]

Elcho agreed and wrote that 'the Castle, which is a very Strong place and cant be taken without battering cannon, of which the Prince had none… Whatever the town might be brought to by threating to burn it or scale the walls, the Castle was impregnable to the Princes army'.[6]

Maxwell added that its strength was even more so because of the weakness of the besiegers, 'As the Prince had no battering cannon, it was hardly possible to reduce the place if it was well defended'. Yet 'as it was a place of great importance in many respects it must be attempted'.[7]

Another Jacobite view of town and castle was:

> The city of Carlisle is quite encompassed with a brick wall the parapet and wall about eight feet high at top but broader at bottom, and generally there is a ditch around the same. The walls are about sixteen feet high, there are three gates by which you enter the city…The citadel is an old fortification almost ruined and stands between the Scots and English gate. The castle is a very large and regular fortification lying on the south west of the Scots gate containing a higher and lower garrison, encompassed with strong walls two moats, almost filled with water over which are two drawbridge and the situation sits on an eminence that the batteries command the avenues leading to every corner of the city.[8]

Yet this was not a universally held view. James Johnstone, a Jacobite officer, wrote that:

> The fortifications are in the old style and have been entirely neglected for several centuries, in consequence of the cessation of the long wars between the two

3 Pat Rogers (ed.), *Daniel Defoe's Tour of the Whole Island* (Harmondsworth: Penguin, 1971), p.556.
4 Andrew Henderson, *History of the Rebellion* (London: Unknown Publisher, 1748), p.56.
5 Maxwell, *Narrative*, p.63.
6 Elcho, *Short Account*, p.312.
7 Maxwell, *Narrative*, p.63.
8 NRS, GD124/10/519, Copy Journal of Prince Charles' Army, describing the taking of Carlisle, November 1745.

> countries, and the final union of the Crowns, on the death of Queen Elizabeth... The castle was formerly a place of considerable strength, but at present its walls, like those of the town, are falling from age into decay.[9]

The castle was certainly not comparable in strength to Edinburgh nor Stirling. Those tasked with its defence were similarly unenthusiastic. When Lieutenant Colonel James Durand of the 1st Foot Guards arrived on 11 October to take command, he noted, 'I found it in a very weak and defenceless condition; having no ditch, no outworks of any kind, no cover'd ways, the walls very thin in most places and without proper flanks'. Folliott commented in 1746 that the defences had not been repaired since 1737 and concurred with Durand, 'it was in a very weak condition, there being neither ditch, covered way, no flankers...he went up to a part of the Rampart between the town and the castle, he was advised not to go too near the wall for fear it should break down'.[10]

Captain John Bernard Gilpin, who had served at the castle since 1738, remarked that it had a circuit of 700 yards, but lacked a defensive ditch, because where it existed it was filled with rubbish and so was passable. A section of the wall, 60 yards long, was low and so scalable. The wall to the right of the gate was very old, thin and decayed, with many cracks and lacked a rampart. The old gateway was easy to open and was undefended by flanking towers. The Lady's Walk section of wall was also very low.[11]

However, preparations for the defence of the city and castle had been taking place since September, even before the Battle of Prestonpans. On 12 September the inhabitants resolved to defend themselves against 'an Insurrection in Scotland by the Highlanders' and 560 of the male residents entered their names in a list of the city's defenders, noting 'We are in apprehensions and preparing for a Defence, which we hope to be able to make against such a force'. [12] On 19 September, Newcastle told Gilpin, 'if they should attempt to make themselves masters of Carlisle, I am persuaded they will fail in it, as I am confident you will do your utmost for the defence of the Place'.[13]

Preparations stepped up a gear after that battle when the place was potentially in the front line of the conflict. The news of the defeat caused concern locally as Alderman Thomas Pattinson, the deputy mayor, wrote to Newcastle on 26 September about the few troops there and so, 'This extream nakedness makes me feel the bad consequences'.[14]

Initial steps to rectify the situation were taken by Pattinson; the city's mayor, James Agilonby, was present but for reasons unknown did not take the lead in the city's defence. On 18 September, an order for 300 muskets and bayonets was despatched to the city and Newcastle sent Pattinson

---

9 James Johnstone, *Memoir of the Chevalier de Johnstone* (London: Folio Society, 1958), p.49.
10 George Gill Mounsey, *Carlisle in 1745* (London: Unknown Publisher, 1846), pp.72, 81.
11 Mounsey, *Carlisle*, p.80.
12 TNA, SP36/67, f243r-52r, Pattinson to Newcastle, 12 September 1745.
13 TNA, SP36/68, f149r, Newcastle to Gilpin, 19 September 1745.
14 TNA, SP36/69, f.105r, Pattinson to Newcastle, 26 September 1745.

commissions for him to appoint officers for the city volunteer force. These arms were soon distributed and men formed into companies.[15] Pattinson, however, was not still confident about the city's defence, writing 'what may lie in my power to encourage the citizens shall not be wanting'. The county's Lord Lieutenant, Viscount Lonsdale (1694-1751) noted that Pattinson 'is in great Distress to know how to conduct himself if the Rebels attack'.[16] What was needed was additional help, Pattinson informing Newcastle on 2 October that 'We are resolved to defend for His Majesty's Government and are not afraid of them, but could wish for some military assistance'.[17]

Meanwhile, the civilian authorities took a number of steps to prepare the city for a siege. Provisions from the neighbouring county were brought into the city so that it might stand a siege. On 30 September the city minute book noted that 100 bushels of potatoes and 30 bushels of wheat 'for the service of the city' be ordered.[18]

A sharp look out was kept on strangers and two men were arrested. Earthworks were erected and deal boxes brought onto the walls to keep the cannons dry. Coals and candles were provided for night watch, to keep the men warm as well as to help them see any enemies approaching the walls.[19]

On 3 October, Newcastle decided to comply with Pattinson's request to a limited degree. He told him that the major military effort was being initially concentrated in the north east of England, 'The King is truly sensible of the importance of Carlisle and would be very glad if it were practicable to send you a succour of Troops, but in the present circumstances you must be sensible that cannot be done till Marshal Wade shall arrive with his Army', but he would send a man (Durand) who was 'a good officer and also a tolerable engineer'.[20] However, Durand was also 'lame with the gout and could not move so nimbly as he otherwise would have done'.[21]

On the same day Newcastle wrote thus to Durand, 'immediately repair to Carlisle... take upon you the command of the Garrison, that's there and of any Troops, that shall be sent there to reinforce it, and for the Defence of the place in case it should be attacked by the Rebels'. He should have the same powers as if he were governor and was reminded that it was of the 'greatest consequence, that you should proceed with the utmost expedition to Carlisle'.[22] Chancellor of the Cathedral, Dr John Waugh (1703-1765) was told, of Durand, by Newcastle on that day, 'I am persuaded he will do the best he can to defend the town; and I am sure he will not want any assistance, or lights, that you can give him'.[23]

---

15 TNA SP44/133, p.142; SP36/68, f151r, Newcastle to Backhouse, 19 September 1745.

16 TNA, SP36/69, ff105r, 270r, Pattinson to Newcastle, 26 September 1745; Lonsdale to Newcastle, 30 September 1745.

17 TNA, SP36/70, f.49r, Pattinson to Newcastle, 2 October 1745.

18 TNA, SP36/70, f49r Pattinson to Newcastle, 2 October 1745; Cumbria Archive Service (CAS), Ca2/6, p.191, Carlisle Corporation Minutes, 1745.

19 Mounsey, *Carlisle*, p.59; TNA, SP36/70, ff.82r-86v, Newcastle to Waugh, 3 October 1745; CAS (Carlisle), Ca4/41, Carlisle Corporation Accounts, 1745.

20 TNA, SP36/70, f.79v, Newcastle to Pattinson, 3 October 1745.

21 Mounsey, *Carlisle*, p.62.

22 TNA, SP36/70, f.82r, Newcastle to Durand, 3 October 1745.

23 TNA, SP36/70, f.84r, Newcastle to Waugh, 3 October 1745.

On the morning of 11 October, Durand arrived at Carlisle. Along with Captain Gilpin, in command of one of the two Invalid companies in the castle, he viewed the defences and was shocked at what he saw, as noted above. However, he told Gilpin 'not to mention our opinion of the weakness of the place for fear of discouraging the militia and inhabitants; but on the contrary, to speak of it as a strong place and very tenable'.[24] However, it was not all bad news; Durand deemed the disposition of what forces there were to be very good. The difficulty was that there were insufficient men to stand a siege; 650 in all, mostly townsmen and militia, Durand later noting 'These appearing to me too weak a garrison for town and castle'. He asked Lonsdale to have the counties' other five companies of militia to be brought into Carlisle. The Lord Lieutenant was in Yorkshire during the crisis, but, on receipt of Durand's letter, he wrote to the deputy lieutenants in the counties of Cumberland and Westmorland to send the militia where Durand desired.[25]

The county militia had been ordered into being in the northern counties by an order sent on 5 September from London and which Lonsdale remitted to the clerks of the peace in Cumberland and Westmorland on 9 September.[26] He was fully aware of their shortcomings, telling Newcastle on 3 October that 'Their arms are extreamly bad and it is impossible to gain new ones in so short a time as they shall probably have'. He added that 'very little service can be reasonably expected from the militia'.[27] Of the weapons of the 282 men that we know about, 57 lacked a sword and seven a musket, 14 lacked a bayonet and nine were entirely unarmed. Of those arms held, almost half the guns and 72 of the swords were faulty.[28] However, on 21 September the city militia were raised and Lonsdale reported that his subordinates 'had proceeded in this service with great chearfulness'.[29] Yet, according to Waugh, 'the [county] militia officers came to our defence with great reluctance and stayed there from the first with great unwillingness and were constantly objecting to ill usage from the corporation who could not say that they did anything to oblige them'.[30]

There were other shortcomings noted about the militia. Apparently 'The Westmorland company came very unwillingly'. Others were there 'tho' much against their inclinations or intentions'. However, some were 'ready and willing to do their best service for the defence of the place'. It should also be noted that Durand 'had no command over them'.[31] And, as Durand later noted, 'The militia were out every morning at exercise'.[32]

A month later there was a crisis. The money to pay the county militiamen their wages expired (only a month's wages had been raised). Some men left

24 Mounsey, *Carlisle*, p.72.
25 Mounsey, *Carlisle*, p.72.
26 Rupert Jarvis (ed.), *The Jacobite Risings of 1715 and 1745* (Carlisle: Cumberland County Council, 1954), pp.230-31.
27 TNA, SP36/68, f199v-200v, Lonsdale to Newcastle, 3 October 1745.
28 Jarvis (ed.), *Jacobite Risings*, pp.249-58.
29 TNA, SP36/69, f21v, Lonsdale to Newcastle, 21 September 1745.
30 RA, CP7/62, Waugh to Cumberland, 21 November 1745.
31 Mounsey, *Carlisle*, pp.59-60, 63.
32 TNA, WO71/19, p.292, General Courts Martial, 1746-1747.

Carlisle to make their way home and others talked of following suit. Sir John Pennington, colonel of the militia, had the militia cavalry round up those who had left and brought them back to the city. There was an emergency meeting of local gentry over the issue of paying the men. Sir George Fleming (1667-1747), Carlisle's elderly bishop, attended the meeting and spoke strongly on the need to do so. Durand offered 50 guineas to the project. The meeting resolved to order the clerk of the peace to advance the money to the militiamen and this worked.[33]

Steps were also taken to improve the artillery complement. Gilpin organised the arrival of 10 cannon of between 2- and 4-pounder calibre from ships at Whitehaven to be brought to Carlisle and these were mounted on platforms on the walls. As there were initially only six cannon balls per gun, orders for more were given and so six cartloads of cannon balls from Whitehaven arrived. There were already 80 townsmen allocated to the 20 guns in the castle and another 40 were set to man the 10 guns on the city walls. The latter gunners were instructed by the castle's master gunner.[34]

However, there was conflict between military and civil authorities over the former's wishes to strengthen the defences. Durand wanted the city's gates blocked up and property near the walls destroyed in order to deny the attackers cover. Yet as regards the former, the magistrates believed it 'would be an infinite prejudice to the city', presumably because it would be a hindrance to commerce and thus the wealth of the merchants. They also objected to the demolition of property near the walls, 'and said it was private property and they could not do it'. The cost of these buildings was £150. If they were destroyed the corporation would have to at the very least reimburse the owners and possibly face further prosecution for such illegal actions. Durand was forced to acquiesce, for 'fear of disobliging the town, upon whose inhabitants I partly depended for the defence'.[35]

However, he was able to make a few improvements. The Scotch and Irish Gates, both of which were single gates with no drawbridge or outworks to cover them, were blocked up, leaving only the English Gate accessible. Here, at least the outward gate was iron and it was flanked by a round tower, on which Durand had a cannon mounted, so that it could not easily be forced. He had sandbags filled and materials necessary for walling up the gates to be gathered together. He had 400 grenades loaded and primed. Provisions from the countryside were gathered in to ensure enough food for the garrison for two months. Ladders within a seven-mile radius of Carlisle were taken in, as were pickaxes and shovels, and it was ensured that there were enough wells for water. A few outlying sheds were demolished. The Horse Militia was sent out as scouts and on one occasion captured a Jacobite quartermaster, who was sent to Newcastle.[36]

The militia and townsmen were to prove less than effective. In the case of the townsmen this was because they were unpaid and so, having paid

33 Mounsey, *Carlisle*, p.72.

34 Mounsey, *Carlisle*, pp.72-73.

35 Mounsey, *Carlisle*, pp.61-62, 73.

36 Mounsey, *Carlisle*, pp.73-74.

occupations, were reluctant to spend time away from the latter, so their drill and other military training was limited. Conversely, the militia may have been too enthusiastic. Durand instituted an alarm system in case any danger was sighted. This was used too much by the nervous inhabitants with the result that the militiamen became exhausted with being called out under arms on every occasion, presumably at night time as well as during the day time. The militia were divided into three reliefs and a picquet, and Durand wanted only a third to be on duty at any one time in order to allow the others to rest. The militia thought they should not be on guard all night and wanted the townsmen to share the burden, but the latter refused. None thought that they should be under Durand's orders and indeed they were not (the townsmen being led by the deputy mayor and the militia by Pennington).[37]

There was, however, the possibility of additional military support. In London Lieutenant General Folliot, the governor, was in discussion with Newcastle and the former applied for 500 men from either St Clair's or Battereau's Regiments which had been despatched to England from Ireland. Waugh claimed that Newcastle had told him that Carlisle was not worth the cost of an express message. If this was true, then it showed extreme short sightedness on Newcastle's part.[38] There was also a request for two companies of Howard's Regiment from Newcastle to be sent, but they never arrived, either.[39]

However, as long as the Jacobites remained in Scotland, morale was high. Pattinson told Newcastle on 7 October, 'The loyal Corporation and Townsmen are in good heart'.[40] Ten days later he wrote 'as to this city we are not in the least afraid of the Rebels, being resolved to defend it to the utmost of our power'. One Dorothy Palmer was equally impressed, 'nor do we think the Rebills will attempt to take Carlisle should they come this way, the place being well provided with all things for a siege and the inhabitants resolved to loose their lives before the surrender'.[41] On the last day of October, Pattinson reassured Newcastle, 'be under no fears for Carlisle, for the Rebels can't take us, if we are honest, which is what I have no reason to doubt, not but that we have some timerous persons amongst us'.[42]

The defenders were composed of the following:

Castle Garrison:

- Two Independent companies of Invalids in Carlisle castle (80 men), described as 'very old and infirm'.
- 37 men from Cope's army who had fled after Prestonpans.

37 Mounsey, *Carlisle*, pp.74-75.
38 Mounsey, *Carlisle*, p.95.
39 TNA, WO71/19, p.293, General Courts Martial, 1746-1747.
40 TNA, SP36/70, f244r, Pattinson to Newcastle, 7 October 1745.
41 TNA, SP36/71, 270r, Pattinson to Newcastle, 17 October 1745; J.P. Dalton (ed.), 'Cumberland and the Forty Five: Some Letters', *Transactions of the Cumberland and Westmorland Antiquarian and Archaeological Society*, 2nd series, Vol.XLV (1946), p.108.
42 TNA, SP36/72, f.396r, Pattinson to Newcastle, 31 October 1745.

City Garrison:

- Cumberland and Westmorland Militia. Elcho thought these amounted to 2,000 infantry and 100 cavalry.[43] However, initially the force was of two companies, numbering 150 men, but a further five companies were brought into Carlisle, totalling in all perhaps 525 men. Apparently 'their arms consisted of different kinds of fowling pieces bad old muskets, which were but in a very bad order'.
- Troop of militia Horse, 70 men
- Carlisle Volunteers; nine companies of 30 men each

Artillery:
Twenty 6-pounders (Durand claimed these were 9-pounders but Captain Gilpin said otherwise and he had been there for several years) in the castle and later the 10 light guns from Whitehaven in the town. Manned by 80 townsmen and supervised by John Steadman, the castle's master gunner and three other gunners. Of the latter, one was 'very old and infirm' and the other two townsmen who were never properly trained. There were also 16 mortars, which seem not to have been employed.

Total: 117 regulars, 525 militia infantry, 70 militia cavalry, 350 armed townsmen, total of 1,062 men.

Lieutenant Colonel James Durand was the castle garrison's commander. The Invalid companies were led by Captains Gilpin (an infantry officer of 22 years' experience, who had been at Carlisle since 1738) and John Cowley, with Lieutenants George Smith and John Houldsworth. Sir John Pennington was the colonel of the Foot Militia and Colonel Dacre in charge of the Militia cavalry.[44]

Besiegers:
- Atholl Brigade (3 battalions totalling 1,000 men)
- Roy Stuart's Edinburgh Regiment (200 men)
- Ogilvie's Regiment (200 men)
- Glenbucket's Regiment (200 men)
- Duke of Perth's Regiment (130 men)
- Elcho's Lifeguards (150 men)
- Kilmarnock's Horse (70 men)
- Pitsligo's Horse (150 men)

  Total, 1,730 infantry and 370 cavalry; grand total of 2,100 men.[45]

43 Elcho, *Short Account*, p.312.

44 Mounsey, *Carlisle*, pp.72, 81; TNA, SP36/71, f271r, Waugh to Newcastle, 9 October 1745; NRS, GD124/10/519, Copy Journal of Prince Charles' Army, describing the taking of Carlisle, November 1745.

45 Elcho, *Short Account*, between p.324 and p.325.

Artillery: six 1 1/2-pounders, four coehorn mortars, two royals (taken from Cope's army after Prestonpans) and six 'Swedish' guns from France.[46] The six guns and two mortars were described as follows on 21 September. The six guns had six-foot-long barrels; two had been made in 1719, two in 1721 and two in 1741. All were 2 ½-inch bore. The two royal mortars had 5 ¾-inch bore and the small coehorns 4-inch bore. They had plentiful ammunition; in total the cannon had 162 cannon balls and 61 bags of grape shot; there were 28 coehorn grenades and 40 for small coehorns, along with 11 barrels of gunpowder.[47]

The besiegers were commanded by the Duke of Perth, who had no prior military experience, 'though brave even to excess, every way honourable, and possessed of a very mild and gentle disposition, was of very limited abilities and interfered with nothing'.[48] However, as Sir John MacDonald later wrote, 'The Duke of Perth, who had learned a little of the art of fortification in his youth, was determined on the siege of this town, and obtained permission to undertake it with his own people, the rest having refused the task'.[49]

On Saturday 9 November it was market day in Carlisle. Because of the impending crisis it was decided that it should still be held but that it should only take place in the suburbs outside the city walls. Drums were beaten and all stood to arms on this day.[50] This was just as well, for a party of 50-60 of Major Baggot's Jacobite hussars were ordered by Charles to reconnoitre Carlisle and stood on Grimber Hill, two miles north from Carlisle. At one o'clock were at Stanwix bank (to the north east of the city), and they then reached the bridge. At first the guns could not fire on them for they were mingled with country people returning home from the market. At three, however, the latter had dispersed and so the guns from the castle fired upon them and they retreated. They reported to Charles, now at Rockcliffe, that 'he could see a good many people upon the walls, that they seemed very alert and that they had no sooner observed them on the Bridge than they fired some of their Guns from the Castle, but without doing any execution'.[51] At three that afternoon, a countryman was despatched with a verbal message from the Jacobites to the mayor, ordering that they provide accommodation for 13,000 infantry and 3,000 cavalry that night (over treble the actual numbers of the Jacobite army) or they would reduce the town to ashes. This was refused, there was cannon fire against them. That night the Jacobites began to encircle the city.[52]

Durand noted that 'the whole garrison appeared in the highest spirits, and seem'd resolved to defend the town to the last'. Even so, he sent an express to Wade, who was at Newcastle-upon-Tyne with a sizeable British-Dutch army, to tell him of the Jacobites' arrival outside the city.[53] In 1748 two Carlisle

46 Elcho, *Short Account*, p.313; Johnstone, *Memoir*, p.49.
47 RA, CP5/318, Inventory of stores taken at Prestonpans, 1745.
48 Johnstone, *Memoir*, p.33.
49 Tayler and Tayler (eds), *1745*, p.91n.
50 Mounsey, *Carlisle*, p.75.
51 Bell (ed.), 'Memorials', pp.238-239; Douglas, *History*, p.51.
52 Douglas, *History*, pp.48-49.
53 Mounsey, *Carlisle*, p.75.

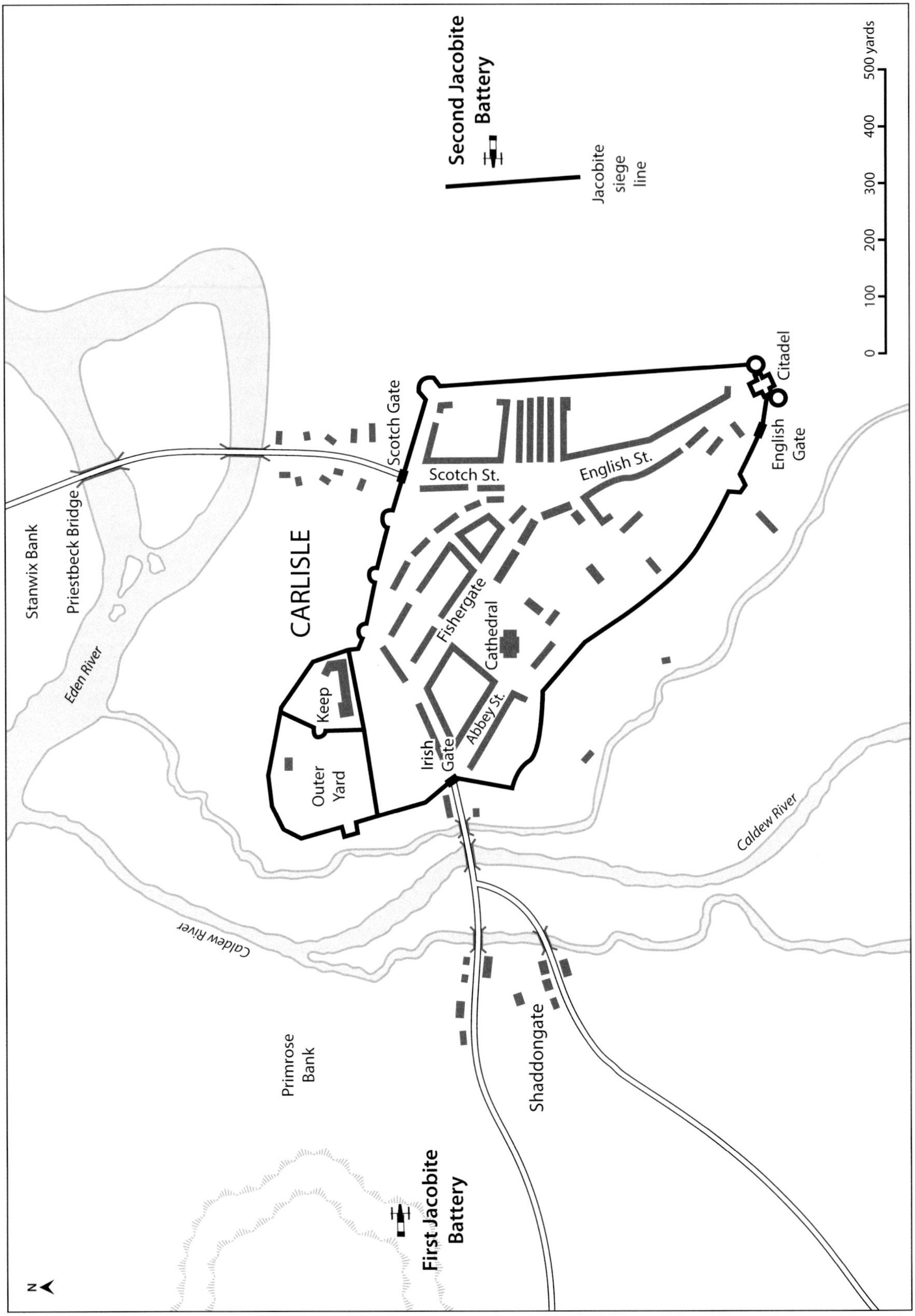

Carlisle and environs, November 1745.

men claimed recompense for having taken letters to Wade; John Porter and Thomas Thompson, as will be noted another messenger was sent later on, but which man carried which message is unknown.[54]

On 10 November, the entire Jacobite army was formed on Carlisle moor to the north west of Carlisle. As time went on, the south and west were blockaded by the column that Charles had led from Edinburgh; the north and the east by Murray's. However, a thick fog had enveloped the place, making reconnoitring impossible. According to O'Sullivan, 'There was such a fog, yt day, yt a man cou'd hardly see his horses Ears'.[55] It did not lift until two o'clock in the afternoon. In the meantime scouts were sent from the city and ascertained that there were several bodies of Jacobites in its vicinity.[56]

At this point a body of Jacobites, including the Atholl Brigade and the MacPhersons, along with the Duke of Perth, O'Sullivan and Captain Francis Geoghegan, approached the walls, at first approaching the west side and then veering towards the south, reconnoitring the place. Some went into the suburbs by the English Gate and as close to the walls as pistol range. They were fired at from both castle and city as some approached the Irish Gate and some were seen on Carlisle Fields; in both cases the Jacobites hastily departed out of range.[57] At two in the afternoon a message was penned in the Jacobite camp and it was received in the city an hour later. It read:

> Being come to recover the King our father's just rights, for which we are arrived with all his authority, we are sorry to find that you should prepare to obstruct our passage. We therefore, to avoid the effusion of English blood, hereby require you to open your gates, and let us enter as we desire, in a peaceable manner; which if you do, we shall take care to preserve you from any insult, and set an example to all England of the exactness with which we intend to fulfil the King our father's declaration and our own. But if you shall refuse us entrance we are fully resolved to enforce it by such means as Providence has put into our hands: and then it will not perhaps be in our power to prevent the dreadful consequences which usually attends a town's being taken by assault. Consider seriously of this, and let me have your answer in the space of two hours; for we shall take any further delay as peremptory refusal, and take our measures accordingly.

It was signed by Charles, styling himself regent of the British Kingdoms.[58] Durand, the militia officers and the chief inhabitants of Carlisle examined the message at the Bush public house. Durand recalled, 'all treated it with the contempt it deserved' and detained the messenger.[59] No answer was sent, except by cannon fire, which continued into the night. There was also a summons to Durand to surrender within two hours of receipt, but a flag of defiance was raised and two cannons fired by way of answer. Meanwhile, the

54 Jarvis, *Jacobite Risings*, pp.393-394.
55 Tayler and Tayler (eds), *1745*, p.92.
56 Mounsey, *Carlisle*, p.75.
57 Mounsey, *Carlisle*, p.75.
58 Douglas, *History*, p.49.
59 Mounsey, *Carlisle*, pp.75-76; NRS, GD124/10/519, Copy Journal of Prince Charles' army, describing the taking of Carlisle, November 1745.

Jacobites decided to erect a battery to the north west of the English Gate, 80 yards from the walls and sheltered by enclosures. Men from Perth's Regiment and the Atholl Brigade were involved in this manual work. Perth desired the command and it was given to him. O'Sullivan went to reconnoitre the best place for the battery 'but found there was no possibility of undertaking any thing there, it was within a small musquet shot of the Castle, [it was 80 yards from the walls] not a picaxe, Shouvel or fascine to raise a Battery, & if there were, it would signify nothing wth our Artillery'. He reported this to Charles and was told that another place to attack from should be found on the next day, somewhere that would be not so exposed to the garrison's fire.[60]

The rest of the Jacobite army were quartered in villages around Carlisle, Murray posting men in such a way that all communications between the city and the outside world be severed. Those not taking part in the siege were predominantly the clansmen, who, as O'Sullivan remarked, 'the highlanders are not fit for Seeges'.[61] Some of the hussars and infantry were at Blackhall. That night, Charles received news that Field Marshal Wade was either on the march or preparing to do set out, from Newcastle, with over 10,000 men. Charles then ordered several of his regiments to prepare to march to Brampton at daybreak, believing that would be the best battleground.[62]

Apparently, however, the garrison expected an assault that evening, as the thick fog returned. The walls were thus lined with men and lights were everywhere. To increase the men's morale, the city and county notables such as Pennington, Dacre and Waugh stood with them. The militia were drawn up in Castle Street, so as to reinforce the men on the wall where necessary.[63]

The attack never came and therefore, on the 11 November, much of the Jacobite army marched to Brampton, seven miles to the east of Carlisle, along the road to Newcastle. They did so with great enthusiasm, as Murray of Broughton later wrote, 'It is almost impossible to describe the joy that was in every bodys' face upon the news of Wade's approach; the Chevalier him self expressed the utmost Satisfaction'.[64] The site for the battle they anticipated was deemed 'a very proper place to wait for Wade (his horse cou'd be of no manner of use), & very fit for Highlanders – Hillocks, morasses, he cou'd hardly find a place to set himself in battle & there we expected to give a good acct of him, if he once come into it'.[65] At ten that day, Charles was at Warwick-on-Eden. A number of Jacobites, taken by the garrison to be the rearguard, were seen at Stanwix Bank. The garrison's artillery fired on them, and they fled. That night they occupied Rickerby and adjacent villages, to the north of the river Eden. They were given orders to march to Brampton. Some stragglers and two supply wagons were allegedly taken by the garrison.[66]

---

60 Tayler and Tayler (eds), *1745*, p.92.

61 Tayler and Tayler (eds), *1745*, p.92; James Duke of Atholl (ed.), *Chronicles of the Atholl and Tullibardine Families* (Edinburgh: Privately Published, 1908), Vol.III, p.81.

62 Bell (ed.), 'Memorials', pp.239-240.

63 Douglas, *History*, p.52.

64 Bell (ed.), 'Memorials', p.240.

65 Tayler and Tayler (eds), *1745*, p.93.

66 Douglas, *History*, pp.49-50.

Earlier that morning, there had been alarm in Carlisle that there were Jacobites near to the Irish Gate. Firing had been heard at two and in the daylight a number of Lowlanders and their horses were found there. They said that they had been forced into Jacobite service, and were detained. In the afternoon there were two other minor victories for the garrison; one of the French officers in Jacobite employ was killed at Stanwix by artillery fire and his fellows retreated, and later in the day two wagonloads of biscuits for the Jacobite army were taken by countrymen and brought into Carlisle.[67]

On 12 November, the Jacobite army stood at Brampton, Warwick Bridge and adjacent places. They had their sixteen guns with them.[68] A party of horsemen under Colonel Henry Kerr of Graden was sent eastwards to ascertain intelligence about Wade's forces, but they learnt that he was not within 30 miles and had not shifted from Newcastle. At a council of war decided to besiege Carlisle with part of the army 'as it was a place of great importance in many respects it must be attempted'.[69]

It had been, naturally, a quiet day for the garrison. They could not perceive any Jacobite movement, so scouts were despatched and they reported that most of the Jacobite artillery and baggage could not be found. There were only a few patrols at Warwick Bridge.[70] It was, however, the calm before the storm. Pattinson and others thought they had beaten off the Jacobites and he wrote a letter to Lonsdale to tell him of this triumph. Lonsdale thus wrote to Newcastle and on 14 November, apparent good news travelling fast, the latter wrote:

> I have sent it to the King... I beg your lordship would be as good as to acquaint the Mayor of Carlisle with the satisfaction that Every Body here, has in the behaviour of the Town of Carlisle, which we hope, will be an Example to other Places, should the Rebels advance further into England.[71]

On 13 November, realising that Wade was not on the march, 'This agreeable prospect being now vanish'd' the Jacobite army marched back to Carlisle, although only some of them took part in the siege. By choice, Lord George Murray commanded the blockading force, to prevent any relief from arriving, 'declared yt for his part he understood nothing of seeges'.[72] Despite the foul weather, Charles was adamant that his army not be idle. Perth was in charge of the siege operations. By night time batteries were erected, using local forced labour and trenches were dug on the east side of Carlisle, between the Scotch and English Gates, within musket shot of the walls, whilst Perth's headquarters were at cannon range from the walls. Scaling ladders were also being made. The Jacobite batteries were fired upon from Carlisle, by 'a Very smart fire from the walls of Cannon and small arms'.[73]

67 Mounsey, *Carlisle*, p.76.
68 Douglas, *History*, p.50.
69 Elcho, *Short Account*, p.312; Maxwell, *Narrative*, p.63.
70 Mounsey, *Carlisle*, p.76.
71 TNA, SP36/73, f363r, Lonsdale to Newcastle, 14 November 1745.
72 Tayler and Tayler (eds), *1745*, p.93.
73 Bell (ed.), 'Memorials', p.240; Douglas, *History*, p.50.

Perth's men were tired and some had to perform guard duty to escort the cannon and ammunition, helping bring it to the front, and in cutting fascines, as did John Roy Stuart's Edinburgh Regiment. He asked Murray for some detachments of men but was refused in this. However, Perth 'did what he cou'd to encourage his men giving 'um money, & by his own exemple'.[74]

Despite the fact that Perth was 'indefatigable in that service and who meets with innumerable difficulties', working on the siege was not popular among the men. According to Murray, 'the men posted upon the blockade of Carlisle will not expose themselves either in trenches or all night in the open air, within cannon shot, or even musket shot, of the town, except be in their turn with the rest of the army'. Murray recommended that drafts of 50 men from each regiment (Perth's, Ogilvie's, Glenbucket's, and the Atholl Brigade) be used in rotation to guard the battery.[75] He was also critical as to the siting of the battery, 'the ground is marshy, and vastly too much exposed…I suspect the place pitched upon will not answer'.[76] According to Murray of Broughton, Lord George Murray's behaviour was exemplary:

> [T]he disposition [was] left to himself, which he performed with so much judgement, that the few French officers then in the army allow'd they had never seen anything of the kind better executed, and regreted that a man possessed of so fine a natural genius for war Should not have been bred a Solger.[77]

Ogilvie's men stood between Rickerby and Stanwix from 13-15 November to blockade Carlisle to the east.[78]

However, events were unfolding on 13 November inside the walls to the Jacobites' advantage. They heard that the Jacobites were using local labour and carpenters to make scaling ladders from trees at Corby Castle and at Warwick, and there was worse news to come. It was three in the afternoon and Durand was sitting down to dinner with the militia officers and gentlemen. An express arrived from Wade, in response to the one that they had sent a few days ago. Durand felt obliged to show the letter to those seated with him. Wade had written that 'I don't hear they have sufficient [artillery] to make a breach in the walls' and that they should not worry, ending the letter thus, 'I wish you all imaginable success'. This was a conventional and unimaginative enough response, for usually a successful siege entailed the besieging artillery making a significant breach in the city or castle walls and the Jacobite artillery was incapable of such. Yet Wade failed to take into account the vital factor of morale. Implicit of course, was the fact that he did not intend to march to their relief.[79] William Fletcher later wrote that 'the militia proposed to keep the Rebels out 8 or 10 days longer if any promise of Assistance in that time' had been given.[80]

74 Tayler and Tayler (eds), *1745*, p.94.
75 Atholl (ed.), *Chronicles*, Vol.III, p.90.
76 Forbes, *Jacobite Memoirs*, pp.49-50.
77 Bell (ed.), 'Memorials', p.240.
78 Anon., *The Miscellany of the Spalding Club* (Aberdeen: Spalding, 1841), p.295.
79 Mounsey, *Carlisle*, p.76.
80 CAS: Whitehaven, YD/Da8, Fletcher to Unknown, 17 November 1745.

Durand and Pennington tried to convince the others that the letter did not mean what it implied and Durand claimed, 'I thereupon earnestly entreated them to continue to do their duty… assuring them that they had nothing to fear from the rebels, that we were in a very good condition of defending ourselves' and if they continued as resolute as they had, 'the Rebels would never take the town'. However, the militia officers came to another conclusion and told him that they wanted to abandon Carlisle that night and asked him to have the English Gate open. He refused and eventually prevailed upon them to return to their posts. Durand then sent another express to Wade, presumably an explicit request for help, but given that the Jacobites had returned and were blockading Carlisle, the messenger could not get through and so returned.[81]

Contrary to Walpole's gibe that he was merely 'a silly race-horsing boy', Perth proved himself an inspirational commander by his example and his activity on the night of 13/14 November:

> The Duke of Perth was all night in the trenches which had been opened and conducted by Colonel James Grant with a dexterity and judgement that demonstrated him to be at the same time an able engineer as well as an expert Gunner. For the communication and parallels were perfected not withstanding a most terrible fire of cannon, mortar and small arms.

This achievement was more impressive because of the prevailing weather, which was 'a prodigious storm of snow, and the frost was so intense that nothing could equal it, but the valour and resolution of the Highlanders animated by the presence and heroick example of the General the Duke of Perth'.[82]

On 14 November, the Jacobite batteries were moved closer to the walls, about 300 yards from the castle, near the horse racing ground. Grenades were thrown at them and a besieger wrote 'the enemy redoubled their fire'. The purpose of all this was more psychological than physical. Murray of Broughton wrote that 'the Cannon were brought up to batter the Town, more to intimidate than from any thought they could peep upon the walls'.[83] Elcho agreed, writing that 'Whatever the town might be brought to do by threating to burn it or Scale the walls, the Castle was impregnable to the Princes army'.[84] O'Sullivan agreed about the potency of the Jacobite artillery, 'wch wou'd hardly beat down a barn'.[85] Johnstone wrote 'we did not discharge a single shot, lest the garrison should be acquainted with the smallness of their calibre, which might have encouraged them to defend themselves'.[86] In all this they concurred with Durand and Wade. Yet some thought the Jacobite artillery was of a higher calibre than it was, a letter of 10 November noting

81 Mounsey, *Carlisle*, pp.76-77.
82 NRS, GD124/10/519, Copy Journal of Prince Charles' Army, describing the taking of Carlisle, November 1745.
83 Bell (ed.), 'Memorials', p.240.
84 Elcho, *Short Account*, p.312.
85 Tayler and Tayler (eds), *1745*, p.92.
86 Johnstone, *Memoir*, p.51.

'it's apprehend'd in case the Rebels attack it as they have a great deal of heavy Artillery they can't hold out long'.[87] Meanwhile, the besiegers put troops near all three gates.[88]

The Jacobite entrenchments and guns had the desired effect on the inhabitants. According to a contemporary historian:

> The Terror of the Highlanders storming the Town Sword in hand, in the Night Time, having raised in their Minds a dreadful Prospect of Blood, slaughter and Rapine. Some fled over the walls in fright, mostly escaping but some being captured by the besiegers.[89]

One reason why morale among the militia was low was because of their poor treatment by the townsmen, who were their nominal allies. A letter from a gentleman in Kendal on 18 November explained the situation, having been told it by a militia captain. Apparently, the townsmen only contributed two or three men per company (out of a supposed 30) for active service. This meant that the bulk of guard duty fell to the militia; 'so that last week they were obliged to be continually upon Duty, and the week before one half reliev'd the other alternatively'. Additionally, the townsmen made the militia men pay high prices for goods they needed; especially for food, and straw on which they could lie on the walls could not be had. One Captain Wilson, an MP's son, paid £1 10s for the use of a cobbler's stall upon the walls. To conclude, 'many of them were so sick through their great Fatigue'.[90] If the militiamen were in this condition there is no reason to suggest that they had any enthusiasm for defending a city whose inhabitants were so indifferent to them.

Durand viewed the Jacobite positions and 'found a great crowd of people, who seemed to be alarmed at it'. He tried to encourage the defenders, by arguing that the Jacobite entrenchment was 'nothing but a poor paltry ditch, that did not deserve the name of an intrenchment; that the rebels had no cannon large enough to make a breach in our walls…it was only done to intimidate; and that if they would but stand by their walls the rebels could never take the town'. He ordered the cannon to fire and that day there was a constant fire from the city walls of both cannon and small arms.[91]

There was a meeting held at the King's Arms pub. The militia officers and Durand were assembled there. Once again, he argued against a surrender, reminding them that the Jacobite artillery was insufficient to blow holes in the walls, and adding that scaling ladders were useless against walls which were manned. It was no good, 'they still persisted in their resolution to capitulate, and said it was to no purpose to argue any longer about it'. Durand, Gilpin

87 Donald Nicholas (ed.), *Intercepted Post* (London: Bodley Head, 1956), p.139.
88 Elcho, *Short Account*, p.313.
89 Henderson, *History*, pp.56-57.
90 Marchant, *History*, pp.168-170.
91 Mounsey, *Carlisle*, p.77.

and the Invalid officers protested. They asked the townsmen to join them in the defence, and the latter tried to persuade the militia not to surrender.[92]

A Jacobite wrote, 'But the governor and citizens observing that our cannon were ready to be placed on the batteries and the scaling ladders brought up to attack, he thought it expedient to send out the flag of truce'.[93]

By now, however, most of those manning the walls had left them and had flung away their weapons. Durand was certain that in this chaotic atmosphere the Jacobites could take the city. He returned to the castle, asking Lieutenant John Hutchinson to go back to the King's Arms to tell the militia officers that he wanted to hold the castle and that they change their minds. In the meantime, Pattinson discovered that the townsmen were planning to join with the militia in surrender. The reason for this was 'it appearing yt no such relief is now to be had, and ourselves not being able to do duty or hold out any longer, are determined to capitulate'.[94]

Still protesting about the capitulation, Durand and his officers retired to the castle. They were probably surprised that the militia officers and 400 of their men joined them, as did some of the city clergy and gentlemen. Apparently, according to Durand, they 'all declared they would join with me in defending the castle to the last'. Before Durand completely abandoned the city, he had the ten cannon on the city walls nailed up as there was no time to move them, but arms and ammunition were transferred to the castle in time. Lieutenant Hutchinson bought up guns and bread available in the city. In the castle, two ovens, a hand mill and a smithy were erected, all preparations for a continuation of the siege.[95]

In the city, that evening a white flag was hung over the city walls. On hearing this, whilst sat down to supper at Brampton, Charles ordered Murray to go to Perth's headquarters and between them to treat with the representatives of the city, who first contacted Lord Strathallan. Furthermore, according to Elcho, in order 'to frighten them more, that the battery would fire red hot balls upon the town next day if they did not Surrender'.[96] This was scaremongering, for as O'Sullivan remarked, 'wch God knows, he was not in a condition to perform'.[97] Charles also 'charged his secretary with instructions not to do business by halves, in treating for the town and citadel w'out including the surrender of the castle'.[98] The mayor and another gentleman told the Jacobites that they agreed to surrender Carlisle on the conditions that the citizenry were unmolested, that the castle was to be given up, that the militia and officers were allowed to go home, swearing not to fight against the Jacobites for a year, that all the militia's horses and the cannon and other weaponry be left intact and delivered to the Jacobites, and that on the next

92 Mounsey, *Carlisle*, p.77.
93 NRS, GD124/10/519, Copy Journal of Prince Charles' Army, describing the taking of Carlisle, November 1745.
94 Mounsey, *Carlisle*, pp.78, 87.
95 Mounsey, *Carlisle*, pp.78, 87.
96 Elcho, *Short Account*, p.313.
97 Tayler and Tayler (eds), *1745*, p.94.
98 NRS, GD124/10/519, Copy Journal of Prince Charles' Army, describing the taking of Carlisle, November 1745.

morning the Mayor would deliver the keys to the city to Charles at Brampton. Jacobite prisoners were to be released and deserters turned over.[99]

At the same time, a Dr Douglas, representing the castle, said that the mayor could not insist on the castle's surrendering, too, and that the city should not blackmail it into doing so. Perth and Murray were contemptuous of this and believed that the terror of the inhabitants would influence the castle into surrendering. They stated that 'it was inconsistent with the Chevalier's honour to accept of one without t'other, positively insisted upon the Surrender of both and threatened that if they did not, they must give orders to fire upon the Town immediatly'. Surrender of both was eventually agreed upon.[100]

This occurred because at one in the morning of 15 November, Gilpin alerted Durand to the fact that there were no militia on the castle walls. Durand and Pennington went to order them back to the walls. Pennington found 30 of the militia and ordered them to return to their duty. This was difficult and he had to promise that they would be relieved in an hour. However, once Pennington's back was turned, the men deserted. The mutiny arose, they 'declared they would do no more duty nor would they stay and defend the castle upon any account whatsoever'. Some men went over the walls and others forced the gates open. Durand pleaded with their officers to stop them, and they promised to do so, but were unable to accomplish that. By eight that morning there were no more militia in the castle.[101] It is not known whether the 80 townsmen who were volunteer gunners had also left at this stage, but presumably they joined this civilian exodus, too.

Some of the garrison tried to escape on the night of 14 November. Jacobite Captain John Maclean noted in his diary, 'We took Severalls that were making their Escape out of Carlisle befor the terms of the Capitulation were fully agreed on'.[102]

Durand thought that the Invalids, due to their age, infirmities and that numerous fatigues they had recently undergone 'were rendered in a manner of no use'. At ten that morning the militia officers and city inhabitants told him that the Jacobites would give them no terms unless the castle surrendered as well as the city. Should Durand refuse, the Jacobites would destroy the city and massacre the inhabitants. Durand continued in his attitude of defiance and referred to 'these threatenings were words of course and meant very little'. He then consulted his officers and they then agreed that they had too few men to defend the castle and therefore had to surrender, 'the Garrison, consisting only of two companys of Invalids amounting to about 80 men, many of who are extremely infirm, and the castle so large, so that there are neither men to manage the guns nor man the walls'.[103]

---

99 Bell (ed.), 'Memorials', p.241; NRS, GD124/10/519, Copy Journal of Prince Charles' Army, describing the taking of Carlisle, November 1745.

100 Bell (ed.), 'Memorials', p.241.

101 Mounsey, *Carlisle*, p.79.

102 Iain Gordon Brown and Hugh Cheape (eds), *Witness to Rebellion* (East Linton: Tuckwell Press, 1995), p.25.

103 Mounsey, *Carlisle*, pp.79, 94.

On 15 November, the mayor and aldermen delivered the keys to the city to Charles, who assured them 'in a very obliging manner, of his future favour and Protection'. Whilst they returned, that evening Perth took possession of the city and castle, the Jacobites marching in at three as the defenders' flags were struck. Durand and Pennington were allowed to leave with their horses and baggage. They and the other officers gave their parole that they would not serve against the Jacobites for a year. However, despite a promise that arms would be left undamaged, the Jacobites found that this was not the case. The arms of the garrison could not be found, the ammunition was damaged, the cannon were spiked, and the cannon balls had been thrown about the vaults. Murray deemed this an infringement of the articles of capitulation and technically under the accepted rules of warfare this allowed Charles to massacre the garrison, though he did not do so.[104] Elcho wrote that the Jacobite army had plenty of weapons anyway so did not seek those that had been hidden.[105] However a contemporary historian claimed that the Jacobites seized three months' provisions intended for the militia and nearly 200 horses; in the castle were 500-1500 stand of arms, 50-100 barrels of gunpowder, the aforesaid artillery, and 'a great deal of military stores', including cannon balls and 300 grenades.[106] Furthermore, there were shovels, pick axes, 900 ladders, and other supplies; wheat, oatmeal, potatoes, and beer, all to have enabled the garrison to have withstood a lengthy siege.[107]

Perth's Regiment took control of the castle. There had been few casualties on either side. Murray of Broughton stated that a French officer had been killed and another soldier slightly injured.[108] This fatality was Captain Dalton of the Irish Brigade. A Gordon sentinel in Ogilvie's Regiment had had a leg shot off by a cannon ball and a 'private Highlander' had been slightly wounded.[109] None of the defenders are known to have been killed; it is unknown whether any were wounded. Given the amount of shot, ball, and shell being fired, these losses are minimal indeed.

There had been a falling out among the Jacobite high command, however. Lord George Murray was unhappy that Murray of Broughton had negotiated with the mayor and that Perth (his fellow lieutenant general) had been given such a prominent role because the latter's Catholicism would bode against him in England. This was unfair; the division of command earlier had been agreed on and the Highlanders under Murray's command would not have been very good troops in siege warfare. Lord George, tactically gifted and personally brave, was arrogant and high-handed and 'was resolved to have the sole Command and therefore represented how improper it was that the Duke of Perth, a Roman Catholic, Should have any Command in England'. He went so far as to offer to resign his commission and serve as a

104 Bell (ed.), 'Memorials', pp.242-243.
105 Elcho, *Short Account*, p.315.
106 Henderson, *History*, p.57.
107 NRS, GD124/10/519, Copy Journal of Prince Charles' Army, describing the taking of Carlisle, November 1745.
108 Bell (ed.), 'Memorials', p.242.
109 NRS, GD124/10/519, Copy Journal of Prince Charles' Army, describing the taking of Carlisle, November 1745.

volunteer. Elcho and others supported Lord George in this, what amounted to blackmail. Despite Perth's dissatisfaction, he was able to swallow his pride for the common good and had Charles' cause uppermost in his mind, so he agreed to relinquish his command, but this 'completed the dryness that had almost from the beginning Subsisted betwixt them'.[110]

Despite this dissension at the highest levels, the outcome of the siege had been a great triumph for the Jacobites and unlike the case with Edinburgh, had been a complete victory at such a cheap cost. It added much to their reputation that they were able to take the city and castle so quickly. On 17 November, Charles rode into Carlisle, welcomed by a discharge of artillery. James III was proclaimed on the next day, though the townsmen seemed far from enthusiastic.[111] However, given that they had 'been taught to expect no less usage than fire and destruction...became reconciled to the politeness, justice and oeconomy of the officers of all ranks'.[112]

There was a great deal of military criticism about the surrender, as there had been after hearing what happened at Edinburgh. In the following month Colonel Joseph Yorke (1724-1792), a staff officer, wrote, after the alleged weak resistance shown in a later siege, 'shews how infamously it was surrendered on the Rebels' approach, who certainly would never have been able to take it at all if the people had done their duty'.[113] Maxwell, wrote of Durand, 'he made but a sorry defence'.[114]

Civilians, too, were loud in their condemnation, safe as they were in London. Miss Gertrude Saville wrote in her diary, 'the braging loyal town, with the Melitia of 2 Countys in it, many Cannon and other Arms, surrender'd (like boasting deceitful Edinburgh), without a Gun shott against it'.[115] Walpole was also loud in his commentary in a letter to Horace Mann on 22 November, writing:

> We were put into great spirits by an heroic Letter from the Mayor of Carlisle, who had fired on the Rebels and made them retire; he concluded with saying "And so I think the Town of Carlisle has done his Majesty more service than the great city of Edinburgh, or than all of Scotland together"...But alack! The next day the Rebels returned...The great Mr Pattinson...instantly surrendered the town and agreed to pay two thousand pounds to save it from pillage. Well! Then we were assured that the citadel would hold out seven or eight days; but did not so many hours.[116]

Not all would have agreed with these assessments. Naturally, Durand was quick to make his explanations, writing to Folliott on 18 November, detailing his opposition to the surrender and laying the blame elsewhere. He

110 Bell (ed.), 'Memorials', pp.242-243n.
111 Maxwell, *Narrative*, p.64.
112 NRS, GD124/10/519, Copy Journal of Prince Charles' Army, describing the taking of Carlisle, November 1745.
113 Philip Yorke (ed.), *The Life and Letters of Philip Hardwicke, Lord Chancellor of Great Britain* (Cambridge: Cambridge University Press, 1913), Vol.I, p.488.
114 Maxwell, *Narrative*, p.64.
115 Saville (ed.), 'Secret Comment', p.262.
116 Lewis (ed.), *Correspondence*, Vol.19, p.165.

concluded, 'We have done all that lay in our power for His Majesty's service and the preservation of the city and castle of Carlisle'.[117] Waugh wrote that 'The surrender of Carlisle in the manner it was done and the Difficultys that were made in the Defence of it are subjects that were so much to my dissatisfaction that I know not how to look upon them'.[118] He put the blame on the militia, writing that 'the inhabitants would have held out as long as they could, if the militia officers would have stood by them'.[119]

Durand left Carlisle and went to discuss what had happened with Wade at Newcastle. He was not the only man who the government deemed was responsible for the fall of Carlisle; the mayor and his colleagues were also scrutinised, but more so for having proclaimed Charles as Prince Regent and thereby committing high treason. On 15-16 September 1746 there was a Board of Enquiry held of senior officers to ascertain Durand's culpability. Much of the session consisted of Durand talking in his defence, but others such as his subordinate officers, Folliot, and local clergy also spoke. They put the onus on the militia officers and stressed that Durand had done all he could have done in the circumstances. He was acquitted and it was stated 'Colonel James Durand has done everything in his power that became an experienced, diligent and brave officer'.[120]

The question to ask is whether Carlisle could have been held in the circumstances. The failure of the government to provide adequate reinforcements must be stressed; a battalion of infantry should have been able to have held the castle and perhaps the city, too. Since this did not happen, as the government failed to see Carlisle as being a military priority, could Durand with the militia and townsmen have done so? They numbered just over 1,000 men, though some were badly armed and the few regulars were elderly. However, there was no overall command, as had been similarly the case in Edinburgh, and so there was dissension between townsmen and militia, resulting in military ineffectiveness as the latter became exhausted and relations were not conducive to unity and high morale. The besieging force outnumbered them two-to-one, but given Carlisle's defences and artillery this was not a significant edge. In some ways the Jacobite position was remarkably weak. Their artillery was very low calibre and never fired a shot. A breach in the walls was not going to happen. The question is, therefore, would the Jacobite non-clan troops have used the scaling ladders to mount the city walls and attack the defenders? If they had tried, would artillery fire, grenades and musketry have deterred them? These questions cannot be answered, because it was never put to the test. What was at stake was morale and that of the various factions defending Carlisle was low; clearly Wade's refusal to march to its aid was one of the final straws that sapped the will to resist. Had he written a different letter, then the militia might have stuck to their guns.

A comparison made by a Jacobite besieger, though partial, has the ring of truth about it, when he commented on their ability 'to ly in trenches or to

117 RA, CP7/44, Durand to Folliott, 18 November 1745.
118 RA, CP7/62, Waugh to Cumberland, 20 November 1745.
119 RA, CP7/62, Waugh to Cumberland, 20 November 1745.
120 TNA, WO71/19, p.338, General Courts Martial, 1746-1747.

attack stone walls yet stood it out during the coldest frosty nights we have for many years past whilst the garrison of the castle supported by large fires and strong liquors could scarce stand upon the ramparts'.[121]

After Charles had been proclaimed by the Carlisle magistracy, a small garrison was left there under John Hamilton and the army marched south through Cumberland, Westmorland, Lancashire, Cheshire, Staffordshire and reached Derby on 4 December. This was the nearest they ever got to London, but once there the decision was taken to turn back, citing a lack of English and French support as well as British armies being within striking distance, though the wisdom of this decision has been criticised. Be that as it may, the Jacobite army retreated the way it had come, pursued by forces (cavalry and infantry mounted on horses, but no artillery) led by the Duke of Cumberland. The Jacobites were able to fight off this advance guard at Clifton on 18 December and fell back on Carlisle. Carlisle was once again potentially on the front line as opposing armies grew near.

Whitehaven magnates had, prior to 16 December, written to the Duke's military secretary to offer him the use of ten 18-pounder cannon then in the town should they be needed to reduce Carlisle and these were accepted. Cumberland agreed that the Jacobites might 'offer to make a stand at Carlisle' and so on 16 December, whilst at Lancaster, had written to Wade to request troops be sent from there to him.[122]

William Augustus, Duke of Cumberland. From a painting by David Morier. (Author's collection)

The retreating Jacobite forces convened at Carlisle on 19 December. They then had to decide what to do about their sole strongpoint in England. A council of war was duly held at Charles' headquarters, but not all were present; Murray, exhausted by recent days' exertions, was not there. The purpose of the meeting was to decide 'every thing for the March, & the garrison, yt was to be left'. O'Sullivan recorded that 'Some people were for leaving no garrison, at all'. O'Sullivan was adamant that one was needed there for to leave it undefended:

> [W]ou'd be the most unreasonable thing in the world, for we had several rivers to passe, & were not sure to find them foardable; if they were not, Cumberland cou'd not passe the river yt runs by Carlille either, he cou'd not passe by the bridge being under the lash of the castle, so yt he'd be obliged to passe by Brampton wch wou'd alwaise give us two days march of 'em; so

121 NRS, GD124/10/519, Copy Journal of Prince Charles' Army, describing the taking of Carlisle, November 1745.

122 Hepburn and Richardson, 'Transportation of Cannon', p.144; RA, CP8/51, Cumberland to Wade, 16 December 1745.

in all respects, it was better to sacrifice a party than the whole, as it is practised on like occasions.[123]

The decision was taken, by the council, including Charles himself, to leave a garrison there, leaving artillery, ammunition and baggage, with Hamilton continuing to be the governor of the castle and Colonel Francis Towneley (1709-1746), leader of the newly formed Manchester Regiment, commandant of the city. This was mostly condemned in retrospect with the benefit of hindsight; Maxwell wrote, 'This was perhaps the worst resolution the Prince had taken hitherto. I cannot help condemning it'. [124] Others agreed, with Elcho writing 'This was done against the Opinion almost of Everybody'. [125] Murray wrote likewise, 'I was clear for evacuating it'.[126] According to O'Sullivan, Murray was against leaving any artillery there, and Charles compromised by taking only the artillery he had had from France with the retreating army; the so called 'Swedish' guns.[127]

Johnstone wrote that he 'could never comprehend the reason for voluntarily sacrificing these unfortunate victims',[128] yet, according to O'Sullivan, the officers who remained had chosen this themselves.[129] Perth ordered Johnstone's company to remain behind. Unlike Towneley, Johnstone replied in the negative, 'I would willingly shed the last drop of my blood for Prince Charles but that I would never allow myself to be marked out as a victim for certain destruction'. Johnstone left the outraged Perth before waiting for his superior's reply.[130] Yet Lord George Murray alleged that 'The Duke of Perth was very unwilling to leave any of his men'.[131] Perth asked why few of the Atholl men were asked to stay, and Murray said that he would stay there with his Atholl men if he was asked.[132]

The reasons ('specious pretexts') put forward were as follows. Although the army was leaving England, Charles hoped to return there as soon as possible with the troops awaiting him in Scotland. Therefore, he wanted Carlisle in his hands in order to make that entry all the easier. It would also add to his reputation in maintaining the place in his hands.[133] Johnstone claimed that some argued that such a sacrifice was 'bait to amuse the Duke of Cumberland and prevent him from pursing us closely'.[134]

Some thought that the place was a mighty fortress, Perth later noting 'he believed it capable of sustaining a siege'.[135] Elcho also claimed that Charles

123 Tayler and Tayler (eds), *1745*, p.110.
124 Maxwell, *Narrative*, p.88; Forbes, *Jacobite Memoirs*, p.73.
125 Elcho, *Short Account*, p.350.
126 Forbes, *Jacobite Memoirs*, p.73.
127 Tayler and Tayler (eds), *1745*, p.110.
128 Johnstone, *Memoir*, p.72.
129 Tayler and Tayler (eds), *1745*, p.110.
130 Johnstone, *Memoir*, p.224.
131 Forbes, *Jacobite Memoirs*, p.73.
132 Forbes, *Jacobite Memoirs*, p.73
133 Forbes, *Jacobite Memoirs*, p.73
134 Johnstone, *Memoir*, pp.72-73.
135 Johnstone, *Memoir*, pp.224-225.

'was sure the Duke could get no Cannon to take it with'.[136] Brown, Maxwell, Towneley and Geoghegan, all who had seen military service in the French army, believed 'yt Cumberland cou'd not take the castle with the Cannon he had, & the season we were in, in a county where his cavalry cou'd not subsist eight days'.[137] However, Towneley later wrote, 'I knew that was a desperate expedient to retard the pursuit of our enemies, and that those left in garrison there could not possibly avoid being cut to pieces in the place, or submitting to the consequences', yet he 'was willing to sacrifice my life to the safety of my Friends'.[138]

To set against this, Charles could not be sure he would return in the very near future; in fact the army was marching with all haste northwards. Secondly, 'the place was not tenable against a few pieces of battering cannon, or a few mortars'. Johnstone recollected that it had fallen quickly to the Jacobites in the previous month and that it could not last four hours against an artillery bombardment. Murray agreed, 'I was sure it was not tenable'. Destruction of the castle would have been equally effective in facilitating Charles' re-entry into England. Murray claimed part of the castle could have been blown up and military stores thrown into the river. Finally, by leaving a garrison there the lives of so many men were being risked 'without an indispensable necessity'.[139] It was also the case that 'The Prince was not overburdened with men'.[140] It was even alleged by some that 'the measure originated in a spirit of vengeance against the English nation', in that no one English Jacobite of substance made good their promises to support the cause, yet this overlooks the fact that the majority of the Jacobite garrison was Scottish.[141]

The question must be who was to blame. John Daniel, an English Jacobite, defended Charles, writing, 'Now some there are, who censure the Prince for leaving them at Carlisle, thinking it was out of disregard and a desire of getting rid of them'. He denied that this was true, and put the onus on Towneley whom he alleged petitioned, on the behalf of his battalion's officers, to be allowed to remain there. However, many of the latter 'never assented to or desired it'. Most wished to remain with Charles and share his fate in Scotland, despite many desertions from the regiment. However, Towneley told them that their staying was Charles' own wish and so 'they all, taking it as coming from the Prince, most willingly acquiesced'.[142] Yet not all of the garrison were so enthusiastic, Murray writing 'The Prince had some difficulty about those who were to stay at Carlisle, who were very unwilling'.[143]

Johnstone, though, wrote otherwise, blaming Charles for the decision, 'the Prince left the unfortunate Mr Towneley' and 'The Prince promised to return to their assistance in the course of a few days, though this appeared

136 Elcho, *Short Account*, p.350.

137 Tayler and Tayler (eds), *1745*, p.110.

138 Anon., *Authentic Copies of the Letters and other Papers delivered at their execution by the nine rebels* (London: Unknown Publisher, 1746), p.10.

139 Tayler and Tayler (eds), *1745*, p.110; Forbes, *Jacobite Memoirs*, p.73; Johnstone, *Memoir*, p.72.

140 Forbes, *Jacobite Memoirs*, p.73.

141 Forbes, *Jacobite Memoirs*, p.73.

142 Blaikie (ed.), 'Origins', pp.186-187.

143 Forbes, *Jacobite Memoirs*, p.74.

to be morally impossible'.[144] Elcho stated that 'the Prince said he must have a town in England'.[145] Murray concurred, 'I found he was determined in the thing'.[146]

It would seem possible that the reason Charles had for leaving the garrison was to uphold his personal honour as prince regent. Retreating in the face of an army led by the son of the man who he deemed a usurper, must have been galling; to not leave a stronghold in his possession must have been more so. This may seem militarily indefensible, but the concept of honour was widely upheld as being very natural, especially for one who deemed himself the heir to the kingdom.

The officers and men of the garrison gave their horses and baggage to their fellows who were returning to Scotland, as they had no more need of them. John Daniel admired their bravery, 'though it is often objected to them that they were not of extraordinary rank, yet they behaved so as to make those of a nobler birth blush…Unhappy Gentlemen! They merited a much better fate than what was awaiting them!'[147]

Apparently their orders were as follows: 'to do all in their power to put up a stout resistance, not to surrender, no matter what the terms offered, unless everything else had failed and they were reduced to the last extremity'.[148]

The Jacobite garrison was as follows:

The remnant of the Manchester Regiment, led by Colonel Francis Towneley. With him were five captains, six lieutenants, seven ensigns, an adjutant, a chaplain and 93 NCOs, privates and drummers. There were also 18 Scottish officers and 256 men from other regiments. These men were taken from Avochie of Strathbogie's men from Lord Lewis Gordon's Regiment (62), Colonel Grant's regiment, Lord Ogilvie's Regiment (39), the Duke of Perth's Regiment (69), the Atholl Brigade (2) and Roy Stewart's Regiment (47), as well as some clansmen (21). There were also a few men from the French army; two officers, a sergeant and four privates from Lally's Regiment of the Irish Brigade, an officer from the Royal Ecossois and an unattached officer. There were also a surgeon and his mate and seven dragoons, presumably deserters from the British army after Prestonpans, though these may have formed part of one of the Scots units already listed above.[149] About 410 men in all.

Artillery: twenty 6-pounders (Durand claimed these were 9-pounders but Captain Gilpin said otherwise and he had been there for several years) in the castle and ten light guns in the town; six 1 1/2-pounders, four coehorn mortars, two royals (taken from Cope's army after Prestonpans).[150] There were also one brass octagon and three brass 4-pounders; a total of

144 Johnstone, *Memoir*, p.72.
145 Elcho, *Short Account*, p.350.
146 Forbes, *Jacobite Memoirs*, p.74.
147 Blaikie (ed.), 'Origins', p.187.
148 Seton (ed.), 'Commentary' p.97.
149 Marchant, *History*, pp.255-257; RA, CP7/415, Jacobite garrison of Carlisle, 1745.
150 Elcho, *Short Account*, p.313; Johnstone, *Memoir*, p.49.

46 guns.[151] The guns were manned by the aforementioned French and Irish together with eight gunners and 17 matrosses assisting, these 25 men presumably being taken from the English and Scottish contingents already listed.[152]

British estimates of the garrison were at odds with reality. Colonel Yorke wrote that there were 500 or 600 men under Hamilton's command. He wrote that the men there had been forced to stay and were 'a few desperate wretches (amongst which are all of their English recruits)' and that their goal was to allow the main Jacobite army to escape into Scotland.[153] Cumberland wrote that he had heard that the Jacobites 'had left there between three & four hundred men, who, according to the best accounts I could have are most of them their English recruits & the rest Gordon of Glenbuckets men commanded by one Hamilton'.[154] Newcastle wrote that the garrison was 'probably made up of the worst of their troops'.[155]

The defenders were led by John Hamilton and Francis Towneley. Hamilton was a factor to the Duke of Gordon and had joined the Jacobite army after Prestonpans. He had been appointed governor of Carlisle following its fall after the first siege. Yet his military knowledge was probably minimal at best for on being given the governorship on 20 November, he was given 'some two three old officers to assist and advise him'.[156]

Towneley was the sole representative of the English Catholic gentry in the Jacobite army. He had been born in Towneley Hall, near Burnley in Lancashire; his uncle, Richard, had fought in the campaign of 1715, was captured at Preston, was tried and acquitted. Towneley was well-educated but went to France in 1728 and joined the French army as a volunteer. He fought in the War of the Polish Succession (1733-1735) under Marshal Berwick at the siege of Philippsburg, fighting bravely and receiving a commission. He returned to England and in 1745 received a commission as colonel from Louis XV. On 30 November, he was appointed as colonel to the newly raised Manchester Regiment, mainly made up of Englishmen.[157]

Meanwhile the besieging army was composed of the following:

- Foot Guards, about 400 men (taken from the two battalions of Foot Guards)
- Bligh's Foot, at least 300 men
- Royal North British Fusiliers
- Sempill's Foot
- Halifax's Foot
- Granby's Foot
- Montagu's Foot
- Bedford's Foot

151 Douglas, *History*, p.78.
152 RA, CP7/415, Jacobite garrison of Carlisle, 1745.
153 Yorke (ed.), *Hardwicke*, Vol.I, p.487.
154 TNA, SP36/78, f.14r, Cumberland to Newcastle, 22 December 1745.
155 TNA, SP36/78, f.226r, Newcastle to Cumberland, 28 December 1745.
156 Bell (ed.), 'Memorials', p.245.
157 Douglas, *History*, pp.284-85.

Ruthven Barracks, Badenoch, which withstood a Jacobite siege in 1745 but was captured the following year. The main barrack building is to the right of the image, and the stable block to the left. (David Beards)

Portion of remaining Edinburgh City Wall. (Author's Photo)

Edinburgh Castle. (Arran Johnston)

Edinburgh Castle from the south, showing the half-moon battery. (Arran Johnston)

Carlisle Castle. (Author's Photo)

Stirling Castle. (Arran Johnston)

The South-West Prospect of the City of Carlisle, hand-coloured engraving by and after Samuel and Nathaniel Buck.
(Anne S.K. Brown Collection)

F THE CITY OF CARLISLE.

King of the Britons (at the time when Solomon began to build his Temple) and so call'd from him, in that Language, Caer-leil. However that may be, that it was
allum, concerning the Etymology of which Word there have been various Opinions, but none so probable, as that which will have it deriv'd from Lugus (which
n its Ruins many Years after the coming of the Saxons, by whom it was call'd Luel, till Egfrid King of Northumberland about A.D. 680. rebuilt it and envi-
. In the 9th Century, when the whole Country was ruin'd by the repeated Invasions of the Danes and Norwegians, this City was again demolish'd & so remaind
rwards (when he removed them into Wales) of Southern Englishmen K. Hen. I. considering how good a Barrier it might be against the Scots, fortified it still better &
when it was dissolv'd, & the Prior & Convent converted into a Dean & Chapter consisting of 4 Canons or Prebendaries. This City was taken by the Scots in the Reigns of K. Step.
n the late Civil Wars it was able to stand a Siege of 9 Months, and was the last Garrison that surrender'd to the Rebels; and whatever Defence it is now capable of making,
f Saturday, and a Yearly Fair on Aug. 15th for 16 days. These Rights & Priveleges have by several succeeding Kings in so many Charters, been confirm'd & Augmented to ye Cor-
rks for their Liberties, as they did the like sum 21 Hen. 3 for having a Corroner of their own. ~~Its present Representatives in Parliamt are the Honble Cha. Howards & John Hilton Esqrs~~
Garden-Court No. 1 Middle Temple London.

1. Scotland
2. Eterby Scar
3. River Eden
4. River Caudey
5. Castle
6. Irish Gate
7. Abby Gate
8. Registers Office
9. Abby
10. Deanery
11. Library
12. Town Hall
13. St. Cuthberts Church
14. City Wall
15. Goal
16. English Gate
17. Cittadel
18. Corby

Outer wall of Stirling Castle, facing the site of the Jacobite battery on Gowan Hill. (Arran Johnston)

Blair Castle. (Guillaume Piolle)

Fort William, Exterior. (Arran Johnston)

Fort William, Interior. (Arran Johnston)

- Liverpool Blues (from 25 December) 8 companies of 70 private men each, perhaps 600 in total
- Infantry and cavalry from Wade's army (units not specified, but including Montagu's Horse, St George's Dragoons, Georgia rangers, and Yorkshire Hunters).
- Ligonier's Horse
- Kingston's Light Horse
- Cobham's Dragoons
- Kerr's Dragoons
- Bland's Dragoons
- Montagu's Carbineers

Artillery: ten 18-pounders from Whitehaven (from 24-28 December), 10 coehorns and 300 shells from Newcastle, with Major Belford and 78 gunners, including 12 seamen and eight Dutchmen.

Total strength about 3,000-4,000 men; James Ray, a contemporary historian, stated the latter number.[158] Each cavalry regiment might have been about 200 men strong, the remainder being infantry. Compared to the defenders they had a significant superiority of numbers, perhaps as many as 10:1, as well as far higher calibre artillery and far more trained gunners.

They were led by the Duke Cumberland, then the foremost soldier in the British army. He had served as an army officer since 1742 and fought at Dettingen in the following year, as a major general. He was wounded but was applauded for his bravery and mercy. In 1745 he was appointed Captain General of the British Army and commanded the allied army at the Battle of Fontenoy. Although he was defeated it was an honourable defeat, the soldiers and their leader having behaved bravely. Later that year he commanded the main army against the Jacobites in November. Although relatively youthful he was brave and popular.

Not all expected a siege, with Colonel Yorke writing on 19 December from Penrith, 'I don't imagine the Rebels will stop at Carlisle in the fright they seem to be in'. He thought that the Jacobite army should not have abandoned the 'strong position' they were in at Clifton unless morale had been low. However, by next day he heard that the Jacobites were unable to cross the Esk because it was swollen, so all their artillery was placed in the castle, while in the meantime Cumberland had requested artillery from Whitehaven and additional troops from Wade, which were now at Hexham.[159]

On 20 December, Cumberland wrote to Newcastle:

> By the best accounts the Rebels are still in Carlisle, & I believe their intention would be to go off to morrow, if the Rivers & floods would permit them, but I flatter myself that they will be hindered & am making the dispositions to invest the Town tomorrow, with the Troops I have here & the detachment from Marshal Wade's army, & ten eighteen pounders will be as today at Cockermouth, & have orders to move on with the whole posse Comitatus which will be assembled tomorrow at Wigton.[160]

158 Ray, *History*, p.202; RA, CP8/120, Account of artillery at Carlisle, 25 December 1745.
159 Yorke (ed.), *Hardwicke*, Vol.I, pp.486-487.
160 RA, CP8/80, Cumberland to Newcastle, 20 December 1745.

Thomas Pelham-Holles, Duke of Newcastle. Drawn by Wm. Derby and engraved with permission by W. Holt. (Author's collection)

The British forces rested at Penrith on 20 December, but on the previous day St George's dragoons had marched on to Hesket from there, and so were within eight miles of Carlisle. Meanwhile at Newcastle, Marshal Wade sent 1,000 men and 50 cavalry (the former taken from a number of different regiments), to join Cumberland in the vicinity of Carlisle, leaving Newcastle on 21 December and arriving at Haltwhistle as their first stop. At four in the morning of 21 December, Cumberland's own command marched northward. They did so in three columns, with the Duke with the infantry in the centre, and with the cavalry in two columns on each flank; one by Armathwaite and the other by Hutton Hall.[161]

Cumberland arrived outside Carlisle at one on the afternoon of 21 December. He soon had the city encircled in order to prevent anyone escaping and explained his dispositions in a letter to the Duke of Newcastle. Major General Humphrey Bland (1686-1764) invested it on the 'Scotch side with St George's Dragoons & three hundred men of Bligh's Regiment with orders only to prevent anybodys passing or repairing the Bridge upon the River Eden which gos directly to the Scotch Gate'.

Major John Adams, with two hundred infantry, was posted in the Suburbs of the English Gate, to prevent any of the garrison escaping from thence at the south gate. Major Mcrae was posted with another two hundred men with the same orders at the Irish Gate, Sir Andrew Agnew (1687-1771) with three hundred men (probably his own regiment, the Royal North British Fusiliers) was at the Sally Port. Cumberland added 'All the horse & the Foot Guards are cantoned round the Town, at a Mile & two miles distance'.

He thought of the defenders, that 'They endeavour to appear resolute & have fired their Cannon upon every body who has shewn himself' and added

> As we can pursue the Rebels no further it is better to wait the Cannon which will arrive from Whitehaven in a day or two, than to expose ourselves to any considerable loss against such an Enemy as this.
>
> We are in want of Engineers, but by such help as we have, we hope to raise a battery by the 24th in the morning, & then in twenty four hours, the Town will be ours, by Storm, I hope, that we at least may have some revenge on these fellows for the trouble they & the rest have given us.
>
> Major General Bland has taken sixteen carts with their tents. Their Cannon is all in the Town except three pieces.[162]

161 Douglas, *History*, pp.73-74.
162 TNA, SP36/78, f.14r-15v, Cumberland to Newcastle, 22 December 1745.

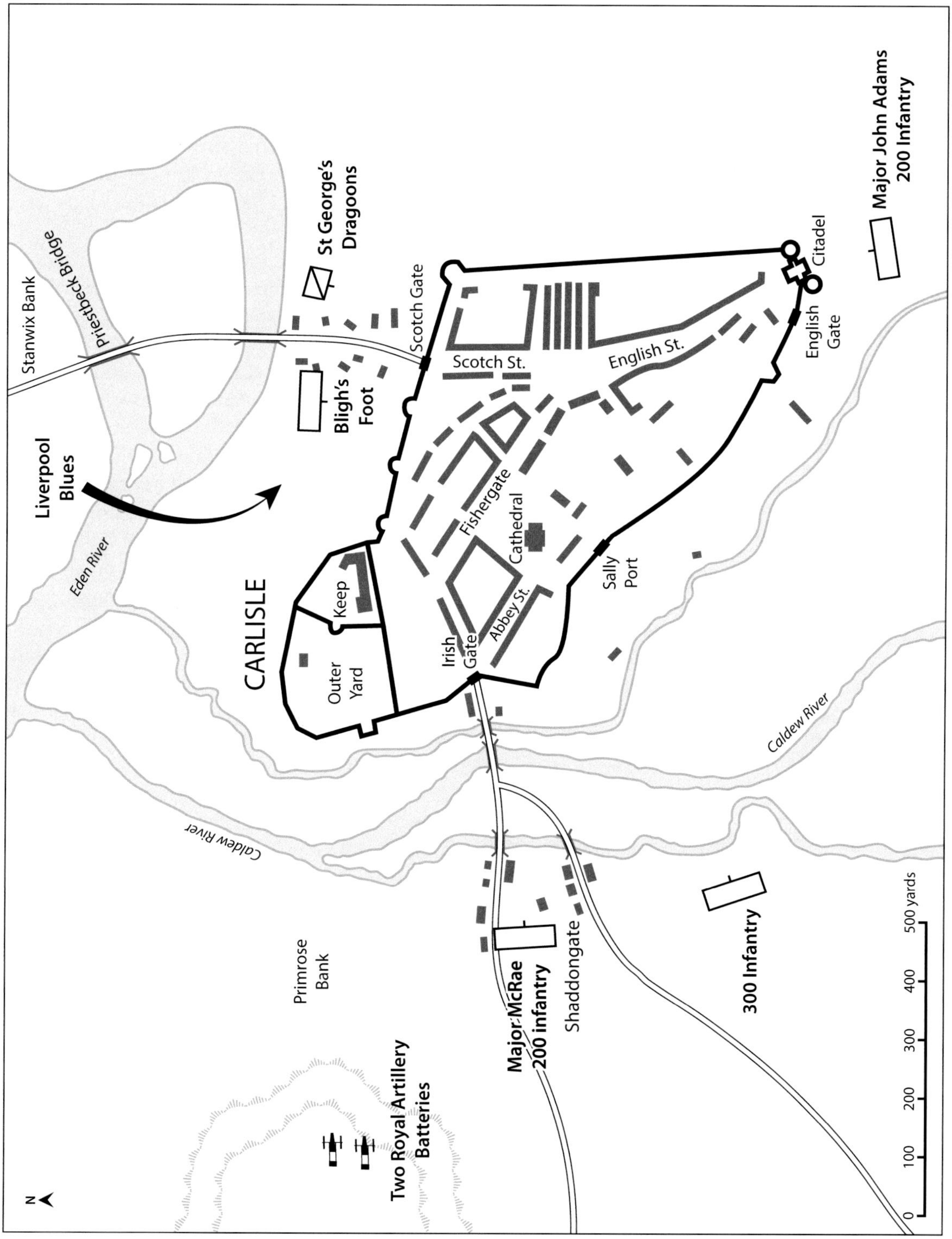

Carlisle and Environs, December 1745.

Cumberland also wrote to summon additional troops. The Liverpool Blues, a regiment of volunteer infantry raised in September 1745, had been at Lancaster when they received an order on 21 December to march to Penrith. They arrived there on 23 December.[163]

Cumberland also requested heavy artillery from Whitehaven. Apparently James Ray was sent there and was met by enthusiastic support, 'thence the People rose in a Body and got Horses and Carriages ready with all expedition'. At least ten horses were needed to pull each of the 18-pounders. Sir James Lowther, the county's richest man, provided 40 horses himself to pull four guns, but in some cases 16 or 18 horses were needed because the roads were very soft due to recent heavy rain.[164]

There was, perhaps, other civilian aid, too. Many countrymen went to Cumberland's headquarters at Black Hall, to the south west of Carlisle 'to assist the King's army with Clubs and Staves and such other weapons as they had: the Game Law forbidding the use of Fire Arms'. It is said that they numbered 10,000 (a number, if true represented almost all the adult men of the county whose total population was only about 65,000), but Cumberland dismissed most of them, considering that they were of no use, except some who were retained to cut fascines for the batteries.[165] Another 50 men from Dalston worked five days on building the batteries and yet another 34 from Weatheral on digging trenches at Stanwix. Others carried cannon balls.[166] Yet another source noted there was 'a great difficulty in bringing the country people to work' and their 'backwardness to serve in the trenches', presumably because they feared Jacobite artillery fire. It was reported that Cumberland was 'resolved indeed to use severity to them'.[167]

With the blockading of Carlisle, the garrison's officers decided to hold regular meetings. Hamilton was appointed as chairman and Captain James Dawson was the clerk. The meetings included Towneley, Captain Brown (styled as a colonel in the Jacobite army, but as his substantive commission was as a captain in the French army this rank will be used of his and other officers in that army) and seven other officers. They decided that each regiment provide a third of their men to mount daily guard, beginning at seven each morning. There would also be a number of other contingents of men. At the castle would be a captain, a lieutenant, two sergeants, a musician (piper or drummer) and 30 privates. The same number, taken from the Manchester Regiment, would form the main City Guard. At both the English Gate and the Scotch Gate would be a lieutenant and 20 privates. The same number should be at the Irish Gate if there were enough men for this. This number amounted to a third of the garrison. Outside the castle, all soldiers had to obey Towneley and Captain Francis Geoghegan, the Fort Major.[168]

163 Jonathan Oates and Katharine Navickas (eds), 'Jacobites and Jacobins: Two Eighteenth Century Perspectives', *Record Society of Lancashire and Cheshire*, Vol.142 (2006), p.27.

164 Ray, *History*, p.202.

165 Ray, *History*, p.203.

166 Jarvis, *Jacobite Risings*, pp.322-325.

167 *Report on Commission of various Collections*, Vol.VIII (London: Historic Manuscripts Commission, 1913) p.156.

168 RA, CP8/209, Records of the Council of war at Carlisle, 22-29 December 1745.

Their aim was to defend Carlisle and alert the governor and others if they came under attack. At daybreak there was to be a parade around the walls. The Main Guard was to patrol on an hourly basis. The guards at each gate were rotated as follows: Irish Gate guards to the English Gate, English Gate guards to the Scotch Gate, Scotch Gate guards to the castle. At night, two officers from the Manchester Regiment were to walk around the walls hourly. In the event of an attack, cannon fire would signal such, with the Manchester Regiment to parade at the main gate (presumably that which was under attack) and the Castle Guard to assemble, too. [169]

Whilst the besiegers awaited their guns, the Jacobite artillery was in action, as a besieger noted, 'They have spared neither powder nor ball, but have kept a continual fire ever since the army invested the town and thank God to very little purpose'. No one was killed and very few were injured. However, on another occasion, a grenadier was killed at Stanwix bank as 'the town played very severely upon them for two to three hours'. Otherwise, however, the Jacobite artillery fire was usually too high and their gunners were deemed 'excreably bad'. In retaliation, four men were hanged; perhaps Jacobite prisoners, on 24 December in sight of the castle 'as a specimen of what the rest may expect'.[170]

Towneley ensured all the garrison was properly armed. He was all for a vigorous defence. The guns fired on all who came into their view. He had had the artillery mounted on the walls. Houses within the batteries' range were burnt. *Chevaux de Frise* (a portable barrier of spikes) were made and erected at the gates in order to prevent the British cavalry from approaching them. He also proposed making sallies against the besiegers, but in this he was successfully opposed by his colleagues.[171]

Charles Lennox, second Duke of Richmond (1701-1750), a lieutenant general of cavalry with Cumberland, thought that the place would be difficult to take, writing to Newcastle on 24 December:

> I don't see how he can reduce them by force without looseing more men than the object is worth. There are miners indeed that are to blow up even the castle, & they are to do it if they can, butt I can see no credit to that, & as for battering them en breche, it will be a long piece of works, & our ammunition is scanty, & I don't believe one real gunner amongst us. Storming & scaling the walls indeed might & I really believe would do, butt it would cost us at least 200 of our best grenadiers, & I am very sure that would not be worth while, for 300 such lowly scoundrels, starving them may be a long & difficulte taske, & opening trenches impossible as they would fill with water, so you may see what real difficultys the Duke lyes under…if he was to aske my advice I do not know what I would give him.[172]

169 RA, CP8/209, Records of the council of war at Carlisle, 22-29 December 1745.
170 *HMC Various Collections,* Vol.VIII, pp.154-155.
171 Henderson, *History*, p.68.
172 McCann (ed.), 'Correspondence', p.199.

Cumberland decided to wait, as Yorke remarked, '[he] chooses to wait patiently…till everything is prepared to attack 'em'. He seemed to believe that the defences were weak.[173]

However, writing on the same day, Yorke noted similar concerns to those listed by Richmond; the lack of artillery and engineers, and the dampness of the ground, but he was also optimistic, 'I hope that our battery will be ready to open tomorrow, and that a very few days will make us masters of this place…I believe we shall soon put an end to it'.[174] Cumberland was confident, too, writing 'As soon as the town is in our Possession, I shall leave Bligh's Battallion in it, order Lord Cobham's Regiment & the detachment from Marshal Wade to joyn his Army & the rest of the Troops to their respective quarters southward.[175]

However, he realised that additional support was required and on 24 December addressed Wade thus:

> [T]he Troops fatigued with forced marches, I was obliged to halt, while they march'd on for Carlisle, where they stay'd but one night to change the Garrison.
>
> We have been waiting here for the ten eighteen pounders from Whitehaven, of which four only are arrived as yet, but I am promised the other six as soon as the horses can draw them up, with them & the assistance I expect from you, I hope soon to put an end to this troublesome, tedious effort & finding there is so small a garrison left in the town, I ordered Brigadier Mordaunt to return back to you as I would not fatigue your Troops more than is necessary.
>
> PS I have just now a report that the Garrison is all retired into the Castle, so that I shall I hope have the Town without any trouble, but this is not yet certain.[176]

There was a degree of civilian discomfort during the siege. John Marchant, a contemporary historian, wrote that the inhabitants were being pillaged by the Jacobites and were prevented by the besiegers of having food supplies brought in from the countryside and were heard crying 'Hunger! Hunger!' from the walls.[177] Cumberland was aware of concerns of civilians and on 27 December wrote to the bishop of Carlisle, to reassure him of this:

> My purpose being altogether to drive the Rebels out of the Town of Carlisle to restore that town to its free obedience to his Majesty, you may be assured I shall in all the necessary steps I may be obliged to that end, have possible regard for the Town & its inhabitants who of all the Kings subjects are most immediately concerned in the success of my enterprise.
>
> What may happen by the unavoidable means of such an undertaking, will I hope be imputed to those who have rendered it absolutely necessary, I shall give all such orders as may most contribute to the preservation & wellfare of his Majestys good subjects, & I must say I cant help wishing that by some timely

173 Yorke (ed.), *Hardwicke*, Vol.I, p.487.
174 Yorke (ed.), *Hardwicke*, Vol.I, p.488.
175 TNA, SP36/78, f.14r-15v, Cumberland to Newcastle, 22 December 1745.
176 RA, CP8/110, Cumberland to Wade, 24 December 1745.
177 Marchant, *History*, p.252.

> & vigorous opposition from the Country, to this detestable Gang of robbers, all proceedings of this kind had been prevented.[178]

Meanwhile, the siege was progressing, as Cumberland told Newcastle on the following day:

> Yesterday arrived Major Belford of the Artillery with Captn [Caroline] Scott the Ingineer, sixty Gunners & several Sailors & this morning we began to batter the four Gun battery with six eighteen pounders & the Artillery Officers hope to have a breach fit to give the assault tomorrow night, so that I persuade my self the thing will now be soon over…
>
> As to Artillery, what they have already with the ten eighteen pounders I have here from Whitehaven will be sufficient. (For those guns would be unsafe at Whitehaven as there is no Fort there, so that the Rebels if they should attempt to return might make use of them to besiege the Town) & for the sufficient horses, the artillery People when the Town is taken shall form an estimate & send it to the Board of Ordnance.[179]

The plan for the artillery, once it arrived, was threefold, or so Yorke imagined on 24 December. Firstly, the great battery would be undermined and blown up, presumably by the miners from local collieries. Secondly artillery fire would be trained on the castle in order to draw attention to that point. Finally pitch barrels would be propelled towards the Irish Gate 'and then slaughter will do his work'.[180]

Richmond had already given some thought to terms of a possible surrender, but wrote on 24 December, 'the Duke certainly cant treate with these rebellious wretches'.[181] Unlike the case with conventional siege warfare, Cumberland may not have sent a summonses to the garrison to surrender at the siege's outset; though one source claimed that he had and that the soldiers taking it had been fired upon with one man being injured. According to Yorke, 'he is for giving no quarter', though Yorke believed that the garrison would be happy to accept terms.[182]

Jacobite artillery had not been quiet, as already noted. According to Yorke, 'The garrison has fired at us ever since we came but without doing any execution'. When Cumberland rode close to Carlisle to reconnoitre, guns were fired on him, but without hitting him, 'may the same good Providence always attend him for the sake of this country' added Yorke.[183] Yorke's father, the Lord Chancellor, was particularly shocked to hear that Cumberland had risked his life, writing on 28 December, 'it is the ardent wish and entreaty of all his faithful servants that he should not expose his person unnecessarily. Carlisle is not an object worth such a hazard. That should be reserved for some greater and more glorious attempt'.[184]

178 RA, CP8/137, Cumberland to Fleming, 27 December 1745.
179 TNA, SP36/78, f219r-220r, Cumberland to Newcastle, 28 December 1745.
180 Yorke (ed.), *Hardwicke*, Vol.I, p.488.
181 McCann (ed.), 'Correspondence', p.199.
182 Yorke (ed.), *Hardwicke*, Vol.I, p.487-488.
183 Yorke (ed.), *Hardwicke*, Vol.I, p.488.
184 Yorke (ed.), *Hardwicke*, Vol.I, pp.490-491.

The besiegers had an unpleasant time of it. Yorke referring to Cumberland's 'vile cantonment'. He himself wrote 'I shall not be sorry when it is over, for we are miserably off now, in worse villages than ever I saw in the mountains in Germany, but as the Duke is as ill off as other people, nobody can repine'. Yorke wrote his letter 'from so dreary a hole'.[185] His father wrote to him to implore that he took care to avoid being sick.' [186] Men had to undergo a great deal of sentry duty at night, as Lieutenant Walter Shairp (1724-1787) of the Liverpool Blues wrote at the siege's end:

> Our four oldest comps had been now upon duty 6 nights running without ever getting any rest or been reliev'd by the younger ones as was first propos'd at which they made great complaints & indeed I must say they had reason for it as they were now growing sick in great numbers & quite Stupid for want of Rest.[187]

There was concern that Jacobites might try and escape from Carlisle. At Stanwix were St George's Dragoons and the Liverpool Blues. On the latter's arrival, Bligh's Regiment marched around to the west of the city. Bland was in charge of the troops at Stanwix. He ordered that four companies of the Blues would stand guard and the other four would be quartered in villages nearby and that they would be rotated. Officers were to go around at night to check the guards were properly posted. Shairp noted that the orders were obeyed because there was nothing else to be done; all the quarters had already been taken by the dragoons.[188]

Nothing noteworthy was seen on the evening of the 25th, but on the next night there was an alarm. At midnight the Blues were alerted that several men had been seen coming over the walls and it was suspected that this might be part of a sally. The dragoons and Blues stood to for an hour and loosed off a few shots 'to let them know we were in readiness to exercise them'. There was nothing more seen or heard so the men were stood down, but a patrol went to the ford to see if any were escaping there, but again without results.[189]

The first four guns arrived from Whitehaven on 24 December (having left Whitehaven on 22 December) and the other six three days later (they left on 26 December).[190] It was also on 27 December, that a wagon with four coehorn mortars arrived from Wade's army. The first battery was erected on the same day. This was on the west side of the castle, at Primrose Bank, 650-700 yards from the castle and consisted of the first six 18-pounders from Whitehaven.[191] A total of 25 mortar shells were fired into the castle and city. The damage done by them is unknown, but it certainly brought swift retaliation, 'a very hot fire upon the place yt the Trench Guard was kept'. Whilst Shairp was visiting there 'they fir'd a round of Grape or Case shott

185 Yorke (ed.), *Hardwicke*, Vol.I, p.488.
186 Yorke (ed.), *Hardwicke*, Vol.I, p.491.
187 Oates and Navickas (eds), 'Jacobites and Jacobins', p.30.
188 Oates and Navickas (eds), 'Jacobites and Jacobins', p.28.
189 Oates and Navickas (eds), 'Jacobites and Jacobins', pp.28-29.
190 Douglas, *History*, p.74.
191 Oates and Navickas (eds), 'Jacobites and Jacobins', p.29; Marchant, *History*, p.251.

Coehorn Mortar abandoned by the Jacobites at Kedleston Hall in Derbyshire and now in the collection there. (Brian Stone)

which fell very thick about us'. The trenches provided shelter and no one was hit.[192]

On 28 December, fire was directed from six of the 18-pounders at eight in the morning against the Jacobite batteries of four and seven guns which were on the west walls of the castle. This target was probably chosen, not only to make a breach prior to a potential assault, but also so as to reduce damage to civilian property, which Cumberland told the bishop was his intention. Apparently 'the Rebel Garrison were as much suprized as if they had felt the Shock of an Earthquake, wondering from whence those roaring guns came, knowing the English Army brought none with them'. Yet they retaliated, 'At first the fire from the town considerably exceeded ours, owing perhaps due to the smallness of their pieces in proportion to the Duke's, but before twelve they failed prodigiously'. James Miller, a member of the garrison, wrote 'We returned this [fire] pritty sharply considering our mettle being but small'. By mid-afternoon, this constant bombardment had resulted in many Jacobite guns being dismounted and these two batteries were abandoned. They retreated to their 10-gun battery which faced eastwards and fired these from late afternoon until the morning of the following day.[193]

That night, coehorns were firing into Carlisle and sailors assisted in working the other guns. Apparently over 1,100 balls and shells had been fired that day by the besiegers. Apart from disabling several guns, they killed and wounded 16 defenders for the loss of one man killed.[194]

This was worrying the garrison and a meeting of the officers was convened. Towneley suggested that the city wall which was being battered should be reinforced by erecting scaffolding behind it. Captain John Burnet of Aberdeenshire was an officer in Grant's Artillery. He said that it was not possible to erect sufficient scaffolding with 'so few hands'. Towneley argued that the scaffolding was needed otherwise with the wall was breached it would be open to the enemy. However, scaffolding would not allow cannon to be mounted on it.[195] Some repairs were, however, effected, by earthern sods being used to shore up the breach.[196]

The artillery had been firing on the castle for two days, though at a reduced rate on the 29 December 'for wee were short of ammunition' as there were only 616 cannon balls and 28 barrels of gunpowder, enough for 480 firings.[197] Cumberland wrote 'On the 29th we were forced to be very moderate in our firing, as our shot failed, till towards evening when a fresh supply arrived, & we had two hours brisk firing which shook the wall very much'.[198] Ray was sent to order 2,000 cannon balls for 18-pounders, which were being made 24 miles distant from Carlisle.[199]

---

192 Oates and Navickas (eds), 'Jacobites and Jacobins', p.29.

193 Ray, *History*, p.203; *HMC Various Collections*, Vol.VIII, p.157; James Miller, 'Diary of James Miller, 1745-1750', *Journal of the Society for Army History Research*, Vol.III (1924), p.209.

194 Ray, *History*, pp.203-204.

195 RA, CP8/209, Records of the council of war at Carlisle, 22-29 December 1745.

196 *HMC Various Collections*, Vol.VIII, p.157.

197 McCann (ed.), 'Correspondence', p.199.

198 TNA, SP36/78, f270r-71r, Cumberland to Newcastle, 29 December 1745.

199 Ray, *History*, p.204.

There was very little, if any, fire from the Jacobite artillery from the castle; an engineer thought there had been none and artillery officers claimed that the enemy fired at them but without shot.[200] However, the batteries which had been dismounted in the previous day were repaired and began to fire again.[201]

On the evening of 29 December, a new battery of three 18-pounders was erected.[202] Major Belford was in charge of the guns, now sited 50 yards from the existing battery, which was completed by the morning of the next day.[203]

The writing was by now clearly on the wall; Carlisle's fall was inevitable, or so some within the walls felt. There was another meeting of the council there. Burnet announced that a breach was imminent. Hamilton put it to the meeting that they had to decide whether to abandon the city and retire to the castle and defend it as long as possible or whether to seek terms immediately. Captain George Abernethy of Banffshire, in Ogilvie's Regiment, thought that the former was preferable, but that most of the garrison felt this was impracticable, due to 'the badness of our men, ye want of arms and no release to be expected from ye army'. It was noted that the fourth article of Charles' instructions to them was that the governor be allowed to negotiate a surrender if necessary. Abernethy suggested that Hamilton should enter into negotiations, but should try to hold the castle if no good terms were offered.[204]

Burnet was of a more pessimistic turn. He stated that on the previous day he had stood on the batteries and had ordered the gunners to return fire. Yet the gunners and matrosses had deserted the guns because of the enemy fire. Furthermore, when advanced parties of British infantry brought their muskets to bear on the French gunners, the other defenders refused to man the walls; not a single man remained. Burnet added that to surrender was not at odds to their loyalty to Charles. They should do so immediately, not wait until they were in extremis. Dawson sided with Towneley who wanted to fight on. The opinion of absent members of the council and junior officers was also sought, but by the day's end the decision had been taken – to surrender.[205] The alternative was to risk the place being assaulted and that meant death and destruction for the garrison.

Hamilton was instrumental in the surrender, perhaps through 'a true fear or promise of his life'. He may have been influenced by one Weir or Vere, a captured government spy. Weir had been invited to dine with Hamilton every day and was clearly trusted by Hamilton. Yet Towneley, always the more energetic of the two leaders, on being told of the intended capitulation, 'endeavoured, seconded by his whole corps, officers and soldiers, to oppose him; but finding by no means effective to hinder the place from being given up, he was obliged to send, by Hamilton's direction, articles of Capitulation to

200 McCann (ed.), 'Correspondence', p.199.

201 Ray, *History*, p.204.

202 Douglas, *History*, p.75.

203 Ray, *History*, pp.204-205.

204 RA, CP8/209, Records of the council of war at Carlisle, 22-29 December 1745.

205 RA, CP8/209, Records of the council of war at Carlisle, 22-29 December 1745.

Cumberland'.[206] Weir claimed that he talked to Hamilton about capitulation and that the latter was receptive to the idea. The two then jointly wrote a letter to Cumberland. They then contacted Abernethy and other Scottish officers who agreed with their plan.[207]

Hamilton may also have been swayed by civilian entreaties. According to Andrew Henderson, a contemporary historian, when the walls were being 'much shaken', the townspeople 'appeared in the most supplicant Manner before the Commandant, and beseeched him to think of preserving their Lives'.[208] Before the surrender, Hamilton took the time to burn all the correspondence that had been left with him by John Murray, leaving only 'some Missive letters he received afterwards that were not material'.[209]

Samuel Maddox, an ensign of the Manchester Regiment, later recalled that Towneley 'seemed to be in a great passion at Colonel Hamilton, for surrendering the place, and not making a defence until the last; saying It was better to die by the sword, than to fall into the hands of those damned Hanoverians'.[210]

A number tried to escape, but most were taken. One man 'a person of Distinction' was being let down the wall and some countrymen who were watching that part of the wall, shot and killed him. On his body were a gold watch and 60 guineas, which they took.[211] That night Sir Francis Geoghegan, a captain of Lally's Regiment, tried to escape from Carlisle. He was captured and brought before Cumberland. He gave the Duke two letters. They were written by the bearer himself, styling himself 'Commander of the French Artillery, and of the French Garrison that was at, or might come to Carlisle, for the defence of the town and citadel'. One was for him and the other was for the commander of the Dutch troops who were alleged to be among the besiegers. This was to remind them that the Dutch troops had been part of the garrison of Tournai which had surrendered in May 1745 under the agreement not to bear arms against the French for 18 months and therefore they should retire from the siege.[212] Some who escaped were more fortunate. Two officers, Captain Brown of Lally's Regiment, and a William Maxwell, a Scot, escaped over the wall on the 30 December.[213]

By the 30 December, the Royal Artillery had been effective, according to Richmond, 'there is a great deal of their wall beat down, & a great crack made in it, I thinke the breach will certainly be made by tonight or tomorrow, & then the whole is ours'.[214] Before that could happen, after the first discharge from the Royal Artillery on 30 December, two white flags were hung out

206 Blaikie (ed.), 'Origins', p.193.
207 Douglas, *History*, p.284.
208 Henderson, *History*, pp.68-69.
209 Bell (ed.), 'Memorials', p.419.
210 Douglas *History*, pp.282-283.
211 Marchant, *History*, p.251.
212 Douglas, *History*, pp.74-75.
213 Blaikie (ed.), 'Origins, pp.192-193.
214 McCann (ed.), 'Correspondence', p.199.

and their drums beat a chamade at the English Gate, indicating a desire for a cease fire.[215]

The Jacobites, on seeing a number of British soldiers approaching the gate, sent a message to Cumberland, desiring that both sides exchange hostages. Cumberland would have no pretence of parleying and sent a message to the Jacobites which read as follows:

> A) His Royal Highness will make no Exchange of Hostages with the Rebels and desires they will let him know by me, and what they mean'd by hanging out the White Flag.
> B) To let the French Officer know, if there is one in the Town, that there are no Dutch Troops here, but enough of the King's to chastise the Rebels, and those who dare to give them any Assistance.
> Sign'd
> Col. Conway
> Aide de Camp to his Royal Highness the Duke.[216]

Two hours later, the Jacobite emissaries returned, with the following message from Hamilton:

> In answer to the short Note sent by His Royal Highness Prince William, Duke of Cumberland, the Governor, in Name of himself and all the Officers and Soldiers, Gunners and others belonging to the Garrison, desire to know what Terms his Royal Highness will be pleased to give them, upon the surrender of the City and Castle of Carlisle, and which known, his Royal Highness shall be duly acquainted with the Governor and Garrison's last or ultimate Resolution, the White flag being hung out on Purpose to obtain a cessation of Arms for concluding such a Capitulation, This to be given to His Highness' Aide de Camp.
> Sign'd,
> John Hamilton.

After Cumberland received the letter, he responded in a way that Yorke and Richmond had already predicted a few days previously:

> All the Terms his Royal Highness will or can grant to the Rebel Garrison of Carlisle, are, That they shall not be put to the Sword, but be reserved for the King's Pleasure.
>
> If they consent to these Conditions, the Governor and Principal officers are to deliver themselves up immediately, and the Castle, Citadel, and all the Gates of the Town, are to be taken Possession of forthwith by the King's Troops. All the small Arms are to be lodged in the Town Guard Room, and the rest of the Garrison are to retire to the Cathedral, where a Guard is to be placed over them. No Damage is to be done to the Artillery, Arms or Ammunition.

215 Yorke (ed.), *Hardwicke*, Vol.I, p.492.
216 Marchant, *History*, p.253.

It was signed by Richmond at half past two.[217]

Little time elapsed between sending this and the Jacobite response, written at three o'clock:

> The Governor of Carlisle, and all Officers composing the Garrison, agree to the Terms of Capitulation given in, and subscribed by order of his Royal Highness, by his Grace the Duke of Richmond, Lenox and Aubigny, Lieutenant General of His Majesty's Forces, recommending themselves to His Royal Highness' Clemency, and that his Royal Highness will be pleased to interpose for them with his Majesty; and that the Officers Cloaths and Baggage may be safe, with a competent time to be allowed to the Citizens of Carlisle to remove their Beds, Bedcloaths and other Household Furniture impressed from them for the Use of the Garrison in the Castle.

The French tried to make separate terms for themselves, under the rules of war, as they were regular forces of another state, but this was turned down. James Nicholson, a lieutenant in Perth's Regiment, tried to escape after the capitulation was made, but failed.[218]

Thomas Sydall (1709-1746), a Manchester wigmaker who was the adjutant of the Manchester Regiment, was adamant against the surrender, later claiming:

> I heartily forgive all who had any hand in the scandalous surrender of Carlisle, for as it was the opinion of every one of the garrison who had been in foreign service that the place was tenable many days, and as the Elector's troops then lying before the town were in a bad condition (which I strenuously insisted upon) would have procured us such terms as to have prevented the fate to which we are now consign'd.[219]

Cumberland was not sympathetic to the pleas for mercy set out in Hamilton's note, as he told Newcastle,

> I wish I could have blooded the Soldiers with these Villains, but it would have cost us many a brave man & it came to the same end, as they have no sort of claim to the King's mercy & I sincerely hope will meet with none. It will be necessary to have his Majesty's pleasure known here soon, as to their destination & as I hope to get away before that can arrive, I shall leave them here under the care of the Duke of Richmond, if Major General Howard does not come up before my departure.[220]

Richmond wrote on 30 December about the issues concerning a possible surrender, 'to be sure the Duke can not treat with them, yet if they putt out

217 Marchant, *History*, p.254.
218 Marchant, *History*, pp.254, 256.
219 Paton (ed.), 'Lyon in Mourning', Vol.I, p.29.
220 TNA, SP36/78, f270r-71r, Cumberland to Newcastle, 30 December 1745.

the White flag, I really cant see how he can out them to the sword after it, 'tho to be sure they ought all to be hanged'.[221]

Cumberland added:

> Brigadier Bligh was ordered immediately to take possession of the Town, & will have there this night four hundred Foot Guards & seven hundred marching Foot, with one hundred & twenty horse to patrole in the streets, so that now we may have the happyness to say, that this part of the Kingdom is clear of all these Rebels
>
> As the surrender of Carlisle to the Rebels was the source of all the distress, this part of the Kingdom has felt from them, & is of so scandalous a nature that it deserves the strictest enquiry & punishment, I humbly conceive it would be greatly for his Majesty's present & future service & for the repose of the Kingdom, if some Examples were made in it. I have taken upon myself to seize both the Mayor & Town Clerk of Carlisle, upon information that they both met the Pretender's son & proclaimed his Father, whether they did it out of fear or disaffection, seems to me to be of the same bad consequence. They both of them own the fact, so that I venture to send them up to Town tomorrow, with an officer & a couple of sergeants, & inclose to you the two affadavits made before the Recorder concerning them, but as I shall be in the Town by tomorrow, I shall have more substantial Evidence against them, which I shall also send to you.[222]

Walpole agreed whilst writing that Cumberland had taken the place, 'but was long enough before it to prove how basely or cowardly it was yielded to the rebels'.[223]

By night fall Bligh had marched with 400 Foot Guards and another 700 infantry, into the city. The streets were patrolled by 120 dragoons. Cumberland went there in person at ten on the morning of the 31 December.[224] Apparently his arrival on horseback, was 'amidst the Acclamations of a rejoicing Multitude'. The county nobility also arrived and so did four Edinburgh councillors who dined with Cumberland, requesting he visit their city. The Duke then walked around the walls to review the defences, and then asked where Charles had stayed when at Carlisle 'in which he took up his Lodgings, and lay in the same bed'. Anything taken from the populace was restored, once proof of ownership was established.[225]

Cumberland ordered that money was not to be taken from the prisoners; only tax money taken from tax collectors by the Jacobites should be confiscated. Prisoners would need what money they had when they were incarcerated. Captain Carey of the Guards was instructed to secure Hamilton and to take control of all the Jacobite papers he could find. Captain Never had the task of questioning Jacobite officers.[226]

221 McCann (ed.), 'Correspondence', p.200.
222 TNA, SP36/78, f270r-71r, Cumberland to Newcastle, 30 December 1745.
223 Lewis (ed.), *Correspondence*, Vol.19, p.193.
224 Douglas, *History*,
225 Henderson, *History*, pp.69-70.
226 Douglas, *History*, pp.283-284.

Once inside, they found 16 pieces of Jacobite artillery, including the guns taken by the Jacobites after the battle of Prestonpans (six 1 1/2-pounders, four brass coehorns and two royals as well as four other guns, including three 4-pounders. There was also the Jacobite baggage and tents. Although a garrison was left in Carlisle, most of the troops were soon dispersed; the Liverpool Blues were sent home, Ligonier's Horse was sent to Chester, Cobham's Dragoons to Newcastle, Kingston's to Nottingham; Kerr's, Bland's and St George's to be stationed around Carlisle and Penrith. Bligh's and the other infantry were ordered to Scotland. The cannon from Whitehaven was placed in the castle.[227] Cumberland left on 2 January. [228]

Ray, who lodged in the George Inn, found a souvenir for himself. This was a 'basket hilted Back Sword of curious Workmanship'. He thought it had been made in France for one of the Highland chiefs. It had Charles' effigy engraved on it, holding a globe and sceptre, and the motto 'Long Live King James the III'. Because of this motto, though 'the whole was a piece of neat work', he felt he could not wear it.[229]

The rank and file of the Jacobite garrison laid down their weapons in the market place.[230] According to Elcho, 'all the prisoners were confined in the Cathedral and were very ill Used'.[231] Miller, who experienced this first hand concurred:

> We were barbarously treated, the souldiers rifling us and taking every thing of value from us, both money and cloaths, they did not allow us any provisions for three days and on the 4th but one biskit per man. They broke open a well in the body of the cathedral which had not been used for upward of 100 years. We were obliged to drink that or die of thirst.[232]

Worse was to come for the seven of the prisoners who had served at Prestonpans with the British Army and then joined the Jacobite army, and for four other army deserters. They were hanged at Harriby under the terms of the articles of war that bound all soldiers. Such was the lot of deserters; it had happened in the campaign already, and later occurred at Edinburgh in January 1746 and again after Culloden in April. [233]

Cumberland wrote to Newcastle, thus:

> I came hither yesterday & was astonished when I had seen the strength of the Town & Castle, which if the Rebels had chose to have held out must have cost us some blood & much time & which renders the delivery of it to them more infamous as well as more criminal.[234]

---

227 Douglas, *History*, p.255.
228 Henderson, *History*, p.70.
229 Ray, *History*, p.212.
230 Ray, *History*, p.210.
231 Elcho, *Short Account*, p.354.
232 Miller, 'Diary', p.209.
233 Ray, *History*, pp.211-12.
234 RA, CP9/13, Cumberland to Newcastle, 1 January 1746.

Similarly, he observed to Wade, 'a fortunate thing it is that it has been taken with so little loss…for I look upon it as being capable of being made as strong a place as is necessary in this island'.[235]

In another letter he told Newcastle:

> There is a plan form'd for rendering it stronger & I hope with a very little expense it may be made a place of great consequence as I set out Post tomorrow morning for London, I shall bring a rough draft of it with me for His Majesty's approbation & I hope to have the honour & great Pleasure of kissing his Majesty hands on Saturday night or Sunday Morning.
>
> PS I shall have Lord Mark Kerr's Regiment of Dragoons here to conduct such Prisoners as his Majesty may please to order from hence. I have discovered here their Military Chest consisting of about £1000, & hope to find some Papers of Remark. I shall leave Sir Everard Fawkener here a day or two to press forward the necessary Examinations & dispositions relating to the surrender of this place, & the behaviour of some of the people which would go on very slow under the Magistrates here, who are backward & slow to what concerns their Countrymen & neighbours.[236]

After the siege was over, Shairp noted that there had been a plan to storm the breach and that 200 of the Liverpool Blues would have been part of the storming party. He wrote in his memoir, 'Butt thank God that it happened as it did else a good many lives would have been lost in the attempt'.[237]

At the beginning of January, when the Jacobite army was beginning to besiege Stirling Castle, news came to them of the fall of Carlisle by Captain Brown of Lally's and Captain William Maxwell, an engineer, who had successfully escaped. At first it was disbelieved, but after a while it was taken as being true. Daniel felt relieved that he had not been there, 'I reflect upon this, I think I may say I have good fortune, in leaving that unhappy town and regiment, that I was not on some gallows or other made a partaker also of his clemency!' It also affected Charles, who 'was extremely troubled, and lamented much the loss of his subjects, especially the English, who were to be made sacrifices of'. Such sentiments were felt by most in the army, even to the extent that they wished they had been there even if they had been taken.[238]

Perth then pardoned his disobedient subordinate, Johnstone, stating that he had been deceived about the place's strength. Johnstone, as with Daniel, was very thankful that he had made the right choice, 'I fervently thanked the Almighty, who had watched over my destiny'.[239] Later in 1746 Johnstone happened to be in London, when he saw a dozen of the Carlisle garrison being led to their execution on Kennington Common.[240] On 30 July 1746, following trials at Southwark, eight officers (including Towneley) of the

235 RA, CP8/154, Cumberland to Wade, 30 December 1745.
236 TNA, SP36/80, ff3r-4r, Cumberland to Newcastle, 1 January 1746.
237 Oates and Navickas (eds), 'Jacobites and Jacobins', p.31.
238 Blaikie (ed.), 'Origins', pp.193-194.
239 Johnstone, *Memoir*, p.225.
240 Johnstone, *Memoir*, pp.224-225.

Manchester Regiment were hanged at Kennington Common; another two soldiers from the same regiment were hanged at York on 1 November that year and another two at the same place seven days later. The regiment's chaplain and a sergeant were hanged at Carlisle on 18 October 1746, three more men died at Brampton three days later, and another at Carlisle on 15 November. Four sergeants were hanged at Penrith on 28 October. Hamilton met his end on Kennington Common on 15 November. However, of the other Scottish officers taken at Carlisle, relatively few suffered the ultimate punishment; only a captain and three lieutenants were executed (one being the aforesaid James Nicholson).[241]

As with the earlier siege the question needs to be asked, could Carlisle have been held? This time it is easier to answer. Unlike the case with the Jacobite army in November, the besiegers were properly eventually equipped with heavy siege artillery which could, and did, blast a hole in the walls. There were adequate numbers to storm the place, though such would have been costly in lives of both sides. Hamilton was probably right to surrender, because a last stand as advocated by Towneley would likely have been poorly supported by the garrison and would have almost certainly have been doomed to a bloody conclusion. The mistake was to have left the garrison there in the first place. Given the relative ease of taking Carlisle in November, the Jacobite command should have known better, but it is likely that Charles' sense of honour dictated his choice, as it was to do so at Culloden several months later, with even more fatal results.

This was the last siege on English soil, and the only one in which the British Army was the besieging force. However, there were to be several more sieges in Scotland before the campaign was over.

241 B.S. Arnot and J.G. Seton (eds), 'Prisoners of the '45', *Scottish History Society*, 3rd series, 13, Vol.I (Edinburgh, 1929), pp.147-151.

5

Stirling: Town and Castle, 1746

Although the defenders of Stirling Castle had been unable to do little more than fire their guns at the passing Jacobite army on 14 September 1745, and to little effect, the garrison did take a more active role in the following month. They were always envisaged as playing more than a purely defensive role. On 30 October, following information about Jacobite forces at Alloa, Captain Abercrombie was sent with troops to disrupt them, and they captured 16 men, as well as taking baggage, arms and animals back to the castle.[1]

There was concern, as soon as it was known that the Jacobite army was on the retreat from Derby, that Stirling might be in danger. Newcastle wrote to Wade on 10 December, 'it is apprehended, they may attempt to force the castle of Stirling and even besiege that of Edinburgh'.[2] Two days later, Major General William Blakeney, lieutenant governor of the castle, issued an order to the county of Stirlingshire to raise five companies of militia, to total about 200 rank and file, to be paid for out of subscriptions and to be in arms for three months. Walter Little of Liberton was one of the company commanders and Sir Michael Bruce was another. Little's company included two lieutenants, two sergeants, two corporals, a drummer and 43 men.[3]

On 15 December, Blakeney received a letter to ask him how many soldiers and militia he had, as well as what quantities of oatmeal and provisions.[4] Fears of a Jacobite attack intensified once Charles' army had returned to Scotland, with Newcastle informing Cumberland on 28 December, 'as the rebels, in all probability, will endeavour to make themselves masters of Stirling castle and Edinburgh Castle, it is extremely to be wished that the army under Lieutenant General Hawley should get into Scotland as soon as possible in order that the Dispositions may be made for the defence of those places without loss of time'.[5]

After the main Jacobite army had crossed the River Esk on 21 December 1745, they marched through the Lowlands of Scotland via Dumfries and

1 Mounsey, *Carlisle*, p.38.

2 TNA, SP36/76, f317v, Newcastle to Wade, 10 December 1745.

3 NRS, GD122/3/17/37, 40, 45, Blakeney to Unknown, 12 December 1745.

4 TNA, SP54/26, 109b, Unknown to Blakeney, 15 December 1745.

5 TNA, SP36/78, ff.228r-29v, Newcastle to Cumberland, 28 December 1745.

Glasgow. During their marches in England, other Jacobite forces had been gathering in Scotland, along with small numbers of newly arrived French forces and heavy artillery. The two armies needed to meet.

As with Edinburgh and Carlisle, Stirling was a town with a medieval castle and it was described thus:

> The castle is not so very difficult of as access as Edinburgh, but it is esteemed equally strong, and particularly the works are capable to mount more cannon, and these cannon are better pointed; particularly there is a battery which commands, or may command the bridge; the command of which is of the utmost importance, nay it is the main end and purpose to which, as we are told, the castle was built.[6]

Ray, writing two decades later, repeated some of this verbatim (and unattributed), adding that the castle was 'built on a very high Rock. The works are capable of mounting more cannon… The walls with variety of casements, and all the outworks, are very firm, and in good condition'.[7]

However, matters inside the castle in the autumn of 1745 were not entirely good. Blakeney had written, on 6 September, about an officer of the garrison who 'seems to be fond of the company of the most disaffected people here, and talks very oddly when he is in liquor as I am informed…I shall only watch him so close as to put it out of his power to put any ill designs in execution'. This was Lieutenant Charles Elphinstone.[8] Worse was to come, for on 25 September he told Guest that Elphinstone, the castle's storekeeper, was in a treasonable correspondence with Mr Cheape, Guest's secretary. Blakeney would not arrest or dismiss Elphinstone but would keep a strict watch on him.[9] Two months later, Blakeney also noted, this time to Lieutenant General Roger Handasyde, then in Edinburgh, that Jacobite forces were gathering at Perth and might attack the castle. This was a concern in light of 'the necessarys that we wanted, and that we had not a gunner who knows how to point a gun'.[10]

Danger was mooted as the new year opened. Fletcher, writing to Newcastle on 2 January,

> The rebels at Glasgow say they are to attack Stirling, and what makes it appear probable is that on Monday at noon they began to move their cannon from Perth to Stirling…two of eight pounders, two of twelve pounders, two of sixteen pounders all brass, besides iron cannon, with these were also carried a good quantity of powder and cannon balls.[11]

The Jacobite army marched north east from Glasgow on 4 January and quartered itself on Falkirk, Bannockburn and Callendar in the following

6 Rogers (ed.), *Defoe's Tour*, p.612.
7 Ray, *History*, p.263n.
8 TNA, SP54/26, 9, Blakeney to Unknown, 6 September 1745.
9 NLS, MS16604, f97, Blakeney to Guest, 25 September 1745.
10 NLS, MS16604, 101, Blakeney to Handasyde, 25 November 1745.
11 TNA, SP54/27, 1a, Fletcher to Newcastle, 2 January 1746.

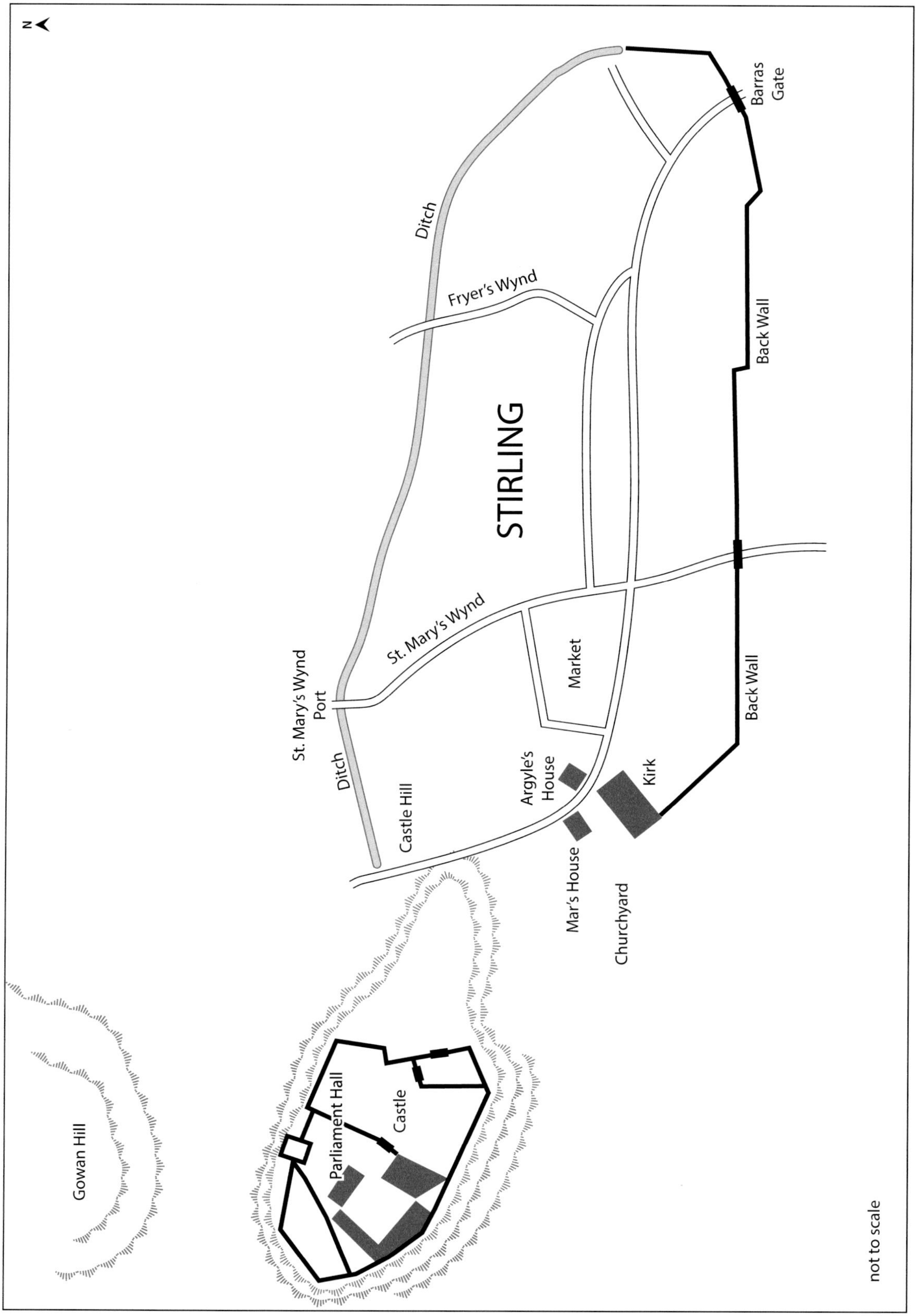

Plan of Stirling.

days.[12] The town of Stirling was summoned to surrender. It refused.[13] The precedents did not look good, though, for the defenders. When it had last besieged, on 6 August 1651, it had surrendered on the same day and the castle the day after, though the latter's defences had been strengthened in the intervening century.[14]

Attackers
Count Francis Mirabelle de Gordon, commandant general
Two companies of artillerymen

- 1st company: Captain de Bodin, one lieutenant, sergeant, corporal, nine gunners and 20 soldiers
- 2nd company: Captain de Marchand, sergeant, corporal, 11 gunners and 20 soldiers.[15]

Defenders

- Town Militia, five companies totalling about 300 men
- Country Militia, six companies (one from Perth) totalling about 320 men
- Castle garrison, 200 men, including two additional companies from Sempill's Regiment.
- At least one 16-pounder, one 12-pounder, nine 9-pounder and four 6-pounder cannon in castle.[16]

Major General William Blakeney (1672-1761) was lieutenant governor of the castle. He had been born in Ireland and saw military service in Flanders in the War of the Spanish Succession and later in the West Indies. He became colonel of his own infantry regiment in 1737, a brigadier in 1741 and a major general in the following year.[17]

Some effort had already been made to prepare the town for a siege. A newspaper later asserted:

> The town walles were all repaired, additions were made where necessary, all the avenues leading up to it built up, several deep trenches made, and everything else so well provided for a siege, that with so great a number of country militia, townsmen, &c., to defend it at all hazards, the town could have held for some months.[18]

Yet the situation was not quite so rosy as the above suggested. In fact the town was also described as being 'ane open defenceless place'. The north

12 Maxwell, *Narrative*, p.94.
13 Elcho, *Short Account*, p.364.
14 Craig Mair, *Stirling: The Royal Burgh* (Edinburgh: John Donald, 1993), p.117.
15 RA, CP7/450, Mirabelle's artillery corps, 1746.
16 Forbes, *Jacobite Memoirs*, p.96n.
17 ODNB, Vol.6, pp.133-134.
18 *St. James Evening Post*, 30 January 1746.

William Blakeney, Baron Blakeney by Thomas Ryley, after George Chalmers, mezzotint, mid-eighteenth century. (Anne S.K. Brown Collection)

Stirling Town Walls. (Matthew Oates)

was certainly 'open and without walls, having only some low fences and accompanying gardens and parks'. The only improvements had been that some slight dry stone walls had been built up and the gates and gardens had been 'stopped up'.[19]

The Jacobite advance guard had arrived before Stirling on 2 January. The town gates were ordered to be closed against them and the militia, townsmen and volunteers were put under arms for its defence. By 3 January Jacobite forces under Lord John Drummond, Lord Lewis Gordon, and the Master of Lovat had arrived. On the following day they began to cut down trees to use as fascines and to raise a battery.[20]

Blakeney had given the militia the following instructions on 4 January. Of the country militia, one company was to be stationed at Barras Gate and another at Fryers Wynd. Captain Erskine's company was to take post at the breast work at the lower end of the Meal Market and were to provide a sergeant, corporal and 12 men for Captain Little's company. Their main alarm post was to be at the upper end of the Meal Market. As to the town militia, their main alarm post was to be at the Cross. A captain, lieutenant and 40 men were to compose the main Guard. At St Mary's Wynd were Captain Finlayson, with two lieutenants and 40 men. Captain Hamilton and a detachment were at Castle Hill alarm post and were joined by a company of Perth Militia. An officer and 30 men were posted at the School Manse. Hamilton was in charge of an alarm to secure communication on both sides of the road from Argyll's house to the castle.[21]

If an alarm was rung, 'speedy succour' was to be given to any post which was in danger. In that case, magistrates were to call upon troops for help against the Jacobites. Blakeney finally declared that 'All the troops to maintain their posts to the last extremity but if over powered, they are to retreat in the best order they can to the castle, the men taking care to prime and load their arms as they march face about and fire which will give a great check to the enemy in their pursuit'.[22]

At nine in the evening of Sunday 5 January the Jacobites sent a drummer to the East Gate with a message detailing terms of surrender. The guards at that gate fired on him several times and he replied 'I'm but a Messenger' and 'ran off with all speed, leaving the Drum by the Gate'. The drum was then taken within the walls.[23] The garrison were 'fully resolved to stand it out, and all in top spirits'.[24]

However, on the next day, doubtless seeing the bulk of the Jacobite army arrive, two magistrates from the town went to the Jacobite camp with proposals to surrender 'to prevent effusion of blood', but these were not accepted. The inhabitants were opposed to the proposals 'not being well informed with the terms'. The Jacobites then began to show what they could

19 Stirling Council Archives (SCA), SBC11/15, Town Council Minutes, 1745-1752.
20 SCA, SBC11/15, Town Council Minutes, 1745-1752.
21 NRS, GD122/3/17, 38, Blakeney to Unknown, 4 January 1746.
22 NRS, GD122/3/17, 38, Blakeney to Unknown, 4 January 1746.
23 SCA, SBC11/15, Town Council Minutes, 1745-1752.
24 Forbes, *Jacobite Memoirs*, p.97n.

be capable of. Under the direction of Colonel James Grant, who had been so effective during the Carlisle siege, a battery of three small calibre guns was erected in a trench near Livelands out of view of the castle, against the town of Stirling. In the evening the militia gave up their weapons to the castle, and some of the militia officers took refuge there.[25]

The townsmen were not all daunted and elected new officers and placed their guards in the town walls. From seven until ten that evening the Jacobite guns fired, but did very little damage. Blakeney was impressed with their bravery and said that any of the militia officers who had taken refuge in the castle could re-join the militia on the walls. One Captain McKillop and some others did so at about midnight.[26]

On the next day, the town received another message and this time it was accepted, at about one in the afternoon. It was from Charles and read as follows:

> Intending to take possession of our Town of Stirling; we hereby require and command you to give our forces peaceable entry into and possession of the said town and... you are expressly required to deliver up to us all their arms, and likewise all cannon, ammunition and military stores presently in the said town assuring you hereby that if you refuse or delay to receive us, or to deliver up the arms and military stores, as aforesaid, and thereby oblige us to use that force which Providence has put into our hands after our discharging of one cannon against the said town, no articles or capitulation or protection shall be given to any of the inhabitants for their persons goods and effects.

The inhabitants were reminded that the town was now entirely blockaded on all sides and anyone caught outside the town that 'they shall be caused to immediate execution'. The council had until two that afternoon to make their reply.[27]

Furthermore, to reinforce the Jacobite message, a trench was opened and guns were pointed in musket range of the town. On 6-7 January men from the Atholl Brigade were paid to make fascines. There was a general order for the Jacobite sentries, 'All the posts that form the blockade of Stirling are to be extremely vigilant to let nobody come in or go out of the town, and the continual patrols, especially at night'. Those taking part were two officers and 50 men from each of the following regiments; Roy Stuart's, Glenbucket's and Ogilvie's.[28]

Stirling's Provost, James Wallace, then called a meeting of the council. Versions of what happened at the meeting vary. According to one, Wallace and a few councillors were in favour of surrender, but the majority were opposed. Another account claims that the decision was unanimous to send two representatives to John Murray, stating that they needed a day to deliberate and could give a reply by ten on the morning of the following day.

---

25 Forbes, *Jacobite Memoirs*, p.97n.
26 SCA, B66/25/335, Memorial of Prince Charles, 2 January 1746.
27 SCA, B66/25/335, Memorial of Prince Charles, 2 January 1746.
28 Anon., *Spalding Society Miscellany*, Vol.I, p.324.

William Christie, a former Provost, and James Jaffray, a merchant, took the message out of the town to go to the Bannockburn residence of Sir Hugh Patterson, (1685-1777) a Jacobite sympathiser, where Charles was staying, and were allowed the time requested.[29]

On the following day the council, possibly with the town's clergy and principal inhabitants, discussed the terms that they could expect from the Jacobites. If they let the Jacobite army in, they and their property would be unharmed. Again, there are two accounts as to what happened in the discussion. One has that at this point, although more councillors were now in favour of capitulation, the majority were still for defending the place until Hawley's relief army could arrive.

The contest at last grew so high. Messrs Stephenson and Erskine headed the party in favour of continued resistance. On the other hand, another account alleged that 'by far the greatest part of those present who are known to be as zealously affected to His majesty King George as any in Britain, Gave it as their Judgement that to continue the defence of the place would be a dangerous and fruitless attempt.[30]

Their reasoning was as follows. Firstly, Jacobite numbers were increasing with several thousand being in Stirling's proximity. They had erected a battery of small cannon and had two larger guns as well, just arrived. There was not a single cannon in the town of any size. The defences on the northern side of the town were meagre indeed. Secondly, the militia and volunteers were in 'want of experience in military affairs, and whose numbers did not exceed 500, which with the addition of a hundred and a few more military, was the whole strength'. In any case, they were much fatigued after three nights and three days of being constantly under arms. If there was resistance and the militia and volunteers had to retreat to the castle, it was uncertain whether they could do so and even if they did, the families of the men would be in danger from the triumphant Jacobite army.

The real fear was the threat of a result of the town being stormed. It was surely better to seek terms than risk Stirling being 'entered by assault the consequences of which must have been that our streets would be strewed with the corpses if the inhabitants and others, and the whole effects of the town became their plunder'. Because of this and attempt at defence must be 'such a risque when in a state of uncertainty as to our relief from the army… neither the publick cause nor any material branch of it depended on the defence of the town'. They concluded 'We must have been quite undone had we stood to the Defence'.[31]

The final decision was 'After long Reasoning from the above Topicks' that Stirling would surrender on the condition that no demands were made on the town's revenues, that it not be plundered and that all arms and ammunition in the town could be sent to the castle. Blakeney heard of these proceedings and he left the castle 'and went round all the Guards exhorting them to this

29 SCA, SCB11/15, Town Council Minutes, 1745-1752.

30 SCA, SBC11/15, Town Council Minutes, 1745-1752.

31 SCA, SBC11/15, Town Council Minutes, 1745-1752.

effect, "Gentlemen, be true to your Religion, King and Country, and defend your posts to the last extremity and if you are overpowered by the Rebels, make a handsome Retreat and I'll keep ane open door for you"'.[32]

A drum was beat and 900 well-armed civilians drew up in the market place and Blakeney addressed them. They gave him a cheer. Meanwhile Wallace and two others left the town to meet the Jacobite negotiators. Once Blakeney heard of this he requested that all the militia depart to the castle. Most did so, but the companies of Captains Main and Erskine remained at their posts and persuaded others to remain with them.[33]

That afternoon, the Jacobites fired 27 cannon balls at the town but only succeeded in breaking a chimney pot. Volunteers and militia in Stirling answered this with musket fire. That evening some councillors went around the walls, sword in hand, 'encouraging the men to stand out'. The only incident of note that night occurred at midnight when Wallace and his two companions returned and were challenged by the guards. They clearly were not recognised or were suspected as being Jacobites for they were arrested and taken prisoner to the main guard room and held there briefly before being released.[34]

Wallace brought with him a letter to be given to Blakeney, outlining the terms of the burgh's surrender. Blakeney was told of this and replied, 'Gentlemen, I received yours. Deliver me up my arms and ammunition'. The volunteers replied, 'if he would leave them with the militia as formerly and head them, they would stand out the siege till our army came up and would give him the disaffected gentlemen as prisoners'. Blakeney told them, 'As your Provost and Baillies think the Town not worth their notice to take care of it, neither can I. I will take care of the castle'.[35]

This was the end of the town's token resistance. Apparently 'nothing but Distraction and Confusion was to be among the militia and was heightened by the loud cries of women and children on learning the place so easily given up to a Band of merciless Villains'. At nine next morning of 8 January, the militia went to the castle with their arms and two hours later the burgh's gates were opened. The Jacobite army began to arrive at four in the afternoon and despite the surrender agreement, 'they were not two hours before they broke the capitulation by breaking up and pillaging the shops of those people who were most noted for their opposition to the Pretender'.[36]

The main reasons later stated for surrender were that the town lacked the provisions and fuel to stand even a few days' siege; nothing had been laid in because the Jacobites were at large in the neighbouring country. Councillors Stevenson and Wright had viewed the Jacobite army and had noted 'the numbers and strength of the rebels'. Therefore, 'in place of holding out against them for some months, we could not have done so for many hours'.[37] There

32 SCA, SBC11/15, Town Council Minutes, 1745-1752.
33 SCA, SBC11/15, Town Council Minutes, 1745-1752.
34 SCA, SBC11/15, Town Council Minutes, 1745-1752.
35 SCA, SBC11/15, Town Council Minutes, 1745-1752.
36 SCA, SBC11/15, Town Council Minutes, 1745-1752.
37 SCA, SBC11/15, Town Council Minutes, 1745-1752.

was a highly critical newspaper article condemning the decision of the burgh council to surrender, claiming 'the town could have held for some months against the Rebels, had it not been for the treachery of the Provost, and the pusillanimity, disaffection and cowardice of a few of the inhabitants'. The council later wrote a defence of their actions against such 'a Representation full of falsehoods'.[38]

Elsewhere, on 9 January, Newcastle wrote to Lieutenant General Henry Hawley (1685-1759), in command of the British army in Scotland which was gathering at Edinburgh, 'By the intelligence we received this day, the rebels seemed to design to besiege Stirling, but His Majesty hopes you will be able to prevent their succeeding in that attempt'.[39] On the same day, Hawley sent what must have been disappointing news, as he wrote that the town 'was not defensible', with the militia and arms being sent to the castle, the town 'opening the gates for fear'. However, he was more confident about the castle: 'I am here assured that Major General Blakeney is very well provided, with men and provisions, to his satisfaction'.[40]

With the fall of the town, the Jacobites then looked to the castle and Charles sent a summons to Blakeney to surrender, and received the polite reply, 'That His Royal Highness would assuredly have a very bad opinion of him, were he capable of surrendering the castle in such a cowardly manner'.[41] The besiegers were, as ever, the non-clan regiments such as the Atholl Brigade, Ogilvie's, Roy Stuart's, Perth's and Glenbucket's, some entering the town under cover. The castle's guns fired on them, on 8 January, on their approach to the town and when they were sighted at Livelands, but on this occasion, according to Elcho, no one was killed or wounded, though the garrison believed this had been 'with some execution'. Whenever the guns had a target they fired, often at mere individuals.[42]

Grant's plan to take the castle was discussed with Charles. This was to open trenches and establish batteries in the churchyard near the castle entrance. Apparently:

> He assured the Prince that this was the only place where they could find a parallel almost on a level with the batteries of the enemy, and that, if a breach were effected in the half-moon which defends the entry of the castle from a battery in the burying-ground, the rubbish of the work would fill the ditch and render an assault practicable.

38 SCA, SBC11/15, Town Council Minutes, 1745-1752.
39 TNA, SP54/27, 11, Newcastle to Hawley, 9 January 1746.
40 TNA, SP54/27, 15a, Hawley to Newcastle, 9 January 1746.
41 Johnstone, *Memoir*, p.83.
42 Elcho, *Short Account*, p.364; NLS, MS17154, f194r, Journal of the Siege of Stirling Castle, 1746.

Stirling Castle from the graveyard. (Postcard of Paul Lang)

There was no realistic alternative, Grant argued:

> [I]t was entirely useless to think of making an attack in any other place, from the impossibility of succeeding, and that as the hills in the neighbourhood of the castle itself, were forty or fifty feet lower than the castle itself, our batteries could produce little or no effect, whilst their batteries would command ours. Besides supposing it even possible to effect a breach on that side, we could never mount to the assault, the rock on which the castle is built being everywhere very high and almost perpendicular, except towards that part of the town opposite to the burying-ground.[43]

Some of the Jacobite forces were placed in Argyll's house near to the castle and other places in order to block communication between castle and town.[44]

The castle, as with Edinburgh Castle four months previously, remained defiant. There was no chance that town and castle would have surrendered together, as had occurred at Carlisle two months ago. On the evening of 9 January, there was firing from the castle 'which alarm'd them much, and did some small execution'.[45] It was left to the Jacobite engineers to decide how it should be attacked. Argyll's house, the meal market and the graveyard were manned by 250 Jacobite troops; the Atholl Brigade initially providing the manpower. Officers were to make nightly rounds and ensure the men's

43 Johnstone, *Memoir*, pp.84-85.
44 Forbes, *Jacobite Memoirs*, p.97n.
45 NRS, MS17154, f.195v, Journal of the Siege of Stirling Castle, 1746.

Argyll's House. (Matthew Oates)

muskets were primed and ready. On later nights, these men were joined by Ogilvies', Glenbucket's, Roy Stuart's and Perth's and, from 14-15 January, men form the Irish Picquets.[46] Apparently, 'There was some dispute among the engineers about the manner of attacking the castle'.[47] On 10-11 January, they began to entrench between Stirling Church and Mar's house, on top of the street, near to the castle's gateway. They worked under cover, so the garrison could not 'disturb' them.[48]

The Jacobites felt that they could undertake the siege of such a strong point as Stirling Castle, which had not been the case in the previous year with the equally well-defended Edinburgh Castle. This was because in the previous November, Lord John Drummond had arrived in Scotland with regular troops and, more importantly, heavy artillery, from France. These were apparently 'sufficient to reduce all the fortresses in Scotland'.[49]

Views about the safety of Stirling castle were mixed. Initially Cumberland was unconvinced it was in danger, writing from London on 11 January 1746:

> Lieut Genl Hawley,
> I was very glad to see by your Letter to the Duke of Newcastle that you was got safe to Edinburg & that you proposed marching on to Stirling as soon as all your Foot should become up, you & I being of the same opinion with regard to that despicable Enemy you have to deal with. I am fully convinced that far from besieging Stirling, they will retire to Perth upon the first appearance of the Kings

46 Anon., *Spalding Society Miscellany*, Vol.I, pp.325-328.
47 Maxwell, *Narrative*, p.94.
48 TNA, SP54/27, 22B, JG to Masterton, 12 January 1746.
49 Maxwell, *Narrative*, p.87.

Lieutenant General Henry Hawley as Colonel of the Royal Dragoons c.1748, oil on canvas by David Morier. (With kind permission from the Hawley family)

> Troops, but how you will be able to come at them there til the Season of the year shall be more favourable, I am not aware.[50]

On 15 January Hawley was confident enough, writing about 'driving the rascally scum out of Stirling to relieve Blakeney… they will go off or they are mad'.[51]

Walter Grossett, the customs officer who had tried to ginger up Edinburgh's defence in the previous September, took a letter from Hawley to Blakeney on 10 January. Hawley had written:

> I had a verball message from you by a man this morning, desiring reliefe. I am getting the foot, who are come up, repaired as soone as possible, for with the nine days marche, after all things others they are good deale harassed butt in good spirits.
>
> I shall move towards you, if possible on Sunday, in the mean time let me know by the bearer or some other way, how long you can hold out, no more now, but I am sincerely yrs.[52]

The difficulty for the castle's successful defence was outlined as follows:

> [T]he garrison lay under Disadvantages in the want of stores and many other things, quite Scandalous to the people who have the management of these affairs…so that if any Misfortune had happened to the Duke's army, so as to allow the Highlanders to come south again, the Castle must have fallen a Prey.[53]

It was not only Hawley and Cumberland who looked forward to either battle or pursuit of the enemy. On 15 January, Major General John Huske (1692-1761), one of Hawley's subordinates, wrote that the Jacobites were 'in a very great pannick and march in the utmost confusion by all accounts'. He believed that they would abandon the siege of Stirling as soon as Hawley began advancing towards them. Huske was concerned about the castle there, 'They certainly will try their best efforts to take the castle of Stirling if possible, the loss of which may be of very ill consequence'.[54]

The lighter Jacobite guns were escorted into Falkirk guarded by the men of the Irish Picquets. However, the four heavy guns from France were at Alloa, guarded by Lord John Drummond and Cromarty's Regiment, having been taken there along the road from Montrose, and because the main bridge at Stirling had already been destroyed by the defenders, these guns would need to be brought along the River Forth. To do so, a vessel had been seized at Airth and brought to Alloa; the other two at the former were burnt by boat

50 RA, CP9/66, Cumberland to Hawley, 11 January 1746.
51 RA, CP9/81, Hawley to Cumberland, 15 January 1746.
52 Blaikie (ed.), 'Origins of the Forty Five', pp.358, 393.
53 Henrietta Tayler (ed.), 'Marchmont Correspondence', *Scottish History Society Miscellany* Vol.V, 3rd series (Edinburgh, 1933), p.350.
54 TNA, SP36/80, f.82, Huske to Newcastle, 15 January 1746.

loads of men from the Royal Navy sloops, the *Pearl* and the *Vulture*, from Leith.[55]

In order to protect this last Jacobite boat, a battery of three 4-pounders under Grant's command, was established on 9 January, but finding the initial position was at a point where the river was too broad, moved the guns to Elphinstone Pans, at a narrow point in the river, to fire on any vessel which would threaten their craft. This was accomplished on 10 January and had a guard of 150 men of Elcho's Lifeguards. On the next day a flotilla of seven vessels, the two largest being of 20 guns, arrived and began to fire. There was also the prospect of 300 troops and sailors being landed under Colonel Leighton. However, despite only 100 Jacobite soldiers being present, more, including the Cameron of Lochiel's Regiment, arrived as time went by and deterred their enemies from attempting to land.[56]

Meanwhile the battery and the ships had been exchanging fire for three or four hours. The battery was unaffected and so the flotilla left when the tide was in their favour.[57] The Jacobite artillery was too light to do much damage, however, but the Jacobites thought that their guns killed ten men whereas they themselves suffered no casualties and no damage to their guns.[58] However, the captain of the *Vulture* recorded in his ship's log that two men from the *Pearl* lost a leg each; one was to die shortly afterwards, and from his own ship John Mitchell was killed, two men lost legs, and several were injured.[59]

These boats had been seen from the castle on 10-11 January; some of them arriving at Polmaise. Outside Stirling Castle, with nothing now to prevent the artillery being brought from Alloa, the guns were put in position.[60] Meanwhile, in the castle, on 13 January, at seven in the morning, the 9-pounders fired on the three houses in the town where the Jacobites had posted men, with additional fire from 11:00 am from the 6-pounders. It was impossible to tell how effective this had been. On 15 January the garrison unfurled a flag of defiance, fired the 9-pounders on property in Broad Street and grenades were thrown from the castle walls. On the next day, two six-pounders from the castle shot at the church steeple, where Jacobites could be seen, whilst another two guns of the same calibre fired at Cambuskenneth Abbey. Under cover of night on 16 January, the Jacobites began to throw up entrenchments at St Mary's Wynd and near Buchan House at the head of the Croft. Lord Lewis Gordon arrived to take charge.[61]

Mirabelle de Gordon was the French engineer officer who was tasked with overseeing the siege. Most Jacobite memoirists were critical of him in varying degrees. According to O'Sullivan he 'was a headstrong ignorant fellow yt wou'd go on his own way & follow no mans advise'.[62] Lord George

55 Maxwell, *Narrative*, pp.94-95. Elcho, *Short Account*, pp.365-366.
56 Maxwell, *Narrative*, pp.95-96; Elcho, *Short Account*, pp.366-367.
57 Maxwell, *Narrative*, p.96.
58 Elcho, *Short Account*, pp.367-368.
59 TNA, ADM52/739, Master's Log of HMS *Vulture*, 1744-1749.
60 Maxwell, *Narrative*, p.96.
61 NRS, MS 17154, f.195v, Journal of the Siege of Stirling Castle, 1746.
62 Tayler and Tayler (eds), *1745*, p.114.

Murray wrote 'we had no good engineers. He who was the principal, a French gentleman, I believe, understood it: but he was so volatile, that he culd not be depended upon'.[63] Johnstone claimed:

> It was supposed that a French engineer, of a certain age and decorated with an order, must necessarily be a person of experience, talents and capacity: but it was unfortunately discovered, when too late, that his knowledge was extremely limited, and that he was totally destitute of judgement, discernment and common sense. His figure being as whimsical as his mind, the Highlanders, instead of Monsieur Mirabelle, called him Mr Admirable.[64]

Another Jacobite was also contemptuous of the Frenchmen in charge of the siege, writing of the, 'two officers…pass'd for engineers, but the one of them was always drunk and the other was a boy, just come from the college'.[65]

Those working on the siege were the Irish and French troops, for 'our highlanders do not like to fight against walls, not to work, so there were only those few regular troops – the lowlanders were employed in it'.[66] Another observer noted, 'The Highlanders…grew tir'd with the siege, which is a service they do not understand, and which drew out longer than they had expected'.[67] There had been some Highland involvement, but 'The Highlanders from the loss they sustained at their first appearance before Stirling castle refuse to enter their trenches'.[68] Lord George Murray was not confident, writing on 16 January, 'We have bad quarters, little provisions and slow advances made towards the siege of Stirling castle'.[69]

On 15 January, news arrived at the Jacobite camp that Hawley and his forces were about to attempt to relieve the castle of Stirling and on 17 January, 1,000 men were left to cover the castle and to guard the guns whilst the majority of the army marched to confront the British army. The resulting Battle of Falkirk was in many ways tactically inconclusive, but Hawley's army retreated to Edinburgh and so the siege at Stirling could continue.[70]

The choice to resume the siege was a controversial decision; some thought that a rigorous pursuit of Hawley's defeated army would have been for the best, but as at Derby on 5 December, conventional military logic was allowed to dictate policy as Maxwell noted:

> [I]t was never heard of that an army employed in a siege, having beaten those that came to raise it, had made any other use of their victory than to take the fortress in the first place; that any other conduct would argue a great deal of levity; that it was of the utmost importance to have the castle; as it opened an easy and

63 Forbes, *Jacobite Memoirs*, pp.95-96.
64 Johnstone, *Memoir*, p.84.
65 William Fraser, *The Earls of Cromartie: their kindred, country and correspondence* (Edinburgh: Unknown Publisher, 1876), Vol.II, p.384.
66 Tayler and Tayler (eds), *1745*, p.114
67 Fraser (ed.), *Earls of Cromartie*, Vol.II, p.393.
68 *HMC Various*, Vol.VIII, p.165.
69 Atholl (ed.), *Chronicles*, Vol.III, p.142.
70 Maxwell, *Narrative*, p.96, 99.

> safe communication betwixt the Prince, wherever he might happen to be, and his friends in the north.[71]

After all, following the French victory at Fontenoy in 1745 they proceeded with the siege of Tournai rather than pursue the defeated allied army and in the siege they were successful. Some Jacobites claimed that the siege was a distraction and that they should have pursued Hawley's defeated army after the battle. Johnstone claimed 'The possession of this petty fort was of no essential importance to us; on the contrary, it was of more advantage to us that it should remain in the hands of the enemy, in order to restrain the Highlanders, and prevent them from returning when they pleased'.[72]

The day after the fighting saw Jacobite cannon move to Abbey Moat, and meal was seen being unloaded from the river. In the town, the Jacobites had the church bells rung for their 'supposed victory'. The castle's guns then fired on the church steeple to disrupt these proceedings.[73]

The news of Hawley's setback led the Duke of Perth to summon Blakeney to surrender on either 18 January at three in the afternoon or 20 January. However, the reply was prompt and resolute: 'He made answer, that he had hitherto been looked upon as a man of honour, that he would always behave himself as such, and would hold out as long as the place was tenable; upon which works already begun were continued'.[74]

There, was, however, one major flaw in the ability of the castle to withstand a lengthy siege: a scarcity of provisions, as noted. It would therefore be a race against time as to whether relief forces could arrive in time or until the Jacobite artillery could batter a hole in the castle walls. On 19 January, work continued in the town. A parapet was raised at the foot of St Mary's Wynd and Buchan House. There was musketry directed from the castle against this. Cannonfire aimed at the houses by the west of the trench and on Lyon's House on Castle Hill. Some of the last firing at targets in the town occurred on the 21 January, when it was believed that the Jacobite leaders had gathered in Mrs McKell's house in St Mary's Wynd. [75]

Yet this scheme, to assault the castle from a site in the town, as advised by Grant, was abandoned. According to Johnstone, this was because 'The inhabitants of Stirling having remonstrated with the Prince against the plan, as fire from the castle would, they said, reduce their town to ashes'. This had been the same issue as in Edinburgh in October 1745 and again the Jacobite command took the humane decision that was hardly militarily sensible. Charles then allegedly discussed this with the despised Mirabelle, in whom he was confident, asking whether there was another option and Mirabelle agreed that there was. Indeed, he claimed that he could 'reduce it in the course of forty eight hours'.[76] Sir John MacDonald noted that Mirabelle was

---

71 Maxwell, *Narrative*, pp.106-107.
72 Johnstone, *Memoir*, p.85.
73 NRS, MS 17154, f.195r-196v, Journal of the Siege of Stirling Castle, 1746.
74 Maxwell, *Narrative*, p.107.
75 NRS, MS17154, f.196v, Journal of the Siege of Stirling Castle, 1746.
76 Johnstone, *Memoir*, pp.85, 96.

opposed to the guns' current siting 'where it was considered wise by Sullivan and Grant, a good man and a clever engineer'.[77]

The siege continued from elsewhere. Work on the battery on Gowan Hill, to the east of the castle, was first noted on 20 January and took place at night, with 50 yards of entrenchments and gabions being put in place on the first night. Some musketry was fired against it, but work proceeded. On the following day's afternoon, cannon fired at the men at work, 'which made them run off, they soon returned'. On 22 January the battery on Gowan Hill moved 30 yards closer to the castle and cannon would soon be hauled up there. This was despite the fact that canister from the castle's 9-pounders and musketry from one o'clock beat the entrenchers away at two in the afternoon, for they later returned to work, under the cover of musketry. Fire was constant in the evening. [78]

This was not without cost. Indeed, a deserter who arrived at the castle, a Mr McLaughlan, 'informed us they were most private with all their designs and took particular care to conceal, even from their own people, the numbers of their killed'.[79] Johnstone lamented the Jacobite dead, 'we lost a great many brave men, particularly of the Irish brigade. What a pity these brave men should have been sacrificed'.[80] Maxwell claimed the siege cost four or five dead men per day, making it the most expensive siege in this campaign.[81]

Ogilvie's men had the burden of guarding the entrenchments after their return from the Battle of Falkirk, beginning on 19 January and carrying on until 27 January, with a break from 22-25. They were then moved to the town, joining Stonywood's men there, whilst Perth's Regiment guarded the entrenchments, but Ogilvie's were back there on 30/31 January with Perth's at Stirling. On 31 January/1 February, Ogilvie's and Stonywood's 150 men formed the town guard.[82] The Atholl men took much of the duty of blockading the castle, too, Murray writing on 25 January that there were 'absolutely necessary for the blockade'.[83]

The Jacobites were experiencing other difficulties with the siege. Murray wrote 'I am sorry it is impossible to go on so quick with the battery of cannon as would have been wished'.[84] Perth told O'Sullivan that 'The difficultys that we lie under are inconceivable...the engineer requires a great number of workmen and a considerable guard and as I said before, the men of Lord Ogilvie's are so scattered to search for victuals even out of town'. There was a lack of horses to move supplies to where they were needed and a lack of fodder for the horses.[85] Apparently the townsmen were slow in the provision of supplies 'Encouraged by the approach of the King's army'. The weather, too,

---

77 Tayler and Tayler (eds), *1745*, p.121.

78 TNA, SP54/27, 41e, Millar and Wright to Unknown, 22 January 1746; NRS, MS 17154, f.196r, Journal of the Siege of Stirling Castle, 1746. .

79 NLS, MS 17154, f.196r, Journal of the Siege of Stirling Castle, 1746.

80 Johnstone, *Memoir*, p.97.

81 Maxwell, *Narrative*, p.109.

82 Anon, *Spalding Miscellany*, Vol.I, pp.329-332

83 Atholl (ed.), *Chronicles*, Vol.III, p.165.

84 Forbes, *Jacobite Memoirs*, p.90.

85 RA, CP9/252, Perth to O'Sullivan, 23 January 1746.

was against the besiegers, 'the heavy rains interfered with his operations'.[86] In the meantime, Charles emphasised the importance of the siege, writing 'I wish with all my heart, as you do, that the siege could be quicken'd, and am continually giving orders about it'.[87] However, though he visited the trenches on the afternoon of 21 January with his staff, that was the only time the men there saw him.[88] One Jacobite wrote despairingly of the progress made, 'the siege of which was carried on with all the vigour that the bad season of the year and the drunkenness of our famous French engineer would allow of'.[89]

Most of the army did not want to be involved with the work of the siege as MacDonald noted: 'there was no labourers…the Highlanders would not undertake this work for fear of derogating from their noble birth, of which they are so proud, and the Lowlanders are too lazy to work in the trenches'. Only the French and Irish troops would undertake it, 'they worked even better than could have been expected and had considerable losses out of their small numbers'.[90]

Concern that Hawley had been reinforced and was expecting Cumberland to take command of the army, led to 'There was no doubt but he would make another attempt to relieve Stirling, if he arrived before it could be taken: therefore orders were given to carry on the works with greatest vigour'.[91] Apparently Mirabelle 'chose such a bad ground full of Stones & very little earth, yt the trinches, cou'd hardly be perfectioned any where, & his battery was so well made, & so well placed, yt it cou'd not resist'.[92]

There was artillery fire from the castle on a daily basis, though it was apparently slight. Both sides fired shells from coehorn mortars at one another. However, supplies in Stirling were few because the bridge had been destroyed and that stopped country people bringing food.[93] On 23 January, Perth ordered 100 'well armed' men from the Atholl Brigade to 'mount garde of the trenches' in order to grant respite to those men who had been doing this unpopular duty already.[94]

On 24 January Hawley heard additional news about the siege and he reported the news to Newcastle. Apparently:

> [A]s to Stirling, by all accounts, they proceed very slow. Mr Blakeney has killed so many they can get none of theyr people to go to theyr battery and they are trying to erect for which reason the men of the Irish Brigade and the Drummond Regiment are employed in the service.[95]

86 Seton (ed.), 'Commentary', p.103.
87 Atholl (ed.), *Chronicles*, Vol.III, p.165.
88 Forbes, *Jacobite Memoirs*, p.98n.
89 Fraser, *Earls of Cromartie*, Vol.II, p.393.
90 Tayler and Tayler (eds), *1745*, p.121n.
91 Maxwell, *Narrative*, p.109.
92 Tayler and Tayler (eds), *1745*, p.121.
93 Elcho, *Short Account*, pp.381-382.
94 RA, CP9/252, Perth to O'Sullivan, 23 January 1746.
95 TNA, SP54/27, 41A, Hawley to Newcastle, 24 January 1746.

Two days later, Hawley reported that the Jacobites 'have as yet made no progress against the castle of Stirling'. He had had two messages from Blakeney, 'he has killed there so many that theyr men are quite rebutted, he is very well in all aspects and has not loste a man, as they have only pickered at him, with small arms out of the houses'.[96] Two days later, Hawley wrote 'every thinge goes well with Blakeney, they had yesterday fired no cannon against the castle, only muskets, from the houses, but he has not loste a man they have many killed'.[97] In London there were fears for the castle, however, with Walpole writing on 28 January, 'A worse loss is apprehended: Stirling Castle; which could hold out but ten days; and that term expires tomorrow'. He hoped that the castle would be relieved.[98]

On the morning of 25 January the garrison saw the flag of Saint Andrew over the Jacobite entrenchments. However, the wind would not let it stand. It was seen on the next day, too, flying proudly. This was too tempting for the castle's gunners and they took aim, de-masting it later that day.[99] A bad omen for the Jacobites, perhaps?

Although the Jacobite cannon was unable to fire, and musketry was wholly ineffectual, they eventually did have a way of firing into the castle at this time. At 11:00 p.m. on 26 January, coehorn mortar fire was employed. The 17 shells fired that night caused no damage. On the next day, in the space of five hours in the evening, 54 shells were fired and five went through the roof of the Parliament House where private soldiers were resting, but none were hurt. Another 56 shells were fired on 28 January and once again, no losses were sustained.[100]

It is possible that all this mortar fire, impotent though it was to be, was for the benefit of the besiegers' morale, as they were being fired on and yet were unable to retaliate. On the evening of 26 January a French soldier deserted to the castle, where he told the defenders that, 'our firing for some nights past has done considerable execution and that the force landed from France under Lord John Drummond are quite sick of their expedition, and many of them would gladly desert, were they sure to be admitted into the garrison'.[101]

Yet despite the incessant fire, day and night, with cannon and musket, on the men at work on Gowan Hill, 'so that it was not in their power to make the least progress', work was moving towards completion in the last few days of January. On 27 January the garrison noted that a battery was being erected with woolpacks to cover it. Despite cannon fire making breaches in the entrenchments, these were being filled up with sand. More woolpacks were out into position on the next day.[102]

On 28 January the battery on Gowan Hill was complete with three heavy guns ready to fire.[103] It was believed that if the guns made a breach 'itt is the

96 TNA, SP54/27, 46, Hawley to Newcastle, 26 January 1746.
97 TNA, SP54/27, 51a, Hawley to Newcastle, 28 January 1746.
98 Lewis (ed.), *Correspondence*, Vol.19, p.204.
99 NRS, MS17154, ff.197v-r, Journal of the Siege of Stirling Castle, 1746.
100 NLS, MS17154, f.197r-198v, Journal of the Siege of Stirling Castle, 1746.
101 NLS, M17154, f.197r, Journal of the Siege of Stirling Castle, 1746.
102 NLS, MS17154, f.197v-198v, Journal of the Siege of Stirling Castle, 1746.
103 Elcho, *Short Account*, p.382.

general Report of the Ribles so soon as they have made any considerable Bretches on the walls that the clans are to enter with sword and pistole in hand'.[104] Apparently this was thought to be imminent, as 'The Ingineer has given assurances 18 hours after he begins he shall be master of the castle'. Yet the informant thought otherwise, 'They are in no great earnest of being masters of the place'.[105]

This battery had been largely undisturbed up to now. According to a memoir, this caused concern about Blakeney's loyalties:

> His inferior officers in the mean time held a consultation, and resolved, that he intended to give up the fort, and were actually in the point of arresting him, when he suddenly ordered all the works to be manned, charging the cannon with bags of musket balls, dispersed after a few moments the whole Rebel rout.[106]

The day of decision was 29 January, though Johnstone claimed it was on the next day. According to him, 'Monsieur Mirabelle, with a childish impatience to witness the effects of his battery, unmasked it as soon as three embrasures of the six of which it was to have been composed were finished'.[107] The newly completed Jacobite battery of two 18-pounders and one 12-pounder opened fire in the morning. There is divergence of opinion as to when this began and when it ceased. A Jacobite account gives it as beginning at eleven o'clock; however, it was 'silenced in a few hours after it began to play; some of the guns were dismounted, and one of the sixteen pounders so bruised, that it could not be of further use'. Another account has the guns beginning their bombardment between five and six and ceasing at ten, 'by the furious playing of our guns and continual showers of small shot upon them'. [108] The guns that were fired from the castle at the battery were a battery of nine 9-pounders and another of four 6-pounders.[109] However, John Miller told how a 16-pounder and a 12-pounder fired 'very hotly' on the Jacobite guns, on both the French battery and Elphinstone's battery. This was despite the many sandbags and woolpacks protecting the guns.[110]

Johnstone described how the battery had been destroyed after a brisk fire from the castle's guns, 'But it was of short duration, and produced very little effect on the batteries of the Castle, which being more elevated than ours, enabled the enemy to see even the buckles of the shoes of our artillerymen. As their fire commanded ours, our guns were immediately dismounted…our guns being pointed upward, could do no execution whatever'.[111] This was not quite the case, with the Jacobite artillery 'shattering two of the ambrasures, one bullet went through the roof of the gaird-room; severals of them went

104 TNA, SP54/27, 55d, Millar to Unknown, 29 January 1746.
105 TNA, SP54/27, 55e, Unknown to Unknown, 29 January 1746.
106 Anon., *Memoirs of the Life and Actions of General Blakeney* (London: Unknown Publisher, 1756), p.12.
107 Johnstone, *A Memoir*, p.97.
108 Maxwell, *Narrative*, p.112; NLS MS17154, f.198v, Journal of the Siege of Stirling Castle, 1746.
109 Forbes, *Jacobite Memoirs*, p.98n.
110 TNA, SP54/27, 55d, Millar to Unknown 29 January 1746.
111 Johnstone, *A Memoir*, p.97.

over the castle, towards the town of Cambusbarron, one of which greased in the middle of the toun'.[112]

Of the Jacobite guns, apparently one gun had 'nine wounds' in it and some of them were so badly damaged 'it was quite surprising'.[113] The memoir cited above claimed that this firing led to 300 Jacobite dead, 'cut down like grass under a scythe', but this is surely an exaggeration.[114] The Jacobite guns were not yet silenced, for at two that afternoon, some gunners crept up to the now abandoned battery and 'fired one gun out of bravado'. The castle's 9-pounders fired canister into the abandoned battery and there was further musketry throughout the day in order to stop the guns being carried off.[115]

There is a myth, as recorded by Johnstone, that Blakeney:

> [P]erceived our ignorance from the position of our battery and did not disturb us whilst constructing it. Convinced that we could do him no injury from that quarter, he remained quiet…and allowed us to go on, that we might lose our precious moments which we ought to have employed in pursuing the enemy. Well he knew he could destroy our battery whenever he pleased'.[116]

As noted, the castle's guns were far from silent throughout the siege.

Lord George Murray put the blame elsewhere, somewhat disingenuously, informing his wife on this day, 'The season hinders the taking of Stirling Castle'.[117] On 31 January, guns from the Nether Bailey and Lady's Hole fired at Jacobite forces to the west of the castle at Rayleburn, hoping to clear them from there. It was also on this day that the garrison's only fatality occurred. An anonymous off duty soldier put his head above the battlements to take a look and was killed, just had had happened to one of Molloy's defenders at Ruthven in the previous year.[118]

According to Elcho, though, the Jacobite guns 'did the walls much damage'. Mirabelle was greatly criticised for beginning the cannon firing when there were only three guns; had he waited a day longer he could have had seven guns firing. Apparently 'people did not hesitate to say he had been bribed'.[119] John Daniel claimed that Mirabelle had 'not been good for any thing' and had wasted three weeks erecting batteries 'in an improper place' and 'we spent three week's labour in vain'.[120]

Yet despite this apparent failure on the Jacobites' part there remained concerns for the castle's safety, with Miller writing 'if they are not speedily relieved they cannot hold itt out any considerable time'.[121]

112 Forbes, *Jacobite Memoirs*, p.98n.
113 Tayler (ed.), 'Marchmont Correspondence', p.350.
114 Anon., *Memoirs of Blakeney*, p.12.
115 NLS, MS 17154, f.198v-r, Journal of the Siege of Stirling Castle, 1746.
116 Johnstone, *Memoir*, p.98.
117 Atholl (ed.), *Chronicles*, Vol.III, p.171.
118 NLS, MS 17154, f.198v-r, Journal of the Siege of Stirling Castle, 1746.
119 Elcho, *Short Account*, p.382.
120 Blaikie (ed.), 'Origins', p.192; TNA, SP54/27, 55d, Millar to Unknown, 29 January 1746.
121 TNA, SP54/27, 55d, Millar to Unknown, 29 January 1746.

The siege had been a costly failure for the Jacobites and caused them more casualties than any had to date. One estimate of their losses was 'above 600 of their best men, almost all French', and though this is certainly a gross exaggeration, the numbers are probably in their scores and would have included Scottish as well as French and Irish fatalities.[122] More realistically, Elcho put Jacobite losses at 30 killed and 50 wounded.[123]

Unaware of all this, Cumberland lost no time in marching towards Stirling, declaring on his arrival in Edinburgh on 30 January:

> I thought it of the utmost importance to move to the relief of Stirling Castle, which we are under some pain for, tho' the Rebels have as yet mounted but three Guns, they have made a seeming disposition for saving their Baggage in case of another affair, but I believe they propose to themselves to retire to Perth without coming to Blows, if they can take the castle before we come up.[124]

The Jacobite failure to take the castle was used by Lord George Murray as a major argument for why the Jacobite army should retreat. In a letter by him to Charles, signed by several of the clan chiefs on 29 January he noted:

> We are afraid Stirling Castle cannot be taken so soon as was expected; if the enemy march before it should fall into your Royal Highness' hands, we dread the most fatal consequences. If your Royal Highness should risk a battle, and Stirling Castle not in your hands, we can foresee nothing but utter destruction to the few that will remain.[125]

The Jacobite army retreated on 31 January-1 February, the decision been based on the additional grounds that the army was too weakened by desertions that it would be folly to stand and fight a superior force. Whether this was indeed the case was another question, but retreat it did, on Lord George Murray's insistence, despite Charles' wishes, just as it had done at Derby in the previous month. The siege of Stirling Castle had ended in dismal failure.[126]

On 31 January, the Jacobites hauled away their disabled cannon and on the same day both sides heard that Cumberland was leading the British army from Edinburgh towards Stirling. In Blakeney's case, an express arrived at the castle from 'that glorious Hero'. Panic appeared to have gripped some of the former besiegers as trenches were abandoned for the final time. On the following day, Blakeney sent 100 men to sally out into the town to take what Jacobite baggage and artillery they could find. The soldiers went further afield to take coehorn mortars, 50 barrels of powder, 100 boxes, 200 cannon balls, meal, and prisoners.[127]

---

122 Forbes, *Jacobite Memoirs*, p.98n.
123 Tayler (ed.), *Jacobite Miscellany*, p.157.
124 TNA, SP54/27/55A, Cumberland to Newcastle, 30 January 1746.
125 NRS, GD126/30, Letter from Lord George Murray, 29 January 1746.
126 TNA, SP54/27/55a, Cumberland to Newcastle, 30 January 1746.
127 NLS, MS17154, f.198r, Journal of the Siege of Stirling Castle, 1746.

At five in the evening of 1 February the advance guard of the relief force arrived. Next day, Cumberland came, to be greeted with wild acclamations in Stirling. He rode through the town and met Blakeney at the gateway to the castle, which had just fired a 21-gun salute in his honour. The aged veteran offered the Duke the keys to the castle and the younger man replied 'in his royal way', 'they were already in good hands'. Blakeney was then thanked in the King's name, 'for his gallant defence' and having done 'no more than was expected of him'. Cumberland then viewed the castle walls and guns and was pleased with what he saw.[128]

Yorke commented on 3 February, now that the British army had arrived at Stirling:

> The attempts they made on Stirling Castle were absurd; for it was absolutely out of their power to take it without the Castle wanted provisions, and General Blakeney had just enough for ten days when we relieved him. The battery which they had raised, and raised so many fears in London, was a bugbear; for it was so commanded that the garrison could pick out the men in the works, and our gunners fired so well that the battery which opened its mouth at ½ past five in the morning, never spoke again after ten; for the guns were battered so much that they were rendered entirely useless. The King owes the safety of this part of the Kingdom to the two castles of Edinburgh and this, and the Governors, in my opinion, should not be forgot.[129]

Indeed, it was not. Cumberland referred to Newcastle's noting 'his Majesty's satisfaction on the Rebels raising the siege of Stirling Castle'.[130] Blakeney was promoted to Lieutenant General, became lieutenant governor of the fortress at Minorca, and on death earned himself a place in Westminster Abbey. As with Guest at Edinburgh Castle he was defending a strong point, but had relief not come speedily it would have fallen due to lack of supplies. He was also favoured by facing an inept opponent and in later sieges the Jacobites would not always be labouring under such a handicap.

Johnstone saw the siege as a tragedy and concluded: 'Thus a work of three weeks, which had prevented us from deriving any advantage from our victory at Falkirk and which had cost us the lives of a great number of brave men, was demolished in an instant, like a castle of cards'.[131] With the benefit of hindsight, some Jacobites believed the place was impregnable, Cumberland writing that 'They were very much disappointed at the defence General Blakeney had made in Stirling Castle, & said it was impossible for Man to take it'.[132]

---

128 NLS, MS17154, f.199v, Journal of the Siege of Stirling Castle, 1746.

129 Yorke (ed.), *Hardwicke*, Vol.I, p.495.

130 RA, CP10/233, Cumberland to Newcastle, 14 February 1746.

131 Johnstone, *Memoir*, p.97.

132 TNA, SP54/28, 1B, Cumberland to Fletcher, 1 February 1746.

6

Fort George and Fort Augustus

Although the Jacobite army marched from Stirling following the failure to take Stirling Castle and was thought incapable of standing against the army led by Cumberland, it were still able to take offensive action. This ability was proved at Ruthven Barracks (as noted in Chapter 2) and was to be so against two of the Highland forts garrisoned by British troops. At the end of the previous year, Duncan Forbes (1685-1747), Lord of the Sessions and a leading Highland loyalist, had made the gloomy prediction as follows, 'they will be able to make themselves masters of the three Forts in a trifle of time, as the regular troops cannot possibly follow them northwards through the mountains at this time of year'.[1]

Inverness had been garrisoned by Lord Loudoun's loyalist Highland troops in the winter of 1745, but on the approach of the Jacobite army he withdrew the majority of his men northwards. However, as he later wrote, 'I laid a good deal of provisions in Fort George, but the arms and what ammunition could be spared I put of ship board'.[2] The garrison commander seems to have been confident, writing 'If they have not heavy cannon, I despise their whole army…We are in no danger as they will disperse'.[3]

Fort George stood on a hill to the south of Inverness and overlooked the River Nairn. There had been a fort there in the 1650s, but it had been abandoned at the Restoration. Defoe wrote that it, 'has been restored since the Revolution; and a garrison was always kept there by King William, for the better regulating of the Highlands'.[4] Johnstone was impressed by it, writing, 'The castle of Inverness was fortified in the modern manner, being a regular square with four bastions, and it was advantageously situated on the top of an eminence which commanded the town…and has been kept in good repair with the view of enforcing the subjection of the Highlanders'.[5] A contemporary Jacobite observer further noted it as, 'a castle of considerable

1 Kingsford, 'The Highland Forts', p.368.
2 RA, CP12/71, Loudoun to Cumberland, March 1746.
3 NRS, GD248/48/3, 45, Grant to Unknown, 10 February 1746.
4 Rogers (ed.), *Defoe's Tour*, p.661.
5 Johnstone, *Memoir*, p.103.

strength, due to both its natural position and to its fortifications' and amply-provisioned, supplying it with everything necessary for sustaining a siege'.[6]

Captain Burt described it thus, 'The castle stands upon a little steep hill closely adjoining the town, on the south side, built with unhewn stone; it was lately in ruins but is now repaired'.[7]

Garrison

The establishment at the fort, as it was also at Fort Augustus, was a deputy governor, an adjutant, a surgeon, a master gunner and two other gunners.[8]

- Major James Grant, in command
- Lieutenant Colonel Innes 'yt was gouty'.
- Captains Master of Ross (Independent company), Grant and Minchin (Guise's)
- Lieutenants Graham, Charles Ross, William Grant
- Ensigns James Grant and David Ross
- Quartermaster Hartley
- Adjutant Major Colquhoun
- About 210 infantry: One independent company of Ross, one company of Guise's Regiment, a company of Grants (each company being about 70 men) and some sick men from other units
- 16 cannon (including nine 3-pounders)
- Master Gunner/storekeeper and two gunners 'but good for nothing'.

They were well supplied with 'Great Plenty of all kinds' of provisions and had no lack of water or whisky. The garrison were regularly paid, or as Grant later put it 'at least he heard no complaints'.[9]

Cumberland felt confident that the Jacobites would be unable to take the place, writing, 'There is another thing amazes me stil more, which is that they should attempt to take a regular & a good fort, as it described to me, with nine three pounders, & in a Country where they can hardly subsist'.[10] On 18 February, Charles had O'Sullivan to lead the advance guard of the MacDonalds with two guns, to clear Inverness of any opposition to him. There were some outposts held between them and the town, but those manning them fled on the Jacobite approach. On seeing this, Charles ordered him to continue his march but to avoid the fort and go straight into Inverness. A man came from the town and told that it had been abandoned and O'Sullivan asked if its erstwhile defenders could be easily pursued. The reply was in the negative 'because the castle commanded the bridge'. The ford was impassable and so the Jacobite march was initially frustrated.[11]

---

6 Seton (ed.), 'Commentary', p.108.
7 Burt, *Letters*, p.37.
8 TNA, WO24/246, Papers concerning establishments, 1745-1746.
9 Elcho, *Short Account*, p.392; Tayler and Tayler, (eds), *1745*, p.134; TNA, SP54/30/30b, Examination, April 1746.
10 TNA, SP54/28, 43A, Cumberland to Newcastle, 25 February 1746.
11 Tayler and Tayler (eds), *1745*, pp.132-133.

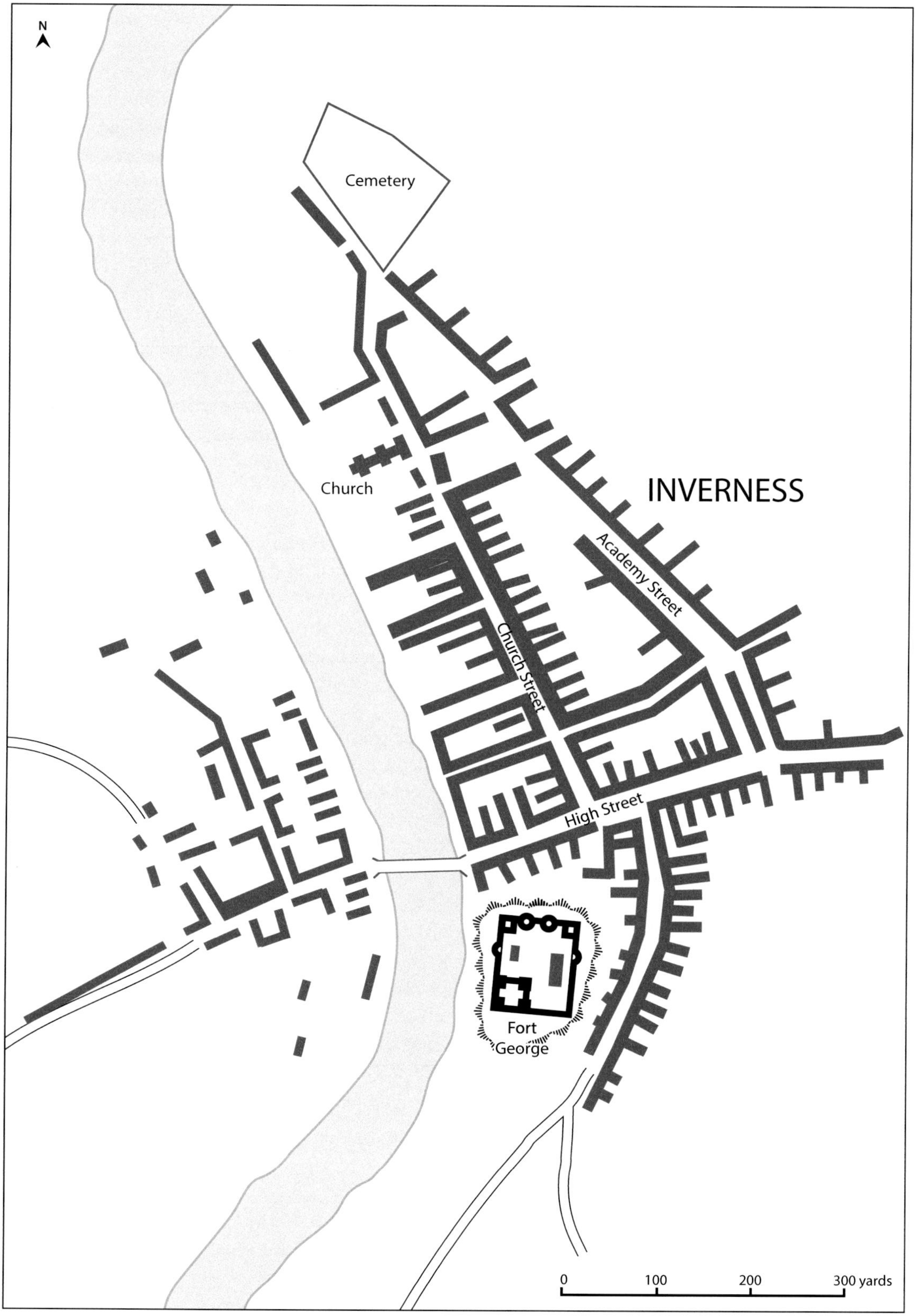

Plan of Fort George.

Charles then ordered O'Sullivan to possess the town and 'to form the blockade & gave him the direction of the Siege'. He marched the men into Inverness and took up posts around the fort, '& examined it yt night as nearly as he cou'd, with a personne well inclined of the Town, yt he was directed to'.[12] At this stage, John Millross, one of the garrison, considered that they should have fired upon them 'they might have done much more execution to the rebels'.[13]

Cannon were planted by the Jacobites behind the entrenchments that Loudoun had previously made. They then sent a drummer to the fort to demand its surrender. The man arrived at the fort with a letter to the governor and was allowed inside, blindfolded, to deliver it. It was refused.[14] Grant was determined to hold the fort against the Jacobite army. As ever, the artillery possessed by the Jacobite army was of too small a calibre to do the fort any serious damage (the heavy artillery used against Stirling Castle had been abandoned there due to transportation difficulties). It was on 18 February that the Jacobite army appeared before the walls. Instead of deploying artillery, they began to lay a mine under one of the bastions so as to blow it up.[15] Apparently, 'the garrison were firing very briskly upon them' on the Thursday.[16]

There was a suggestion that the Jacobites in Inverness be fired upon by the guns, but they did not do so 'for fear of demolishing the houses and not seeing any of the Rebels and being afraid of being called to account if he had done it'. Most of the officers were opposed, too, especially Innes. Oddly enough it was said that the guns of Edinburgh Castle had not fired on the city, but, as stated, they had done so after having received explicit orders to do so if necessary.[17]

There may have been some additional negotiation at this point, and a cease fire was agreed upon. This, however, was broken by the Jacobites who used the night to move their guns about 21 yards closer to the fort. A loyalist in Inverness managed to have information about this brought to the fort. Then, 'The Guns were brought to bear upon the Trench, whence the Rebels were driven off with precipitation, scarcely taking time to carry off their Wounded Men'.[18]

On the early morning of 19 February, O'Sullivan examined the fort again and 'found it was too well fortified for one Smal cannon'. The coehorn mortars were present but were never used. Nor 'wou'd it be no easy matter to escalled it because of a double enceinte it had'. However, he did detect where it was vulnerable. They could not go over or through the walls, but there was the possibility of going under. The bastion that faced the bridge was the potential

12 Tayler and Tayler (eds), *1745*, p.132.
13 TNA, SP54/29, 14D, Millross to Bury and Bruce, 15 March 1746.
14 Henderson, *History*, p.102; TNA, SP54/30/30b, Examination, April 1746.
15 Elcho, *Short Account*, p.392.
16 Douglas, *History*, p.151.
17 TNA, SP54/30/30b, Examination, April 1746.
18 Henderson, *History*, p.102.

weak point and he told the Marquis d'Eguilles, an envoy from France, of this and then went to inform Charles.[19]

There may have been some artillery fire against the fort. Lord Glenorchy wrote on 24 February, that a spy told him that eight cannon had been set to work against its walls, and had been fired upon by the fort's guns, but that the Jacobite cannon 'had done no execution when he came away'.[20] However, Major Colville claimed that the Jacobite guns did not fire at all.[21] Charles told O'Sullivan to set about laying a mine. The latter began to have pickaxes and shovels collected and d'Eguilles found workmen to make more. Planks were obtained to sustain the mine tunnel and baskets and tubs were located to carry away the earth that was dug out. Work commenced that night. Everything seemed to be going well.[22]

The Duke of Perth, as usual, took the command of the siege. He summoned Grant to surrender or he would blow the bastion up on the next night. Grant sent the Master of Ross to examine the mine, but this was refused. He returned and then the fort's guns began to open fire. They fired on a guard house near the mine entrance, and damaged the chimney and the roof 'for it was too low, yt they cou'd point their Cannon, on the windows or doors'.[23]

That night there was mortar fire from the fort against those working on the mine, 'wch obliged those yt worked at the mine to abandone it'. However, O'Sullivan, James Grant, and two others continued the work there. When the bombardment ceased, the men returned to work. One of the sentries fired on O'Sullivan and the musket ball pierced his hat but did not injure him otherwise. Meanwhile, the Jacobites established a battery on Bara hill and on the following morning, it opened fire on the barracks inside the fort.[24]

Initially Grant refused to surrender on account of his orders from London.[25] However, realising that 'his Grenads & all he cou'd do, did not hinder us to continue the mine, [Grant] propos'd to Capitulat'. It was later noted 'the people were all seized with a pannick on hearing of a mine'. The Master of Ross went out to capitulate. The Jacobite guns had disturbed the garrison's water supply and 'all the officers in the Garrison were for it' [surrender]. Grant said that they should put this in writing as a council of war, but Innes said that there was no need for all the officers would vindicate him.[26]

Perth would not negotiate terms; the garrison must surrender at discretion or not at all. Grant decided to surrender the fort at discretion.[27] Thomas Sheridan wrote on that afternoon, 'The Garrison left in ye castle has this afternoon begun to parley. If they do not surrender before this time tomorrow night they will in all appearance take a flight upward'.[28]

19 Tayler and Tayler (eds), *1745*, p.133.
20 RA, CP11/58, Glenorchy to Cumberland, 24 February 1746.
21 RA, CP11/138, Colville to Napier, 27 February 1746.
22 Tayler and Tayler (eds), *1745*, p.133
23 Tayler and Tayler (eds), *1745*, p.133.
24 Tayler and Tayler (eds), *1745*, pp.133-134.
25 RA, Stuart Papers (SP) Miscellany, 11, p.215.
26 TNA, SP54/30/30b, Examination, April 1746.
27 Tayler and Tayler (eds), *1745*, p.134; Elcho, *Short Account*, p.392.
28 RA, CP11/282, Sheridan to Stuart, 28 February 1746.

John Millross thought that more could have been done against the attackers, 'and would have fired more, but the Governor and Lieutenant Minchin were very backward and hindered them from firing'.[29] Mr Thomson, the master gunner, apparently thought so too, and later recalled:

> [T]he force to reduce it was nothing at all, the officers in the garrison proposed to sally out upon the besiegers, and both Lieutenant Graham and I laid down a method to undermine them, if they proceeded to a sap. All was in vain; the governor was against everything; his brother vassal (the Grants) had embraced a neutrality with the enemy; he got very good terms for himself, but the rest of the garrison, and I amongst others, have been stript of our all.[30]

The Jacobites found useful stores within the fort. According to O'Sullivan:

> We found no mony, but a good quantity of Armes & ammunition; a great quantity for such a garrison, of meal, salt beef [100 barrels], Ches, bear, Wine &ca but there was a very ill acct given of it for the most of it was plundered, notwithstanding all the precautions yt cou'd be taken.[31]

The officers were allowed to retain their personal possessions but the surrender agreement did not extend to the men whose property was plundered.[32] The Master of Lovat, who was Grant's nephew, suggested that he could personally parole Grant if the latter agreed to go home and swore not to fight against the Jacobites.

The prisoners were troublesome and expensive to feed and guard. The Grant clan came to claim their own clan members who were among the prisoners and guaranteed that these men would no longer fight against the Jacobites. This was agreed to, though some hostages were taken for the men's future behaviour. The Rosses taken regained their liberty by promising not to serve against the Jacobites, too. The Master of Ross wrote to let the Jacobites know that he would guarantee his men's actions and sent a pair of pistols to Charles. The other officers including Grant, swore that they would not act against them either.[33] Many of the Grants enlisted with the Jacobites, though some deserted shortly afterwards.[34]

There was much criticism of Grant. Henderson wrote that the surrender 'was solely owing to Grant whose cowardice and bad conduct cannot but reflect Dishonour on himself'.[35] A statement made by one of the garrison suggested that a more prolonged resistance was possible. John Millross claimed that the surrender was against the wishes of most of the garrison, 'But they were obliged to submit to the governor'. Lieutenant Minchin was

---

29 TNA, SP54/29, 14D, Millross to Bury and Bruce, 15 March 1746.
30 Andrew Henderson, *The Life of William Augustus, Duke of Cumberland* (London: J. Ridley, 1766), p.266
31 Tayler and Tayler (eds), *1745*, p.134.
32 TNA, SP54/30/30b, Examination, April 1746.
33 Tayler and Tayler (eds), *1745*, pp.134-135.
34 TNA, SP54/29, 14D, Millross to Bury and Bruce, 15 March 1746.
35 Henderson, *History*, p.102.

apparently drunk at the time but Lieutenant Grahame of Guise's wanted to fight on and 'came boldly up and called up to the private soldiers to stand by him and he would stand by them as long as he had a bit of life in him, for he was ashamed to see so little done in defence of the castle'.[36]

Apparently there were very few fatalities, as Johnstone recorded:

> The Prince immediately gave orders to raze the fortification and blow up the bastions. Monsieur L'Epine, a sergeant in the French artillery, who was charged with the operation, lost his life on the occasion. This unfortunate individual, believing the match extinguished, approached to examine it, when the mine was sprung, which blew him up into the air, with the stones of the bastion, to an immense height.[37]

A contemporary historian noted:

> Their Chief Engineer, who laid the Plan for blowing up this Fort, was mounted up into the Air by one of the Blasts and killed, whose Dog fared better than his Master, for although he was also blown up at the same Time, a great Height, and thrown near to the other side of the River, yet lived, but was sadly lamed.[38]

The incident of the dog also excited the interest of another contemporary historian, who noted that the engineer was also the man who was responsible for the blowing up of St Ninian's church earlier in the month, and looking down at the artillery: the dog was looking down too, standing on a large stone, and was flung onto the other side of the river by the blast 'where he fell into a Yard newly digged, but received little Damage, being preserved from suffocation by the Stone on which he stood'.[39] Cumberland, writing on 14 March, mistook this sergeant for Colonel Grant, writing 'They have blown up their chief of Ingineers, Colonel Grant'.[40] Elcho noted that two or three men were killed on each side.[41] Three of the garrison were killed by musketry.[42]

News of the fort's fall reached Edinburgh by 28 February, as noted by Fletcher.[43] On 27 February Cumberland wrote to both Major General Campbell and the lieutenant governor of Fort William, referring to 'the hasty surrender of Fort George'.[44] On the next day he informed Newcastle, 'I suppose that before this you will have had the bad news of Fort George's having fallen into the rebels' hands. I am no way able to explain how or by what neglect it is so, but a silly affair it is.' He went on to express his fears

36 TNA, SP54/29, 14d, Millross to Bury and Bruce, 15 March 1746.
37 Johnstone, *Memoir*, p.104.
38 Ray, *History*, p.366n.
39 Henderson, *History*, p.103
40 TNA, SP54/29, 10b, Cumberland to Newcastle, 14 March 1746.
41 Elcho, *Short Account*, p.392.
42 RA, CP11/138, Colville to Napier, 27 February 1746.
43 RA, CP11/156, Fletcher to Newcastle, 28 February 1746.
44 RA, CP11/139-40, Cumberland to Major General Campbell and Captain Campbell, 27 February 1746.

that other forts might also be lost.[45]. Newcastle replied on 6 March: 'The first account that Fort George had fallen into the rebels' hands came from your Royal Highness. The Lord Chief Justice Clerk has sent the Duke of Argyle some particulars, which do not do great honour to the Garrison'.[46] Loudoun was unable to supply an answer, having 'heard so many accounts of this that I cannot tell you what is Truth'.[47] Cumberland concluded on 5 March, 'I am very sorry my Accounts were so Sanguine concerning Inverness, but I was entirely misinform'd, as well with regard to the State of the place, as Lord Loudons strength, yet as it cost them so little trouble to take it, I hope it will not cost us more to retake it'.[48]

When Cumberland later heard more news about the fort's fall from three officers who had escaped the Jacobites, he was unimpressed, as the men gave:

> [S]o bad Account of the Governor's particular Behaviour & of the whole Defence of Fort George, that if His majesty approves of it, when I get to Inverness, I shall fetch him away from his own House, where He is upon his Parole, & make him give an Account before a Court martial of his Reasons for surrendering the Fort in so extraordinary a Manner. [49]

The Jacobite success here meant that Inverness was theirs and it would prove to be their base of operations for the next two months; indeed, until the end of the campaign. It was a useful place because it was accessible by sea and was a sizeable town, providing supplies and shelter. The fort had been isolated and there was no possibility of any relief.

Major Grant was held by the Jacobites as a prisoner until the battle of Culloden on 16 April. After the battle, Hawley, Huske, Lord Albermarle, and Major General Humphrey Bland were ordered to enquire into why the fort was surrendered.[50] They took evidence from all concerned. On 23 April, Cumberland wrote:

> Major Grant Deputy Governor of this fort having been tried by a general court martial (whereof General Huske was president) & broke. I sent a copy of the sentence, which I have taken the liberty to approve. The proceedings of the court are so voluminous, that I have not time to get them copied, & it is necessary to keep the original here for the trial of Lieutenant Colonel Innings [Innes]. I should be humbly of opinion that as this lieutenant governor is vacant, Major General Blakeney would be more usefully employed, if he had this lieutenant governorship then he can be in that of Plymouth, if it were given to him with a particular manner of inspecting the works, & to command all the troops in this chain, as the governor in chief will be seldom present.[51]

45 RA, CP11/159, Cumberland to Newcastle, 28 February 1746.
46 RA, CP11/239, Newcastle to Cumberland, 6 March 1746.
47 RA, CP12/71, Loudoun to Cumberland, 2 March 1746.
48 TNA, SP54/29, 2A, Cumberland to Newcastle, 5 March 1746.
49 RA, CP12/353, Cumberland to Newcastle, 21 March 1746.
50 Douglas, *History*, p.189.
51 TNA, SP54/30/24, Cumberland to Newcastle, 23 April 1746.

There was, initially, a board of enquiry held concerning Grant, Innes and the three captains, as the senior officers. Hawley, Albermarle, Huske, and Bland investigated the five officers at the end of April and concluded that they 'are guilty of misbehaviour in not doing their duty in defence of the fort'. They would then by formally charged at a court martial of the same offence.[52]

The court martial was held before the Judge Advocate, David Bruce, with Huske also being present. They concluded:

> The court after mature deliberation & weighing the Evidence both for and against Lieutenant Governor Grant, are of opinion that he is guilty of a breach of the fourteenth article of war, in misbehaving himself before the Enemy and shamefully abandoning Fort George to the Rebels, and do therefore ajudge him to be dismissed from his Majesty's service & rendered incapable of ever holding any further military office or employment under His Majesty.[53]

Thirty-two miles to the south west of Fort George was Fort Augustus. At the beginning of the campaign, in August 1745, the Jacobite army had avoided the fort's guns.[54] They did not do so now. French and Scottish Jacobite forces took cannon from the former towards the latter. This fort was described thus: 'Fort Augustus, is a regular Fortification, which was built by General Wade, near the south end of Loch Ness, to awe the Highlanders, and prevent them from disturbing his soldiers, whom he employed in making a road here'.[55] To the east of the fort was Loch Ness, to the north was river Oich and it had to be approached from the west, where Kiliwhimen Barracks was.

Defenders

- Major Hugh Wentworth
- Captains James Molesworth and Robert Scott
- Lieutenants Hamlet Wade and Desvorces
- Ensigns Lovegood Watson and Patterson
- Three companies of Guise's Foot (170 men 'fit for duty').[56]
- Gunners 'good for nothing'.[57]
- Sixteen 4-pounders, two 6-pounders, six coehorns.[58]

All these officers had been appointed to their current commissions in 1742, with the exception of Scott who was commissioned as captain in 1741.[59]

---

52 TNA, SP54/30/30b, Examination, April 1746.
53 TNA, SP54/31/24G, court martial, 22 May 1746.
54 Tayler and Tayler (eds), *1745*, p.64n.
55 Marchant, *History*, p.355n.
56 Douglas, *History*, p.166.
57 NLS, 3412, f.96r, Examination, 1746.
58 TNA, SP54/29, 27h, Hart's report, 1746.
59 TNA, WO64/9, Army List, 1736-1751.

Remnant of Fort Augustus (bottom-centre). (Author's postcard)

Attackers

- Brigadier Walter Stapleton
- Major Launcelot Colbert
- Major James Grant
- Irish Picquets
- Royal Ecossois
- Four guns of unknown calibre
- Two 3-pounders
- Three mortars [60]

Colonel Yorke wrote to his father on 9 March, 'Another detachment has been sent with four French picquets to Fort Augustus; the Old Barracks was taken but I did not hear that the fort has yet submitted'.[61] Fletcher, who thought that the fort was 'laid out there for ornament rather than strength', considered that the fort's guns should 'demolish all sort of cover near the fort, it would greatly distress even the rebels'.[62]

60 Elcho, *Short Account*, p.394; NLS, MS 3412, f.100r, Examination, 1746; TNA, SP54/29, 27h, Hart's report, 1746.
61 Yorke (ed.), *Hardwicke*, Vol.I, p.511.
62 RA, CP11/154, Fletcher to Cumberland, 28 February 1746.

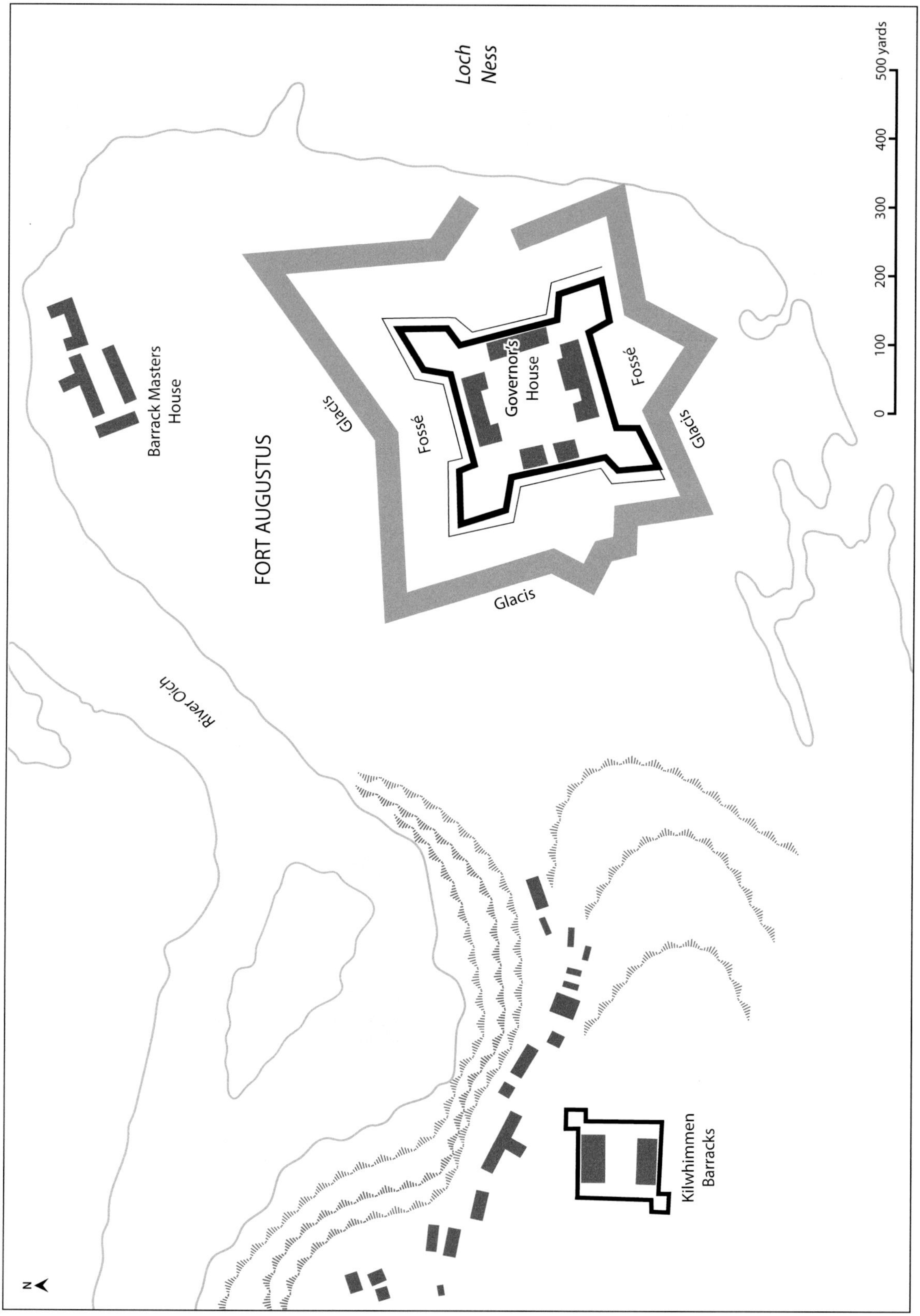

Plan of Fort Augustus.

There may have been some dissension between the French and Scottish Jacobites, for, according to Yorke, 'The French have been forced to do all at [Fort] Augustus, for they could not get the Highlanders near the works, no more than at Stirling; it is not to be conceaved how the French hate 'em'.[63]

There were two outposts for the Jacobites to take; the old barracks and the more recently built fort. An officer, writing before the siege, was unimpressed with the fort, writing:

> [A] new thing, where the public money has been thrown away profusely. They say it cost £30,000 on spacious buildings, a governor's house etc., but it is no fortress and one would be amazed at the folly and profusion that appears there. Twas this year erected into a Government with an establishment for gunners etc…half their garrison are left out of the new fort and quartered in a barrack a quarter of a mile from them.

Yet when it came to the crisis, the lieutenant governor, Major Wentworth, was confident enough, stating that they 'hoped to give a very good account of them' and that the Jacobites, lacking artillery, could not win as long as the defenders 'should al show ourselves true Englishmen and fight boldly in a good cause'.[64] However, he had also written, on 9 August 1745, 'In case they attempt ye Barracks we cannot hold out long they being well armed'.[65]

Four days later he wrote a somewhat mixed letter to Tweeddale:

> I have taken all possible care to arm against the worst that can happen, as far as lys in my power, but…our men have had very hard duty, having both the old and the new barracks to defend. But I thank God we are in good spirits, having a very good Train of Artillery, but I can't find one man who knows how to point a gun, or ever saw a shell fired out of a mortar, there being only two gunners and they not having been much accustomed to it.[66]

At least they were well supplied, with no want of provisions or ammunition. However, they had few picks and shovels. Medically, their needs were certainly deficient, though. One Wilson, an ale seller, had been appointed by Dr Brown, who was supervisor of the three forts' medical needs, was stationed at Fort Augustus. Just prior to the siege, Wilson left, leaving his son to stand in for him, but the young man 'knew nothing of the business'. He only had a box of Mellilot's plasters, two yards of coarse cloth and 'one lancet or two' and apparently later joined the Jacobites.[67]

Apparently according to an anonymous Jacobite chronicler 'Mr Stapleton attaque en arrivant et sans attendes son artillerie' (attacked on arrival and without waiting for his guns) and this was beaten off.[68] The next attack came

63 Yorke (ed.), *Hardwicke*, Vol.I, p.511.
64 Speck, *The Butcher*, pp.31-32.
65 TNA, SP54/25, 72b, Wentworth to Tweeddale, 9 August 1745.
66 TNA, SP54/25, 79b, Wentworth to Tweeddale, 13 August 1745.
67 NLS, MS 3412, f.97r, Examination, 1746.
68 RA, Stuart Papers Miscellany, Vol.11, pp.216-17, Anon, Account of the Forty Five.

on the barracks, which stood to the west of the fort, on 26 February, when the Jacobites moved the guns from the village to within 200 yards of the barracks, hidden behind a small hill. The garrison in the fort could see what was happening when they stood near the garret's windows. At four that afternoon, the Jacobites' six guns opened fire, according to Captain Scott, though the Master Gunner of the Fort claimed it was only one 4-pounder and one 5-pounder which did so. After two hours, they had not damaged the building, but two of its occupants were wounded, one being hit in the face.[69]

As darkness was falling, a 'large body' of Jacobites advanced up to the barracks' walls. The assault was fierce, as Captain Scott, in charge of the soldiers in the barracks, described 'with a great fire some attempted to wrench iron bars that secured the lower windows, but the good behaviour of a handful of men under my command obliged them to retire beyond the bowling green'. There lay a wounded Jacobite officer and others 'lie dead under our walls and upon the bowling green'.[70]

The Jacobites continued to fire for another hour, albeit under cover. The Jacobite guns then began to fire on the southern flank of the barracks. This may all have been cover for the Jacobites' principal plan. It was at eight that evening that sentries heard what they thought was the work of miners at work under the brew house to the south west of the barracks. Lieutenant Desvorces went to investigate it and confirmed that it did indeed sound like digging.[71]

Scott only had himself, his lieutenant, two sergeants, three corporals, a drummer and 48 privates in the barracks and so concluded, 'it was impracticable to defend a breach'. He sent a messenger to the fort to inform them of the situation and his plan to retreat to the fort was approved. He and his men then left the barracks and went to the fort, without any losses. A few minutes later the barracks were blown up as the mine was sprung. The Master Gunner later stated that two barrels of powder on the east side of the barracks had blown up.[72]

On the following day, the Jacobites built on their success by breaking ground 150 yards from the south west of the fort, digging two trenches on rising ground to provide cover for the gunners. As had not been the case at Stirling, Grant was given command of the siegeworks ('Mr Grant etait ingenieur en chef au lieu de Mr Mirabel' [Grant was engineer in chief instead of Mirabelle]).[73] The garrison commenced fire with artillery and coehorns, 'but with little effect owing chiefly to the unskillfulness of our Gunners', wrote Scott. At 11 o'clock that that night the garrison thought they could hear the working of another tunnel beneath them, but this time it was a false alarm.[74]

Scott recalled meeting Wentworth at Cope's bastion by chance. Wentworth took Scott to the guard room, and showed him the windows, which had been

69 NLS, MS 3412, f.100v, 103r, Examination, 1746.
70 NLS, MS 3412, f.100v, 103r, Examination, 1746.
71 NLS, MS 3412, 100r, Examination, 1746.
72 NLS, MS 3412, 100r-100v, Examination, 1746.
73 RA, SP Miscellany, Vol.11, p.217, Anon, Account of the Forty Five.
74 NLS, MS 3412, 100v, Examination, 1746.

reinforced with large, loose stones. Wentworth then made the following comments to the junior officer:

> [T]hey never would be able to resist the Enemy's Guns when they begun to play and if the rebels should storm the fort under the cover of their canon and coehorns as our bastions was commanded from the rocks it was his opinion that it was not in our power to prevent their taking the fort by storme and I knew the consequences of that.[75]

Scott was then asked if he thought, after all that, that it was worth surrendering there and then. He later recalled: 'I told the major I was not judge enough to know what effect the enemys guns would have, but it was my opinion it was too soon to think of surrendering and desired him to be very careful what he did'. Wentworth then canvassed the other officers for their thoughts on the matter. Scott was again asked for his opinion. This time he said that it was hard to answer and that he could not judge his commander. The officers continued to discuss the matter again over dinner.[76]

Wentworth believed 'such an affair should be well considered upon before we come to any determination'. Molesworth suggested that a better method of defence be undertaken. Wentworth disagreed, 'insisting upon the weakness of the fort and arguing the absolute necessity of our surrendering'. If the Jacobites made a breach, no terms would be given and they had already refused to surrender when the initial summons had arrived. It was therefore best to surrender early and so on honourable terms because 'the fort was not tenable'.[77]

At this point Scott was in agreement with Wentworth. Later the suggestion was made to him that he (Scott) could have had Wentworth arrested for his defeatism. Scott may have thought about this but reasoned against it thus: Wentworth had been sent to command the fort by special commission; Wentworth had experience of siege warfare being at one in the West Indies as aide to Major General Thomas Wentworth whereas Scott had no such experience. He thus concluded 'the major must be a much better judge in regard to the strength and further defence of the fort'.[78]

There may have been opportunities for the garrison to have inflicted serious damage to the Jacobites before the siege began, but these were missed by Wentworth, according to the Master Gunner. He later stated that the garrison's guns could have fired on the Jacobites when they first marched towards the fort from Inverness, 'They might have done execution'. There was no fire until the Jacobite artillery reached the bottom of a hill near the fort and then the garrison's guns killed several horses and two to three men.[79]

Grant was in charge of the artillery on this occasion. The Jacobite guns were well protected against counter fire from the fort because of the earth

75 NLS, MS 3412, f.102r, Examination, 1746.
76 NLS, MS 3412, f.102r, Examination, 1746.
77 NLS, MS 3412, 102v, Examination, 1746.
78 NLS, MS 3412, 102v, Examination, 1746.
79 NLS, MS 3412, f.103r, Examination, 1746.

bank protecting them; a defence that prior to the siege the master gunner recommended that Wentworth had levelled, but his comments fell on deaf ears. However, the small calibre guns 'did not do much mischief as they were small', and according to the master gunner, no platforms were erected, they did not cannonade the bastions and the embrasures were only to frighten the garrison. Yet the coehorns, which fired 150 shells at the fort, were to prove more effective as shall be seen.[80]

Fortune smiled on the Jacobite cause in this instance, as a Jacobite observer noted:

> [I]ts capture was facilitated by a stroke of luck. For while the walls were being bombarded by the artillery, a shot fell into the powder magazine. The powder ignited, and large pieces of masonry being blown up, a breach was made in the fort on this side, so that the garrison was forced to surrender.[81]

The Master Gunner later stated that the Jacobite guns blew up the powder barrels and cartridges on the turret of Wade's bastion. There had also been a shell on the court room and damage to the roof on the north side. No one had been injured, though, and the well was undamaged. He suggested that resistance was still possible, 'That the major and the other officers of the Garrison were mistaken in their assertion when they say there was no place of safety for the men to retire to or to boil their pots, for it appears that besides the vaults their common barracks were proof against any shells the rebels had to throw into the fort'. He concluded that it was 'ignorance and panick that seized them all'.[82] On 5 March Wentworth surrendered the fort.

According to Elcho, who was not present, about three men were killed on each side.[83] However, Wentworth, who was there, noted that 'They had none killed and only one wounded'. Ensign Watson stated there were two men wounded and that their doctor 'quite disabled them'.[84]

The articles of capitulation resulted in all the garrison (including women, children and gunners) being made prisoners of war and sent to Inverness. All their personal effects were to be retained by their owners. All the fort's arms, ammunition and provisions were to be handed intact to the victors. The fort was to open its gates to the besiegers at nine in the morning.[85] The Jacobites took the guns, much of the ammunition, 200 bolls of oatmeal and 200 pounds of beef, and mined under the remaking bastions so they could destroy them if needed.[86]

Private James Hunt later recalled that the rank and file were given but a pound of meat per day in captivity but were offered twice that if they enlisted into the Jacobite army. He and another 29 men did so and were marched to

---

80 Elcho, *Short Account*, p.394; NLS, MS 3412, f.100v, Examination, 1746.
81 Seton (ed.), 'Commentary', p.108.
82 NLS, MS 3142, ff. 100v, 107v, Examination, 1746.
83 Elcho, *Short Account*, p.394.
84 NLS, MS 3142, f.96r-97v, Examination, 1746.
85 NLS, MS 3142, f.98r, Examination, 1746.
86 TNA, SP54/29, 27h, Hart's report, 1746.

Fort William along with 150 men of the Irish Brigade on 12 March. Hunt deserted two days later.[87]

The Master Gunner of the fort later made a number of criticisms of Wentworth's preparations for and then his handling of the defence. He claimed that he had failed to order enough sods to strengthen the fort and had laid in no material for the repair of any damage to the fort. No dykes had been levelled, except towards the loch and that was not where the Jacobites attacked from. The Master Gunner had suggested demolishing the huts near to the barracks but Wentworth had said no, because he had no explicit instructions from the government to destroy civilian property with impunity, which had been an issue at Edinburgh and Carlisle in the previous year.[88]

Cumberland was not surprised at the fort's fall, writing on 14 March, 'by the plan I have seen of the fort, it was impossible it should defend itself long, as the curtain was composed of council Rooms and lodgings'.[89]

With the fall of two forts within a fortnight, allied to the withdrawal of Lord Loudoun's loyalist forces, the prospects for the Jacobite cause, despite the retreat from Stirling to Inverness, looked impressive. As a Jacobite historian later wrote, 'The enemy having thus been driven from the most strongly fortified places in the neighbourhood, Edward's [Charles'] prospects looked much brighter'.[90]

Fort Augustus then became a prison for anyone taken by the Jacobites, until 15 April, when it was blown up. The taking of this fort gave their cause much prestige among the country people, who, 'dazzled by these Instances of Success, brought them Provisions, and did what Kindness they could to the Rebels'.[91]

A grim discovery was made: 'The bodies of nine soldiers were found in a cistern in the old barracks at Fort Augustus. A letter from this place, of May 26th said, that they were all drowned by the rebels, after having been made prisoners, that the bodies were then floating'.[92]

As with Major Grant of Fort George, an examination into Wentworth's conduct was subsequently held; the same four senior officers presiding. This took place on 7 May. Having heard the testimonies of all the garrison's officers, they concluded, 'We are of Opinion from the Plan of the Fort, now lying before us, & from the narrative annexed…that the fort was defenceless. But do think that they ought to have delayed capitulating until the batteries had been playing upon them'. They further proposed that Dr Brown should be tried for his misbehaviour and neglect for the lack of medical facilities in the fort at the time.[93]

Having taken Forts George and Augustus, the Jacobite forces had a strong complement of artillery, albeit relatively light guns, though these would be easy to move. They had both regular and Highland troops, and a competent

87 TNA, SP54/29, 27h, Hart's report, 1746.
88 NLS, MS 3142, 103r, Examination, 1746.
89 TNA, SP54/29, 10b, Loudoun to Stair, 2 March 1746.
90 Seton (ed.), 'Commentary', pp.108-109.
91 Henderson, *History*, p.103.
92 Douglas, *History*, p.228.
93 NLS, MS 3412, f.97v, Examination, 1746.

engineer. Having had this success so far, morale was high. There remained one more Highland fort to take. What could prevent Forbes' prophecy coming true? Lord John Drummond with some of his Royal Ecossois were left at Fort Augustus and Stapleton took the remainder, the Irish Picquets, the Camerons and MacDonalds of Keppoch with him against '*le principale fortresses du Nord de l'Ecosse*' ('the first fort in the north of Scotland').[94]

94 RA, SP Miscellany, Vol.11, p.217, Anon, Account of the Forty Five.

7

Fort William, 1746

Fort William was the first purpose-built fortress to be erected in Scotland following the deposition of James II. It had been the brainchild of Major General Hugh Mackay and had been hastily built in 1690. It had been the base for the operations in February 1692 known as the Massacre of Glencoe, and despite concerns in both 1715 and 1719 it had never been attacked by the Jacobites in these campaigns. All this was to change in 1746, however, following the successful Jacobite sieges of Fort George and Fort Augustus.

It was thought to be a difficult strongpoint to take, with Maxwell writing:

> Fort William is the strongest fortress in the north of Scotland; it's situated on the western coast, at the mouth of the river Nevis; it's partly defended by that river and the sea, and that side which is accessible from the land has a good wall, ditch, counter scarp, and bastions at proper distances, and a kind of ravelin before the gate.[1]

Burt thought it strong enough, too: 'It stands in a most barren rocky country, and is on one of the faces of the fortifications by a navigable arm of the sea. It is almost surrounded, on the land sides, with rivers, not far distant from it; which though small, are often impassable'. Although the timber dwellings of Maryburgh were nearby, in case of a prospective siege, 'to the end they might be more suddenly be burnt, or otherwise destroyed by order of the governor, to prevent any lodgement of an enemy that might annoy the fort, in case of rebellion'.[2]

Yet there were concerns as early as 7 August 1745, with news of the Jacobite challenge reaching the garrison. Captain Alexander Campbell, the lieutenant governor, wrote that it would be 'unhappy for us in this place if we are attacked…the inner gate which was pulled down some time ago not yet rebuilt, but all hands are now busy at work to make it up'.[3]

Later that month Campbell could report that improvements had been made to rectify the defences. The gates and the bridge had been repaired,

1 Maxwell, *Narrative*, p.120.
2 Burt, *Letters*, Vol.I, pp.252-253.
3 TNA, SP54/25, 59b, Captain Campbell to Cope, 7 August 1745.

the stockade, palisade and ramparts had been worked on. There were 22 cannon and two mortars in good order with plenty of ammunition for them. The garrison consisted of three companies of Guise's Foot, but they had been depleted by 37 men who were on detachment elsewhere, 'so that there are far too few men to defend the fort'. On 8 August a party of soldiers with a corporal were on a scouting mission but were captured by the Jacobites. Apparently 36 workmen in the fort and 40 townsmen from Maryburgh had offered their services to defend the fort if needed, but there were insufficient arms, ammunition and provisions for them. There was also a shortage of money to pay the garrison and money was owed to the workmen. As to food supplies, the picture was mixed, there being a 'tolerable quantity of meal and salt herrings in customs house', but the brewery was not within the fort and a ship bringing malt to the garrison turned back due to the Jacobite presence.[4]

The lack of men and proximity of the enemy was another concern, as Campbell wrote on 13 August, possibly to Cope or Tweeddale: 'You know the strength of the garrison which is but 130 private men and I am informed it is the first place they intend to attack and the enemy is not above three day' march from this place'.[5] Similarly on 17 January 1746, it was found that there were only 140 soldiers fit for duty at the fort, with six in hospital. However:

> [T]ho' our numbers are few I have yt honour to assure you they are very alert and willing and show'd a brave spirit when we were in ye greatest danger, every one, both officer and soldier lent a ready and a cheerful heart to put this place in ye best posture yt time would admit of.

Even, so, eight days later it was stated, 'it is very probable the lieutenant governor of Fort William will want a reinforcement'.[6]

These failings may have been rectified, but even so, the fort's defences did not impress John Russell, an engineer, writing on 4 March 1746. He noted the four curtain walls, the three bastions, the two demi-bastions, the ditch and the ravelin but concluded, 'They are not in so good a repair as I would have wished. The parapet being too low and some of the walls very old'. He reported that the artillery consisted of eight 12-pounders, twelve 6-pounders, two 10-inch mortars and ten coehorn mortars, with plenty of gunpowder and ammunition.[7] These figures for artillery contradict those given below (and earlier), however. Given that in the previous year Campbell had listed 22 cannon and an inventory gave 22 cannon, it would seem probable that Russell was wrong.

The fort was being used at the year's onset as a base for offensive action against local Jacobites and their sympathisers. This had been advocated in the previous year, as Stephen Poyntz had written to John Weston:

4 TNA, SP54/25, 84e, Report, August 1745.
5 NLS, MS 7069, f3, Captain Campbell to Unknown, 13 August 1745.
6 NLS, MS 3733, f.96, 17 January 1746, f.114, Unknown to Campbell, 25 January 1746.
7 NLS, MS 3734, 173, Russell to Unknown, 4 March 1746.

> An old officer of Wade's regiment tells me that if the small garrisons of Inverness, Fort Augustus and Fort William were ordered immediately to lay waste the cottages and possessions of the Highlanders who are marched southward, they would meet with no opposition, and that they will certainly occasion a desertion from the Pretender's army.[8]

At the end of August 1745, Maxwell had written, 'The garrison at Fort William had sallied out, when the Prince was gone, seized what had been left here, burned some of the people's houses, and carried off their cattle'.[9]

On 22 February, Cumberland sent a message to Alexander Campbell, 'Send out Parties to burn & Destroy all the Country belonging to the Rebells in your Neighbourhood, as far as you dare go with safety to your Garrison'.[10] Apparently 18 houses belonging to members of the Clan Cameron, who were 'mostly rebels' were later burnt. Cattle were also confiscated. Campbell had already anticipated these orders and concluded, 'I flatter myself that we shall be so happy as to have your approbation for these proceedings…for the good of His Majesty's service and the safety of the garrison'.[11]

In early February the fort was reinforced with two companies of Argyll Militia, who came bearing their own bedding, meal and beef. Another company had arrived by 22 February.[12]

The danger to the fort became apparent towards the end of February. Alexander Campbell wrote on 18 February that, with a Jacobite force only 32 miles away, 'I am persuaded they will use their utmost efforts to get this fort into their possession'.[13] On 22 February, he noted that Inverness had been taken by the Jacobites 'last Wednesday' and that Fort George was about to be attacked (as noted it had already fallen), that the Jacobites would then be on the march towards Fort Augustus and his own fort.[14]

Despite the reinforcements of the militia companies, the garrison's officers agreed that they needed more men. If Fort George fell, they would be faced with additional artillery. Despite all this, Campbell wrote 'We are making all the proper dispositions for our Defence and nothing will be wanting on our parts. Pray God send us success'. [15]

Over the next few days they began to prepare for an assault. Maryburgh, that village to the south of the fort, was ordered to be partially destroyed 'as they may not harbour our enemys'. Inhabitants were given time to remove their effects to inside the fort. Some came in and 40 offered their services to defend the fort. Expresses were sent to the sheriff of Argyll and any ships

8 Black, *Culloden*, p.99.
9 Maxwell, *Narrative*, p.28.
10 RA, CP11/82, Cumberland to Captain Campbell, 22 February 1746.
11 NLS, MS 3734, f.285, Captain Campbell to Unknown, February 1746.
12 NLS, MS 3734, 141, Captain Campbell to Unknown, 10 February 1746, 155; Captain Campbell to Unknown, March 1746.
13 NLS, MS 3734, 140, Captain Campbell to Unknown, 18 February 1746.
14 RA, CP11/79, Captain Campbell to Archibald Campbell, 22 February 1746.
15 NLS, MS 3734, 155, Captain Campbell to Unknown, March 1746.

on the Mull for assistance.[16] Major General John Campbell, on 1 March, approved of the demolition of the town, but told Campbell he could not send more men because of the lack of provisions in the fort to feed them all. However, he promised to send a boatload of oatmeal when possible, and would despatch one Mr Russell, 'a very clever indefatigable young fellow… bred an Ingineer'.[17]

The danger became apparent to others, too. On 23 February, Lieutenant James Mackenzie of the Royal Navy sloop HMS *Serpent* was informed, 'Having receiv'd certain intelligence that very large Bodies of the Rebels are already assembled in the neighbourhood of Fort William and that they Design to attempt that Importance Place'[18]. Another sloop, HMS *Baltimore*, arrived on 26 February and *Serpent* arrived on the next day. The latter lent four gunners to the fort.[19]

The reasoning behind the fort's hoped for capture by the Jacobites was that 'Lochiel having determined that whilst it is in His Majesty's possession neither the Camerons nor MacDonalds can be kept to their duty'.[20] Maxwell added, 'These people were particularly interested in the success of it, as Fort William commands their country; and during the Prince's expedition to England, the garrison made frequent sallies, burnt their houses, and carried off their cattle'.[21]

Apparently Charles was opposed to the expedition. According to O'Sullivan:

> The prince was altogether again it, in as much as he had certain accts yt part of the enemy was already arrived at Perth, but the Clans looked upon it, to be so essential a thing for them, & for the good of the cause, yt the Prince consented, tho' it was exposing himself & them & even the Cause to have the Army so scater'd; the best troops at Forte William.[22]

Cumberland was very concerned for the fort's security, too, writing from Aberdeen on 27 February to Captain Campbell:

> As by the hasty surrender of Fort George the Rebells may be incouraged to attempt the siege of Fort William, I have thought it for the Kings service to send Captain Caroline Scott [of Guise's Foot] to take the command of the Garrison as well of what may be there at present, as of what may hereafter be judged proper to be thrown in, & he having served as an Engineer he will be the better qualified, and a better judge of provisions ammunition, &c necessary to be laid in in case of a siege wherefore I desired he may be let into the state of all stores now there, &

16 NLS, MS 3734, f.158, Captain Campbell to Unknown, 24 February 1746; f.162, Captain Campbell to Unknown, 27 February 1746.
17 NLS, MS 3734, 167, Major General Campbell to Captain Campbell, 1 March 1746.
18 RA, CP 11/51, Major General Campbell to Mackenzie, 23 February 1746.
19 NLS, MS 3734, f.165, Askew to Unknown, 27 February 1746.
20 RA, CP11/51, Major General Campbell to Mackenzie, 23 February 1746.
21 Maxwell, *Narrative*, p.120.
22 Tayler and Tayler (eds), *1745*, pp.136-137.

> that what he finds necessary be immediately provided in the most expeditious & cheapest manner possible.[23]

The Duke of Newcastle agreed with Cumberland, writing on 6 March, 'But he has taken great care to secure, I hope, Fort William'.[24] Yorke felt confident it would hold, writing, three days later 'Fort William is what they have a view at next, but I hope they will find that harder at digestion than the other two, as I am told it is a much better place and His Royal Highness has sent an officer there for whose behaviour I would answer for with my head'.[25]

Fort William was seen as a crucial place to hold. Yorke wrote to the Lord Chancellor, Hardwicke, his father, on 31 March: 'The thing which seems to give your Lordship some concern is the apprehension that the Rebels, after taking Fort William, should have it in their power to scour down again to the South, and by that means be for ever giving us the slip'.[26] Yet Yorke was confident that this would not be so, writing on the last day of March:

> In the first place, I don't think it likely they will be able to make themselves masters of Fort William; for by the last accounts come in from those parts, they have given over, or are on the point of quitting, that undertaking, and should they even persist, it will be too much for them to execute before we shall be able to move to its relief; by this means that bridle to the West coast will still continue.[27]

It was at the end of the month that the Camerons and MacDonalds began to march towards the fort, but the siege proper did not begin for some weeks later, despite some skirmishes hitherto.[28] Lord George Murray, in writing his memoirs, was apparently opposed to the action, 'the resolution of besieging Fort William, I did not approve, as I always had heard it was a strong place, and regularly fortified'. However, after the entreaties of Lochiel and the MacDonalds, 'I did not oppose it, though Brigadier Stapleton and I had no hopes of success, by what had happened at Stirling Castle, which was not so strong'.[29]

On 22 February, Campbell summoned the garrison's officers 'to consult on ye properest methods to make a vigorous defence'. They decided unanimously that a detached company should be summoned back to the fort; one from Clifton had already arrived back 'to my Great Joy'. However, Campbell was concerned about the Jacobite artillery, fearing that it consisted of 14 cannon; including six 8-pounders and, that being so, 'I much fear the fate of Fort George will soon be determined, which will still add to their strength'. He thought that 'We must expect to lose numbers by the bad situation of the Fort' and so troops should be sent to the island of Stalker

23 RA, CP11/140, Cumberland to Captain Campbell, 27 February 1746.
24 McCann (ed.), 'Correspondence', p.208.
25 Yorke (ed.), *Hardwicke*, Vol.I, p.511.
26 Yorke (ed.), *Hardwicke*, Vol.I, p.514.
27 Yorke (ed.), *Hardwicke*, Vol.I, p.514.
28 Elcho, *Short Account*, pp.410-411.
29 Forbes, *Jacobite Memoirs*, p.106.

in case the garrison at Fort William needed reinforcements.[30] He also wrote to Archibald Campbell, asking for the company sent to Airds Castle to be ordered to Fort William.[31]

One of the first steps taken to support Fort William's defence was to send naval assistance there. It was decided on 23 February that 'it [was] absolutely necessary that you remain at Fort William'. Lieutenant Mackenzie (presumably the ship's captain was absent) and HMS *Serpent* were to give Campbell 'all the assistance imaginable consistent with the safety of your ship and crew'. The provision of intelligence and the services of men despatched in boats was thought to be useful. Mackenzie was urged to use his judgement to best help the garrison. The lack of gunners in the fort was deemed a concern, 'He wants gunners sufficient, so if you can spare any I am persuaded you will let him have them'.[32]

The fort began to be menaced from 24 February. The Jacobite troops included the Royal Ecossois under Brigadier Stapleton and Cameron of Lochiel commanding men from his own clan, the MacDonalds of Keppoch and Glencoe and the Stewarts of Appin, perhaps 1,500 men in total. Initially their presence was of limited danger, firing at the fort on a daily basis until 20 March, albeit from a distance.[33] Despite all this, Campbell wrote that his concerns were not fully appreciated elsewhere, writing to Major General Campbell on 4 March, 'I profess to you all my apprehensions (or Fears as you are pleased to call them) are not groundless for self preservation, but entirely for the good of His Majesty's service'.[34]

On 4 March an inventory of the fort's resources was made. There was enough beef for the three companies of Guise's for three weeks from 9-30 March and for the two companies of militia up to 16 March. There was enough meal to make bread for 400 men for eight weeks from 4 March. Stores on board the sloop *Serpent* were sufficient for 120 men, from 4 March as follows, bread for 53 days, beef, pork and pease for seven and a half weeks, seven weeks of cheese, six and a half weeks of oatmeal and six weeks of butter. As for military stores, there were twelve 12-pounders and ten 9-pounders; 200 muskets and 2,000 weight of musket shot. There were also two iron thirteen-inch mortars and six smaller coehorn mortars. In both cases these figures contradict those already given by Russell but as the number of guns agrees with that given by Captain Campbell in the previous year it seems probable that this is correct; furthermore Scott (below) refers to 9-pounders which Russell does not. There were 130 barrels of gunpowder, 600 roundshot for the guns and 150 shells for the iron mortars and 120 for the smaller ones. There were also 200 grenades.[35] On the same day, Russell, the engineer promised by Major General Campbell, arrived at nine in the morning and after having taken stock of the fort's defences, concluded 'So that if this Garrison do their

30 RA, CP11/79, Captain Campbell to Archibald Campbell, 19 February 1746.
31 RA, CP11/78, Captain Campbell to Archibald Campbell, 22 February 1746.
32 RA, CP11/51, Major General Campbell to Mackenzie, 22 February 1746.
33 Douglas, *History*, p.162.
34 RA, CP11/257, Captain Campbell to Major General Campbell, 4 March 1746.
35 RA, CP11, 263-264, Inventory of ordnance at Fort William, 4 March 1746.

duty we shall not be taken by the Rebels', though he was dismissive of the credence taken about news of the Jacobite forces, believing it to be put out by themselves and so was a 'continual packet of lies'.[36]

Captain Scott deemed that additional supplies were needed; 800 roundshot for the 12-pounders and 600 for the 9-pounders; 200 bags of grapeshot for the former and 300 for the latter. The cannons needed another 160 barrels of gunpowder and 60 barrels of fine powder. Another 200 shells for the coehorn mortars were needed and another 400 grenades. He also felt that another 100 barrels of musket shot were wanting. One hundred five and a half inch fuses for the mortars were also wanted. As to other materials, the fort's defences needed strengthening and this would require tools; 50 wheel barrows, 50 hand barrows, 200 shovels, 150 spades and 200 pick axes.[37]

On 6 March Scott wrote to Major General Campbell, noting the fall of Fort Augustus and the investment of Fort William, 'I must beg the favour of you to order a number of hands together, to cut fascines and pickets'. He hoped that Duncan Campbell would be able to order the country to undertake such work as soon as possible. He also needed equipment to strengthen the fort's defences; 3,000 fascines, 12 feet long, 400 gabions three and a half feet in diameter and four feet high, 5,000 stakes, five feet long, 1,200 stakes, seven feet long, 200 hurdles, six to eight feet long and three feet broad, 3,000 pallisades, 10 feet long, 500 mallets, 3,000 baskets and 500 planks 10 to 12 feet long.[38] Major General Campbell replied quickly, 'I am persuaded you will find mallets, rams, hand baskets and such like at Fort William. It is a long time since the Deputy Governor was under apprehensions of a visit from the Rebells. He is a carefull, good man, so I'm in hopes that you will find what you require within the place'. In the meantime he assured Scott that Lady Airds would provide wood for the gabions and fascines, and that a sloop was bringing additional provisions for the fort and had been sent on 7 March.[39] This was actually a wherry, with 24 bolls of oatmeal, 2,000 weight of biscuits, guarded by an officer, 16 men and four guns. More was promised.[40] Eight days later 400 pounds of beef, 400 pounds of pork and 12 bushels of pease arrived by boat.[41]

Scott arrived at Castle Stalker from Dunfermline on 6 March. However, he could not progress any further, because the Jacobites, 'I am told', were guarding both sides of the Carron. Boats were thus unable to traverse this towards Fort William. He wanted a tender from a naval vessel to take him to his destination. He hoped to arrive there in a couple of days should such aid be forthcoming. He also looked forward to a favourable wind to take him there.[42]

However, despite his hopes, he was still forced to date his letters from Castle Stalker on 8 March. Although he had sent call for a boat from Mull, he learnt that none were expected there. Jacobites remained on both sides of the

36 NLS, MS 3734, 173, Russell to Unknown, 4 March 1746.
37 RA, CP11/264, Inventory of ordnance at Fort William, March 1746.
38 RA, CP11/266, Scott to Major General Campbell, 6 March 1746.
39 RA, CP11/267, Major General Campbell to Scott, 6 March 1746.
40 NLS, MS 3734, 176, Major General Captain Campbell to Unknown, 7 March 1746.
41 NLS, MS 3734, 189, Inventory of supplies, 15 March 1746.
42 RA, CP11/274, Scott to Napier, 6 March 1746.

Carron. Scott hoped that the *Furnace* sloop or the *Inveraray* wherry could take him to the fort. He was disappointed and four days later was no further in his journey, with the weather now his enemy as the wind prevented boats travelling there. He wrote, 'I am almost crazy not knowing to what saint to vow or how to mend my self'. News from spies was uncertain.[43]

Meanwhile, Russell had set to work on strengthening the defences in the best possible manner given so short a time frame. On 6-8 March he had blinds erected to protect the gunners; mortar shells were filled and fuses fixed to them. On the following day was the first of many sallies against the enemy, indicative of an aggressive form of defence which had rarely been witnessed in the sieges of this campaign to date. Three officers and 70 men were sent out to burn three Jacobite encampments which were a mile from the fort. They did so, and also captured nine horses, 29 cows and 202 goats. The party was chased by 100 Jacobite soldiers, but on the latter coming into the range of the fort's mortars, two shells were fired which dispersed the pursuers.[44]

Yorke noted the importance of Fort William and its strength, writing to his father on 9 March: 'I hope they will find that harder of digestion than the other two, as I am told it is a much better place and H. Royal Highness has sent an officer there for whose behaviour I would answer with my head'.[45] However, he had heard rumours. Jacobite artillery was imminently expected to be put into position and the Appin Stewarts were on their way to besiege the fort. He was concerned that 'they have the best of Gunners from France and will fairly take the place after which they will try to make an inroad into Argyleshire and lay all before them to waste'. On the other hand, he had encouraging news about the state of the garrison, who he had heard were:

> [V]ery cheerful, alert and full of spirits that they have six weeks full provisions that great and small have been busy'd in filling casks in lieu of gabions, raising such works, mending inclosures and have no lack of anything but malt which they have only 30 bolls.

However, the men were apparently receiving a quart of beer per day in lieu of whisky. There were also sufficient supplies of pick axes, shovels, coal, guns and ammunition.[46]

On 11 March, the Jacobite artillery could be detected two miles away from the fort. Meanwhile sandbags and fascines were made at the fort. On 13 March the first shots were fired by the Jacobite artillery. When the fort's guns returned fire, a Cameron officer was wounded.[47] Work began on 14 March to strengthen the defences, with the parapets of the walls facing the landward side being heightened. This work carried on for the following week until the two faces of the bastion were raised until they were seven feet high.[48]

43 RA, CP12/47, Scott to Noble, 8 March 1746; f.83, Scott to Napier, 12 March 1746.
44 NLS, MS 3734, 196, Russell to Unknown, 16 March 1746.
45 Yorke (ed.), *Hardwicke*, Vol.I, p.511.
46 RA, CP12/83, Scott to Napier, 12 March 1746.
47 NLS MS 3734, 196, Russell to Unknown, 16 March 1746.
48 Marchant, *History*, p.358.

It was on 15 March that Scott finally arrived at the fort, with Captain Campbell informing Fawkener, 'Nothing could have given me more pleasure than the arrival of Captain Scott'. He also now saw action as being imminent, 'We are hourly in expectation of being attacked by the Rebels, I flatter myself that the actions will more evidently demonstrate the zeal of this Garrison than anything I can offer on that stead'.[49] Scott dismissed Russell, claiming that he was needed at Dumbarton Castle, and so he went back to Inveraray on 16 March.[50]

Scott had in the meantime, drawn up a list of thoughts about defending the fort and he wrote to tell Fawkener of these. In the first place, he wanted all 'useless mouths', presumably civilians, both male and female, dismissed and sent to Dunstaffnage. This proved impossible to do so because the Jacobites had already surrounded the landward side of the fort and there were no vessels available for evacuation by sea. He then wanted an exact list of all provisions, stores, brandy, wine and whisky in the fort to be made. The garrison was to be divided into four parts; one to guard the walls, one to act as picquets, one to form a reserve and the other to rest. Half of the men were to be under arms at night time, with the others to sleep.[51]

Cumberland was pleased with the defensive measures taken to preserve the fort, informing Major General Campbell on 18 March:

> I have received yours of the 5th & am very glad to see the assistance you have given Captain Scot. As you are already apprised of the march of Captain Pattan with his detachment, I have only to give you notice of that of two Companys of Johnson's from Edenburg for Glascow who are to take in a quantity of Biscuit & Potatoes there & then throw themselves into Fort William. My Lord Chesterfield has been also written, to send directly more ammunition of all kinds. As I look upon Fort William to be the only Fort in the Highlands that is of any Consequence, I have taken all possible measures for the security of it, as by your letters you seem to have done on your part, & I doubt not but you will continue to do every thing that is in your power for the preventing its falling into the Rebels' hands. I am very glad you have sent thither Mr Russell as he may be of great service to Captain Scot, & the precautions we have taken, put me at ease about this important place, but if it were possible that all this should fail I would have you as you will know it long before I can immediately communicate it to my Lord Chesterfield to prevent the stores being sent. You will likewise acquaint the officers of his Majesty's ships or sloops stationed there it is expected of them that they will give all the assistance possible to his Majesty's Garrison there, & annoy the Rebels in all manner of ways.
>
> As to your present situation, tho a disagreeable one I hope it will not be found so, to the extent you seem to think, for I flatter myself that the Rebels will not be in a condition to make any attempt upon you tho I would have you

49 RA, CP12/103, Captain Campbell to Fawkener, 15 March 1746.
50 NLS, MS 3734, 196, Russell to Unknown, 16 March 1746.
51 NLS, MS 3734, 119, Scott to Fawkener, March 1746.

continue to take all kinds of precautions, & I heartily wish you success if it should come to a tryal.[52]

I also enclose Captn Scots Letter to Colonel Napier, which makes me very easy about Fort William.[53]

Defenders:

Table 2 lists the number of Officers and specialists who should have been in the garrison; whether these were the numbers on duty at this time cannot be ascertained.

Table 2 Establishment Strength and Pay, Fort William Garrison

Rank	Number	Daily pay
Governor (also governor of Forts Augustus and George)	1	£2 3s 10d
Deputy Governor	1	
Storekeeper and marshal	1	2s 6d
Master Gunner	1	2s
Gunner	2	1s
Smith	1	1s 6d
Wright	1	1s 6d

Source: TNA, War Office (WO), 24/246, Papers Concerning Establishments, 1745-1746

The three companies of Guise's Foot included the 21-year-old John Cobb from Banbury with three years' military service, 40-year-old William Dawson from Stirlingshire, with two years of army service, George Grach, from Invernesshire, aged 24 with three and a half years in the army, James Dunston from Manchester, aged 30 with a year and a half of army life behind him. All four had been weavers in civil life. Then there was William Moss, aged 23 with two and a half years of military experience, once a smith from Warrington, Joseph Hall, aged 24, who joined the army aged 20 having been born in Henley and finally an Irishman, James Smith, aged 28 from Ballymore, with almost three years of soldiering behind him. Both the latter had been labourers.[54] With the three Argyll Militia companies, the infantry totalled 300 men.

As noted there was disagreement as to how many guns were in the fort, so the numbers below reflect the range noted by contemporaries.

- Twelve 12-pounders
- Ten 9-pounders
- Two mortars
- Six to ten coehorn mortars
- 2 swivels.[55]

52 TNA, SP54/29/31B, Cumberland to Captain Campbell, 18 March 1746.
53 RA, CP12/353, Cumberland to Newcastle, 26 March 1746.
54 TNA, WO116/4, Royal Hospital Chelsea, Out Pensioners' Admission books, cavalry and infantry, 1745-1746.
55 Marchant, *History*, p.359; TNA, SP54/30, 10e, .

The following warships o the Royal Navy provided support to the garrison:

HMS *Serpent*
Commander Robert Askew, Lieutenant James Mackenzie
100 men
12-14 guns
Commissioned 1742; last cleaned, 1745

HMS *Baltimore*
Commander Richard Howe, Lieutenant James Cope
110 men
12-14 guns
Commissioned 1742; last cleaned 1745

Both part of the 'Convoys and Cruizers'.[56]

Attackers:

- Brigadier Stapleton
- Major Grant
- Irish Picquets
- Royal Ecossois
- Cameron of Locheil's Regiment
- MacDonalds of Keppoch.
- MacDonalds of Glencoe
- Stewarts of Appin [57]
  Total: about 1,500 men

The Jacobite artillery comprised three 4-pounders, six 6-pounders, and between seven and nine coehorn mortars

The arrival of Captain Scott heralded the beginning of a more aggressive from of defence by the garrison and the two sloops nearby. On 15 March men from the garrison and the sloops were sent out in armed boats to try and destroy the Killmallie barns, usually known as the Corpach. Jacobite forces moved against them 'in great Numbers'. Despite firing the swivel guns of the boats and exchanging musketry fire, a sailor was killed and three others were wounded. Finally, the tide being against them, the boats retired with their mission unaccomplished.[58]

Three days later there was another attempt at the same. This time the *Baltimore* under the command of Commander Richard Howe, went up towards the barns in order to assist the smaller boats in landing their parties. Despite firing several shots and using coehorn mortars, which set a small building on fire, no landing was practicable because the Jacobites were too strongly entrenched by a hollow road and were in significant strength. The

56 TNA, Admiralty (ADM), 8/25, List Book of ships.1746-1747.
57 Maxwell, *Narrative*, p.120.
58 Marchant, *History*, p.358.

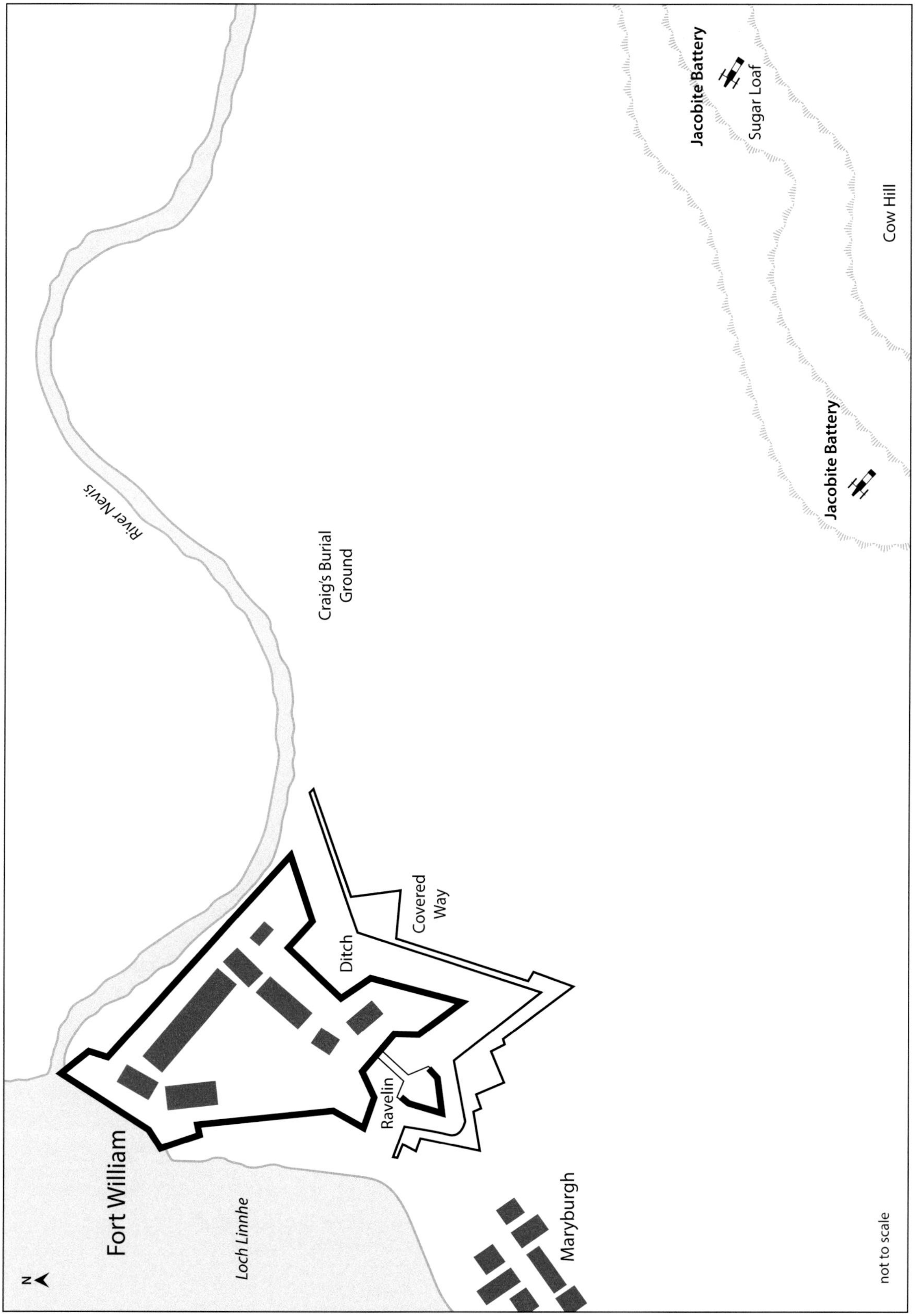

Plan of Fort William.

Baltimore's guns were only 4-pounders and could not damage the stone walls of the barns. So the expedition returned, albeit with no casualties.[59]

Yet these two expeditions had some success, if not that which was intended. Grant was in charge of the siege and he realised that his 6-pounders would never make a breach in the walls. However, the south east of the fort was dominated by a hill, 'whence one can discover everything that passes in the fort' and this was seen as a weakness, '*mais il est domine pour une montagne au sud-est*' (but it is dominated by a hill to the south east) and Grant proposed to have a battery sited there.[60] Grant also noticed that one of the fort's bastions projected so far out that it could not be defended by the fire of the fort's other guns. Therefore, he proposed to have trenches dug nearer and nearer to this bastion and then plant gunpowder there and blow up the bastion, thus creating a practicable breach. However, at that point, he was injured by a cannon ball's blast frightening his horse, being thrown from his horse and being injured in the ribs, suffering a contusion. Stapleton lacked any other engineer and so sent a message to Inverness, to summon Monsieur Mirabelle, who was presumably in disgrace after his failure at Stirling two months ago. Characteristically, Mirabelle continued the siege using a different plan.[61]

Meanwhile, another four Jacobites had been killed. The garrison also had the benefit of four men (three privates and a drummer) from Guise's joining them; men who had been captured at Fort Augustus but who had escaped. On 20 March there were skirmishes between soldiers who were outside the fort, digging for additional sods to be used on the defences, and forward parties of Jacobites. Both sides took cover from rocks and no casualties occurred on either side.[62]

It was not until eleven o'clock at night on 20 March that the siege began in earnest. Batteries were raised and that night they began to fire 'a great many' coehorn mortars; apparently 17-18 five-inch-and-a-half inch bombs, weighing 16-18 pounds each and loaded with 14 ounces of gunpowder. These were fired from a battery on a small hill called the Sugar Loaf, about 800 yards away, but the distance was great and many fell short. They did no physical damage. The garrison retaliated, firing eight 13-inch bombs in return.[63] The bombardment also caused consternation within the fort, 'which put our people into some confusion because of the militia officers made the Guard drummer beat to arms and five guns were fired which was soon put a stop to and the Garrison sent to their beds' excepting a picquet guard who stood by the fire engines.[64]

On 21 March, the Jacobites, finding the first battery to be too far from the fort, erected a new one at the foot of Cow Hill, only 400 yards from the walls. By noon the guns there were in operation and continued so for the next four

59 Marchant, *History*, p.358.

60 RA, SP Miscellany Vol.11, p.218, Anon, Account of the Forty Five.

61 Maxwell, *Narrative*, p.120; Tayler and Tayler (eds), *1745*, p.135n.

62 Marchant, *History*, pp.358-359.

63 Douglas, *History*, p.163; Marchant, *History*, p.359.

64 NLS, MS 16636, 222, Journal of the Siege of Fort William, 21-27 March 1746.

hours. In all, 84 mortar bombs were hurled towards Fort William, some of which crashed through the roofs of several houses inside the walls. This was despite orders given to have the buildings' roofs and floors shored up with beams and earth to protect them. Apparently 'These orders through laziness or carelessness were neglected so that in the evening a shell came through and wounded a man of Argile's in the shoulder and gave another a thump on the nose which bled him and frightened the others'. Some work was carried out on making a parapet and covered way but lacking tools, little could be achieved. Nine coehorns fired 20 bombs, and five 6-pounders and one of the swivel guns also returned fire. This time, though, there was no firing of Jacobite guns in the night.[65] There was fire in the daytime from a battery of three guns. In the evening the mortars fired again, perhaps 60-70 shells being fired.[66]

The morning of the next day saw, renewed fire from the battery on the Sugar Loaf Hill, from three guns, either 4- or 6-pounders. They fired only seven times and caused no damage. Furthermore, one battery moved 100 yards closer to the fort. At noon, rather belatedly, a French drummer came before the fort with the formal summons to surrender. Scott asked him what he had come about and he answered, 'That general Stapleton, who commanded the Siege, by Directions from the Pretender's son, had sent him with a letter to the commanding officer of the Garrison, requesting him to surrender'. He was not admitted into the fort, nor were his credentials examined. Scott replied, 'That he would receive no Letters from Rebels, and that he was determined to defend the Fort to the last Extremity'. He returned and hostilities recommenced. As on the previous day, the guns fired on both sides in the daytime, but eventually those of the Jacobites fell silent. Between 10 that night and three in the morning both Jacobite batteries totalling six guns and several mortars fired 194 shells. As on the previous day, several roofs were damaged. None of the garrison were killed; most of them being indoors. Some were wounded: a picquet standing by the fire engine and the governor, the lieutenant of the Maryburgh volunteers and a tax collector's daughter. Most of the officers had been on the ramparts.[67]

According to Elcho, 'The greatest damage done to the fort was by the Shells and red hot balls and pieces of Iron which struck in the roofs of the houses with a designe to Sett them on fire'.[68] For some reason, Scott did not approve of counter fire, which made the militia uneasy.[69]

There was further cannonading in the morning of the 23 March. This time the garrison fired nine of its guns and two mortars, which temporarily silenced the besiegers' guns.[70] The Jacobite cannon fire cost Argyll Militiaman Donald McIndeor, of Ballinbay's company, his leg shot off. At three that afternoon, some boats arrived with additional supplies for the garrison. Later

65 Marchant, *History*, p.359; NLS, MS 16636, 222, Journal of the Siege of Fort William, 1746.

66 Douglas, *History*, p.163.

67 Douglas, *History*, p.163; Marchant, *History*, p.359-360; NLS, MS 16636, 222, Journal of the Siege of Fort William, 21-27 March 1746.

68 Elcho, *Short Account*, p.411.

69 NLS, MS 16636, 222, Journal of the Siege of Fort William, 21-27 March 1746.

70 Douglas, *History*, p.163.

that afternoon, eight 12-pounders, two 6-pounders and several coehorns belonging to the garrison fired at one of the Jacobite batteries, levelling it, and 'they visibly occasion'd the greatest confusion amongst them'. Several of the Jacobites fell, either wounded or killed. That evening, under the cover of darkness, they began to erect another battery at the foot of Cow Hill, only 300 yards from the fort.[71] At the end of the day, a member of the garrison wrote, 'Thank God we are all in high spirits and in not in the least afraid of our Enemys as we have plenty of provisions and our Garrison in a Good posture of Defence'.[72] Some supplies arrived that day, butter, cheese, malt and meal and the garrison cheered when it did. These came by sea and were brought ashore on the following day.[73]

Little firing on either side took place on 24 March. The garrison spent much of their time unloading the supplies brought by the boats. They also made sure that their shells were in a place of safety so there was less risk of accidents. On this day, Scott wrote a letter, requesting additional supplies and another doctor: 'We may have more wounded, so I would be glad to have the young man for a surgeon's mate. Captain Askew hath lent us his surgeon, but still another would be better and to be of ease to those we have'. He also noted 'We are sadly in want of tooles'.[74] On 25 March the garrison sent a party to a place six miles away to attempt to bring in some cattle. Batteries from both sides meanwhile began to fire upon on one another. In the afternoon, the raiding party returned with 29 bullocks and cows, as well as four prisoners. That evening another party was despatched, consisting of 40 men, to seize more cattle from Jacobite estates.[75]

On 26 March there was further cannon fire from the fort against the Jacobite batteries. Only two guns from the latter replied, suggesting that the others had been incapacitated by the fort's previous fire. According to one witness, the Jacobites' powder magazine had been blown up. In the afternoon, the boats sent out the day before returned. They had been to the country near Ardshiel and brought four prisoners, one of whom was wounded, after the men had burnt two villages belonging to the Stewarts of Appin.[76] Despite one man being killed, one wounded and two bruised that day, morale remained high, 'We are in good spirits and hope to give a good account of ourselves'.[77]

That evening, Scott had the drains near the fort's walls dammed up, in the hopes that if rain came, it would create a moat around the fort. The parapet was raised to seven feet, but there was insufficient wood to create a covered way.[78]

Another Jacobite battery was erected on 27 March, of four embrasures, but only with three 6-pounders. This was placed on the high ground above

71 Marchant, *History*, p.360.
72 NLS, MS 17514, 215, Unknown to Unknown, 23 March 1746.
73 NLS, MS 16636, 222, Journal of the Siege of Fort William, 21-27 March 1746.
74 TNA, SP54/30, 2h, Scott to Cumberland, April 1746; NLS, MS 16636, 222, Journal of the Siege of Fort William, 21-27 March 1746.
75 Marchant, *History*, pp.360-361.
76 Marchant, *History*, p.361.
77 NLS, MS 16636, 222, Journal of the Siege of Fort William, 21-27 March 1746.
78 NLS, MS 16636, 222, Journal of the Siege of Fort William, 21-27 March 1746.

the governor's garden, about 200 yards away. This battery and the other of three guns, fired 250 shots at the fort that day. Two thirds of this fire was from the 6-pounders. Mortar shells, to the extent of 50, were fired and there was also musketry aimed at the fort. Apart from two of the garrison being wounded, no one else was injured.[79] The fort's guns fired back, silencing one of the Jacobite guns before eight in the morning. At about nine there was a hit on the Jacobite magazine, which was afire before blowing up.[80]

Meanwhile, Captain Melvill of the Argyll Militia was sent to Inveraray with letters for Cumberland. These probably included one by Scott, who requested additional supplies of cartridge papers for muskets, musket ball moulds and additional shot for the 6- and 12-pounders, as well as wadding. Presumably the rate of fire was consuming the garrison's ammunition and shortages were feared. That may be why, in the fort, all the splinters from the cannon balls which had been fired at the fort, were gathered up to use as grape shot. It was not just ammunition that was a concern, but 30-40 ankers of brandy or whisky were also requested – equally important to maintain a successful defence, it would seem.[81] Morale cannot have been helped within the garrison by there being insufficient money to pay the militia, who were on the same footing with the regulars as to provisions.[82]

On 28 March Grant, who despite his wounds was clearly not wholly incapacitated, finding that the guns were not making a breach in the walls, erected a new battery of three 4-pounders on high ground called the Craigs, only 100 yards from the fort. According to Elcho, 'As this battery swept the whole parade, Brigadier Stapletons Scheme was, by firing partridge shott, to destroy their men and make them Surrender that way'.[83] There was also firing with the 6-pounders at the fort, too. At some stage in that day, a party of soldiers from the garrison left the fort to bring in water from the surrounding countryside and in this they exchanged shots with some of the Jacobites, driving them up the hill and then returning with the water unmolested.[84]

On the next two days firing on both sides was 'very brisk', but the Jacobite scheme did not provide immediate results.[85] Red hot shot was fired from the guns in the burial ground and many landed within the fort. Apparently these burnt 'some of our fellows fingers, who went to lift the shot, till they became more wary'. Thirty mortar shells were also fired at the fort that day. The garrison only replied with its 12-pounders and its mortars. The 6-pounders were not employed because the cannon balls from these guns could have been fired back from the Jacobites' guns of the same calibre.[86]

By seven that morning the four-gun Jacobite battery had been temporarily silenced, though the garrison's gunners could not see the Jacobite gunners

79 Douglas, *History*, p.163.
80 Marchant, *History*, p.361.
81 TNA, SP54/30, 17n, Scott to Cumberland, April 1746; NLS MS 3734, 226, Scott to Unknown, 27 March 1746.
82 TNA, SP54/30, 18e, Campbell to Argyll Militia, 31 March 1746.
83 Elcho, *Short Account*, p.412.
84 TNA, SP54/30, 17b, Scott to Napier, 2 April 1746.
85 Elcho, *Short Account*, p.412.
86 TNA, SP54/30, 17b, Scott to Napier, 2 April 1746.

in the churchyard, nor their guns' muzzles, but fired mortar shells in their vicinity. From 10 until noon more fire directed was on the Jacobite batteries. This was a prelude to the water parties leaving the fort. Whilst they were doing so, Captain Campbell, the lieutenant governor, crossed from one side of a bastion to another and was shot at and wounded by Jacobite musketry. The Jacobite fire continued in the afternoon, with their cannon firing iron bars and gate hooks made red hot in furnaces.[87]

On 30 March, sentries in the fort called the hour each hour and added 'and all's well'. They were answered on one occasion with fire from the four-gun Jacobite battery: 'Yes, God damn you, too well'. Jacobite guns in the churchyard fired red hot cannon. The water party was fired on by guns using grapeshot and roundshot, but this was ineffectual. The men returned to the fort and were brought inside by ladders being hauled over the walls for them. Jacobite gunfire continued until the evening. Fire was returned, sometimes from the garrison's 6-pounders, which fired the splinters that had been previously collected.[88]

As usual, on 31 March, the watering party left the fort. It was fired upon by grapeshot made up of old nails. It fought a skirmish with the Jacobites 'according to custom'. Two of the garrison were injured, one being shot through the arm.[89]

The garrison believed that there were disputes between the French and the Scottish. At dinner time that evening, they could hear the Jacobites' drums being beaten. This could have been on the occasion of a general review of all the troops or could have been the signal for a retreat. It was decided to fire as many guns as possible at the place where they thought they were, as they could not see them, so swivels, small arms, mortars and grape shot was fired.[90]

Scott was determined on a sally. Choosing a sergeant and 12 men out of two of Guise's companies, they marched out against the Jacobite battery on the Craigs. Lieutenant George Foster with 25 men supported by a picquet, and a group of pioneers with tools followed them. These latter were spikes and hammers to use to disable the Jacobite guns.[91]

Achieving surprise by their rapid advance and after some fighting and the loss of Sergeant Duncan Stewart of the Argyll Militia, they were masters of the French battery on the Craigs. They carried away into the fort three brass 4-pounders and two 6-inch coehorns, as well as rammers, sponges, ladles and other equipment. There was a 6-pounder that they tried to bring in as well, but it was too heavy, so it was only dragged near to the fort, in full view of its guns. It was spiked, and later dismounted by artillery fire. The other artillery they found was spiked and two prisoners, a French gunner and a deserter from Barrell's Regiment, were taken.[92]

---

87 TNA, SP54/30, 17b, Scott to Napier, 2 April 1746.
88 TNA, SP54/30, 17b, Scott to Napier, 2 April 1746.
89 TNA, SP54/30, 17b, Scott to Napier, 2 April 1746.
90 TNA, SP54/30, 17b, Scott to Napier, 2 April 1746.
91 TNA, SP54/30, 17b, Scott to Napier, 2 April 1746.
92 TNA, SP54/30, 17b; Scott to Napier, 2 April 1746; Marchant, *History*, p.362.

There was another attack on another battery, but this failed. Lieutenant Paton was sent from the fort to reinforce the sally parties and succeeded in driving the Jacobite forces up a hill. However, from the fort could be seen hundreds of Jacobite forces converging on them from a mile distant. It was impossible to communicate with the sally parties from the fort, so Scott despatched Ensign Whiteaway to order Paton's return. This he succeeded in doing and the party returned without the loss of one man on the retreat, though in total two men had been killed and nine wounded.[93]

The sally was deemed successful and it was noted 'This gives us [the garrison] great spirits and our men would willingly try fortune again if they could get leave'. On the next day Stapleton could be seen, at sunset, on horseback 'to get news of us'.[94] Campbell, on 1 April, paid tribute to the garrison's de facto commander, 'We are Extreamly Happie in so good a man as Captain Scott who acts on every occasion with prudence and judgement'.[95]

Apparently, another effect of the sally was to foment dissension between the besiegers. Colonel Yorke wrote that a spy reported that, 'there is a coolness between the Camerons and MacDonalds, occasioned by something which happened at the sally made by the garrison. The MacDonalds complain the others did not come time enough to relieve their guard, and the others complain of them for going away before they came'.[96] The Jacobites were now left with only five cannon and low morale.[97] However, firing on both sides continued on the first two days of April.

Writing on the same day as the sally, Yorke stated that the odds on holding out were good:

> I don't think it likely they will be able to make themselves masters of Fort William; for by the last accounts come in form those parts, they have given over, or are on the point of quitting, that undertaking, and should they even persist, it will be too much for them to execute before we shall be able to move to its relief; by this means that bridle to the west coast will still continue.[98]

Other Whigs were impressed with the garrison's defence. Major General Campbell wrote to the officers and men of the Argyll Militia on 31 March, 'your brave and gallant behaviour in the defence of Fort William...and your resolution to defend it to the last, which gave me the utmost satisfaction'.[99] Cumberland was pleased, too, writing on 4 April 'The siege of Fort William goes on as I could wish and [Scott] seems to have acted in the manner I expected he would and I hope he will have an opportunity of recommending himself to His Majesty's favour'.[100]

93 TNA, SP54/30, 17b, Scott to Napier, 4 April 1746.
94 TNA, SP54/30, 17b, Scott to Napier, 3 April 1746.
95 NLS, MS 3734, 242, Captain Campbell to Unknown, 1 April 1746.
96 Yorke (ed.), *Hardwicke*, Vol.I, p.519.
97 Marchant, *History*, p.362.
98 Yorke (ed.), *Hardwicke*, Vol.I, p.514.
99 TNA, SP54/30 18e, Major General Campbell to Argyll Militia, 31 March 1746
100 TNA, SP54/30, Cumberland to Newcastle, 4 April 1746.

On 3 April the besiegers decamped, leaving their five remaining cannon and seven to nine mortars, all of which were spiked. Stapleton realised that 'he could not take it with the Cannon he had'. The besiegers had lost about 30 men killed or wounded.[101] Lord George Murray wrote 'They endured much fatigues and hardships in the attempt and found the thing impracticable'. Eventually, 'but the Siege of Fort William was going very ill…so our people were obliged to abandon it'.[102] Furthermore, when Lochiel left the district, he could only take 400 men with him.[103]

With the benefit of hindsight, Maxwell condemned the attempt to take the fort, 'it was a rash undertaking from the beginning'. He thought that using Highlanders was problematic:

> I must observe here that it is hard to make Highlanders do the regular duty of a siege, though they are excessively brave in an attack, and when they are allowed to fight in their own way; they are not so much masters of that sedate valour that is necessary to maintain a post, and it is extremely difficult to keep them long in their posts, or even in their quarters, without action.

He also condemned Mirabelle, who 'miscarried after ten or twelve days firing without any effect'.[104] Likewise, O'Sullivan noted, 'Yt misfortune was attributed to Grants being wounded in the beginning of the siege & the ill conduct of the French Ingenier who they were obliged to send there, Grant not being in a condition to act'.[105] Bizarrely enough, Johnstone wrote an entirely inaccurate paragraph about the siege: 'He began the siege on the 20th, and it lasted only a few days. It was the last of the Highland forts that remained to be taken, and when it came into our possession, it was immediately razed like the rest'.[106]

The consequences of the failed siege, according to loyalist Lord Glenorchy, was that the Jacobite army could not persuade all its followers to join the main army at Inverness. Apparently 400 Camerons refused to join their leader and the MacDonalds of Keppoch were also reluctant. The Jacobite high command, though, quite naturally, downplayed the significance of the siege. On 4 April, Sir Thomas Sheridan, writing on behalf of Charles to Lochiel and Keppoch, said that 'His Royal Highness looks upon what has happened at Fort William but as a fleabite and would not have any body be cast down about it'. The siege was now old news and the real danger was, as it had been for some weeks, the main British army under Cumberland in and around Aberdeen, especially now that the river Spey was fordable, so Sheridan continued, 'What he desires of you is to come away as soon as possible and bring with you all the men you can'.[107]

---

101 Elcho, *Short Account*, p.412.
102 Forbes, *Jacobite Memoirs*, pp.106, 116-117.
103 Yorke (ed.), *Hardwicke*, Vol.I, p.519.
104 Maxwell, *Narrative*, pp.133-134.
105 Tayler and Tayler (eds), *1745*, p.142.
106 Johnstone, *Memoir*, p.110.
107 RA, CP13/351, Sheridan to Lochiel and Keppoch, 4 April 1746.

Maxwell noted that the failures to take Blair Castle and Fort William as two of the Jacobites' setbacks following a string of successes. The third calamity was the failure of French gold to arrive in order to pay the army and to pay for supplies to feed them. This led to desertions and so when Cumberland and his army marched from Aberdeen they faced a reduced and weakened Jacobite army on Culloden Moor.

Table 3 lists the garrisons' casualties. Included amongst their number were the lieutenant governor and a Sergeant Train, both of whom were wounded. One of the militiamen had been shot dead when at a window: Major General Campbell gave his widow a pension of £12 per annum.[108] Of those wounded, James Dunston had suffered from a rupture, George Crach was lamed in the groin, William Dawson was pensioned off in the following year due to wounds at the siege. William Moss lost his left arm, Joseph Hall and James Smith had both been disabled by being hit by a cannon ball; all these three were discharged with pensions later in 1746.[109] Jacobite casualties are unknown, but were presumably likewise fairly light.

Table 3 Casualties, Fort William Garrison

Unit	Sick	Wounded	Killed	Died of wounds
Guise's	5	13	1	1
Argyll Militia	4	6	1	2
Volunteers	1	0	1	0
Total	**10**	**19**	**3**	**3**

Source: TNA, SP54/30, 10a, Fletcher to Newcastle, 8 April 1746.

Among the Whigs there was much congratulation about the fort's holding out. Fletcher wrote to Cumberland on 8 April, 'I beg leave to congratulate your Grace on the noble defence of Fort William, the success of the sally of 31 March, and of the rebels being obliged to totally abandon the siege and to leave their cannon and mortars and trophy to the besieged. This I hope will effectually strike Terror into the rebels in the neighbourhood of Fort William.'[110]

Newcastle wrote to Cumberland on 17 April, unaware yet of the greater triumph of the day before, 'the King looks upon [the siege] to have been greatly owing to the courage and good conduct of Captain Scott, whose Behaviour has given the King great satisfaction'. George II was also impressed with the behaviour of the Argyll Militia, who 'had done their duty and been of great service on this occasion', in contrast to their being taken before Blair in the previous month.[111]

108 TNA, SP54/30, 18e, Major General Campbell to Argyll Militia, 31 March 1746.

109 TNA, WO116/4, Royal Hospital Chelsea Out Pensioners Admission Books, Cavalry and Infantry, 1746-1754.

110 TNA, SP54/30, 10a, Fletcher to Newcastle, 8 April 1746.

111 TNA, SP54/30, 20a, Newcastle to Cumberland, 17 April 1746.

8

Blair Castle, 1746

We now shift from the western Highlands eastwards. Blair Castle was the principal seat of the Murray family (from 1703, Dukes of Atholl) since the Middle Ages. It had been held by the Jacobites in the summer of 1689 and this had led to the Battle of Killiecrankie on 27 July of that year. It is situated in Perthshire, to the east of the River Garry and close to the village of Blair Atholl. To the south east were fields between the river and the hills, before reaching the Pass of Killiecrankie, a narrow pathway between the river and the wooded hillside; almost impassable for four wheeled traffic.

Blair Castle was not unknown to the Jacobites of 1746. Charles had stayed there at the end of August 1745 on his advance to Edinburgh and for a further few days in early February 1746 on his retreat from Stirling.

Once Cumberland had reached Stirling on 2 February, he decided that his main forces would advance along the coastline towards Inverness. He ordered smaller forces elsewhere. One of these commands was given to Lieutenant Colonel Sir Andrew Agnew, who had assisted in the siege of Carlisle only a few weeks previously. He was to be based at Blair Castle, and send out patrols to 'annoy the rebels', gain intelligence and to round up cattle belonging to the Jacobites in order to feed his men. He was also given unambiguous orders, 'If you are attacked, you will defend yourself to the utmost, as the Rebels have no artillery but three pounders to annoy you, and as succour will be sent you'. He was also given permission to execute any soldiers without recourse to court martial if they refused to 'defend the house to the utmost'.[1]

Agnew and his men took possession of Blair Castle on 12 February, just a few days after Charles had vacated it for the second and last time. Cumberland intended that it would be a useful base from which Agnew's troops could scour the countryside for up to eight miles, seizing all Jacobites, taking their corn especially, as well as burning and destroying their houses. James Murray, 2nd Duke of Atholl, the castle's owner, was not happy with this activity, writing this to Agnew on 14 February, 'I am sorry to understand that the men under your command are committing so many disorders at my house'. Atholl was unable to live in the house at this time and he was unhappy

1 Atholl (ed.), *Chronicles*, Vol.III, p.193.

The Pass of Killiecrankie. (Author's postcard)

that the garrison's supply needs were being taken from his own enclosures. Hawley told Atholl that 'It is absolutely necessary for the service that the Troops continue at Blair Castle for some little time longer'.[2]

There was the issue that 'not only he and all the officers are quartered in it, but every one of the private men, you may easily imagine what sort of a house they will make of it'. Furthermore, all the cattle taken from Jacobites were corralled in Atholl's enclosures, 'so that there is as great devastation without doors as within'. Atholl and his agent saw no need for any of this because, 'there are houses belonging to rebels in the neighbourhood of Blair, sufficient and large enough to contain all the troops under your command both officers and private men and that perhaps would be making better use of them at present than burning them'.[3]

Unlike the subjects of all the other sieges in this book, Blair Castle was not one of the fortresses or castles under the Crown but a private home, though a robust one. There was, thus, no regular garrison with artillery and a knowledge of the locality. This was a scratch force which was not expected to deal directly with Jacobite forces.

The first few weeks seemed untroublesome enough for the garrison. On 8 March Agnew told Cumberland, 'There is nothing extraordinary of any consequence has happened since I came here'. He mentioned, though, that the state of the garrison was less than perfect; four men had died, two had

2 Atholl (ed.), *Chronicles*, Vol.III, pp.204, 206, 208.
3 Edinburgh University Library (EUL), Dc 37 (1), 1-2, Atholl Papers, Unknown to Atholl, 17 and 25 February 1746.

Blair Castle. (Postcard from author's collection)

deserted and 33 were ill in the infirmary. It is unknown whether they had the services of a surgeon, but declared 'Wee are in great want of medicines and in case anything extraordinary should happen'. There was also a lack of gunpowder and musket balls.[4]

Attackers:

- Lord George Murray
- Atholl Brigade
- Cluny MacPherson's Regiment
- Lady Mackintosh's regiment
- Two 4-pounders[5]

Total 700-800 men

The defenders under Agnew were from his regiment, the Royal North British Fusiliers. The junior officers included Captains Peregrine Wentworth, Stratford Eyre, Captain Lieutenant Jocelyn, Lieutenants/Ensigns Lawson, Colville, Beckwith, Robert Mawhood, and Surgeon Vance. There were 270 rank-and-file, for a total force of 300 all ranks[6]

Lieutenant Colonel Sir Andrew Agnew (1686-1771) was the 5th Baronet of Lochnaw. He had served in the army since 1704, first as a volunteer, then as

4 RA, CP12/153, Agnew to Cumberland, 8 March 1746.
5 Tayler and Tayler (eds), *1745* p.142.
6 NRS, GD126/30 Heads for John Home, 1801

a commissioned officer from 1705. He fought at Ramillies, Oudernarde and Malplaquet. Although in Ireland at the time of the 1715 Jacobite campaign, he had risen to the rank of lieutenant colonel of the Royal North British Fusiliers and served at the Battle of Dettingen in 1743. On 11 January, Lord George Murray had written that 'A garrison of 50 men will be enough at Blair castle'.[7]

Relieving force under Lieutenant Prince Frederick of Hesse and Major General Lord Crauford:

- St George's Dragoons
- Hamilton's Dragoons
- Naison's Dragoons
- One battalion of Hessian Guards
- Hessian Regiment Mansbach
- Hessian Regiment Prince Frederick
- Hessian Grenadier Battalion
- Hessian Regiment Prince Maximillian
- Hessian Regiment Donop
- One company of Hessian Hussars
- One company of Hessian Artillery; 160 men, 100 horses and eight 3-pounder cannon
- Staff of 18 men
  Total 4,908 men; though 256 were sick or with the baggage train. Each Hessian regiment had one battalion, made up of 10 companies; each company had 2 captains, 2 lieutenants, 2 ensigns, 3 sergeants, a Fournier, a captain des armes, a surgeon and 52 privates.[8]

In March 1746 the bulk of the Hessian troops, who had arrived in Scotland several weeks earlier as a reinforcement for the British army, were stationed in Perth, in order to prevent any Jacobite thrust into the Lowlands and England. This was because most of the British army was stationed in and around Aberdeen, waiting for the weather to clear to make an advance on Inverness possible. Lord George Murray proposed that he would advance to Blair Castle, knowing that there were '30 Dragoons & some foot of the English troops in garrison' there. He would either blow up the castle or capture those inside and take possession of it. Charles did not approve of the plan, because:

> [H]e did not like to have his army so dispers'd, Part at Dornoch [in pursuit of Loudoun and his men] & Don Robin above three days march by the ferry's they had to passe: Another considerable part of it at Fortewilliam & what he woud carry with him to Blear, & the enemy in March towards him, for he had certain accts that Cumberland was to arrive at Perth. But Ld George insisted.[9]

7 Atholl (ed.), *Chronicles*, Vol.III, p.138.
8 NLS, MS 17526, 162, List of Hessian troops, 1746; Andrew Bamford, (ed.), *Rebellious Scots to Crush: The Military Response to the Jacobite '45* (Solihull: Helion, 2020), pp.202-203.
9 Tayler and Tayler (eds), *1745*, p.142.

Lord George wrote otherwise, 'I was ordered at that time to go to Atholl' and that to clear the district of the posts of Argyll Militia, who, it was feared, would increase in number and together with the Hessian forces and others, would march north into Badenoch and harass the Jacobites there.[10] However, another Jacobite account rationalised the strategy thus, 'If he had managed to get possession of that castle he would have gradually succeeded in besieging Cumberland and preventing him from obtaining forage'. [11]

Murray also believed that taking the castle would be of huge strategic benefit:

> [J]oining that castle to those of Inverness and the barracks of Ruthven the enemy could have harboured in no part of the Highlands except Fort William and so [the Jacobites] always [would have] had the communication free of Perthshire, good part of Stirlingshire, Dunbartonshire, Argyllshire, Moray, Banff, Aberdeenshire, the Mearns of Angus [and] by this means an army of 12,000 Highlanders could never have wanted subsistence, it would have taken three armies equal to the Duke of Cumberland's to oblige them to fight, and even in that case they would have had the choice of which army to have fought.[12]

Lord George Murray was a brother of the Duke of Atholl, the castle's owner. His brother, James, was deemed the rightful duke by the government, but the eldest brother, William, was a Jacobite. Lord George had joined the Jacobite army in early September 1745, from Blair.

Murray was allowed to take his own regiment, which he collected at Strathspey on about 14 March and marched to Atholl. En route he took command of Cluny MacPherson's men and the Mackintoshes. He had also been allocated money for pay and supplies and was given two guns. They were to pass by the castle of the Laird of Grant, to take him prisoner or to force his clan to join the Jacobites, but Grant had already left to join Cumberland. Murray passed the castle and did not remove any of the guns from there, perhaps because there were no horses to pull them. In fact, on arriving at Ruthven, on 16 March, Murray left the two guns he had there, and continued to march to Blair.[13] They marched quickly indeed; in one day and night they covered 30 miles, according to Murray.[14]

Murray and his men had to brush past the opposition posed by detachments of about 200-300 of Argyll Militia stationed in scattered outposts several miles distant from another, to the north of Blair, at Blairfettie, Kynachan. Most were quartered in houses. There were also patrols of regular troops at the bridge of Tilt and the house of Lude. During the hours of three and five in the morning of 17 March, he achieved total surprise without much difficulty, killing about 10 of them and capturing the others whilst asleep and sending them as prisoners to Inverness. None of the attackers were killed or

10 Forbes, *Memoirs*, pp.106-107.
11 Seton (ed.), 'Commentary', p.109.
12 Duffy, *Fight for a Throne*, pp.410-411.
13 Seton (ed.), 'Commentary', pp.142-143.
14 Forbes, *Jacobite Memoirs*, p.107.

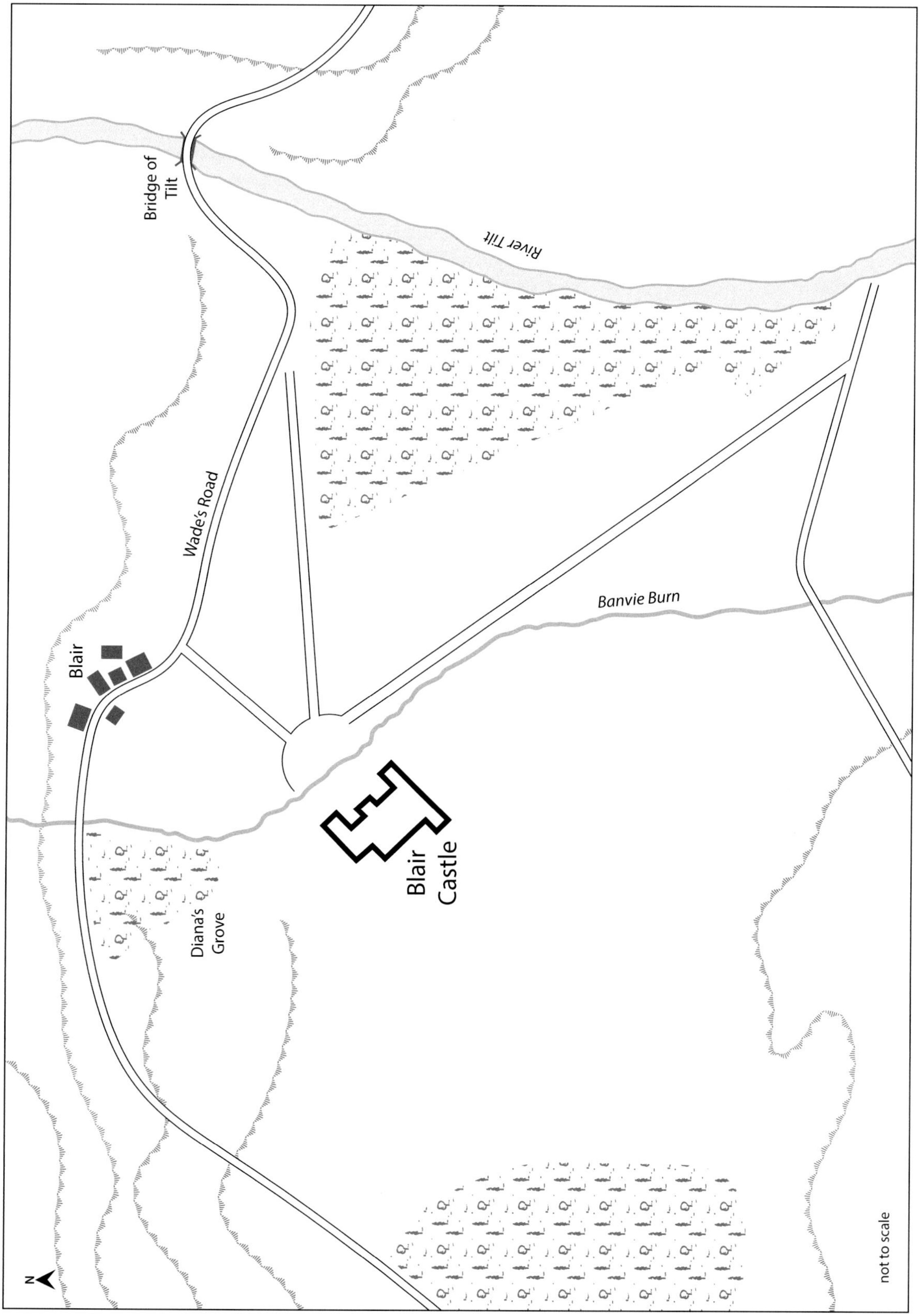

Plan of Blair Castle and environs.

wounded. Also taken were copies of their orders from Cumberland, signed by their colonel, John Campbell, ordering them to attack the Jacobites and disarm them, and in the case of meeting resistance, to show no quarter. Murray and Cluny then established themselves in the village above Blair and they also secured the pass of Killiecrankie, thus encircling the castle.[15] None of the militia were able to warn those in Blair Castle. The surprise was due, according to Agnew, to 'a plain Demonstration what a villainous country this is'.[16]

Later that day, Murray wrote a formal notice for the garrison to surrender, 'I am ordered by His Royal Highness the Prince Regent to dislodge and take all the Garrison in this Country. In consequence of which I send this summons Desiring you will deliver up immediately the castle of Blair, with all arms, ammunition and horse'. The note was 'written on a very shabby piece of paper', but none of the besiegers would deliver it, knowing 'the outrageous temper of Sir Andrew Agnew', he could not be persuaded to do so. Instead they found a tavern maid, by the name of Molly, 'being rather handsome' and who was well known and popular among some of the castle's officers who frequented the establishment in Blair Atholl she was employed in.[17]

Apparently, the besiegers claimed that if the garrison resisted, their guns would batter down the castle and destroy all the defenders. The officers of the latter replied that the attackers would be driven off should they attempt an assault. However, none of them wished to give the summons to Agnew. Eventually a lieutenant was persuaded to do so and on reading it, 'he furiously drove the lieutenant out of his presence…vociferating after him strong epithets against lord George Murray, with threatenings to shoot through the head any other messenger whom he should send'. Molly then returned, unharmed, to Blair churchyard where Murray, Lord Nairn and Cluny awaited her.[18] Agnew, who believed that the Jacobites were 2,000 strong, thought that it had been 'a very ode summons sent to me'.[19]

Agnew wrote to Cumberland that day, 'I shall make the best Defence I can and I question not but I shall have assistance sent me in due time. I am in great want of arms as I told you before'.[20] Evidently the Jacobites had not wholly encircled the place at this time. Meanwhile, Murray was confident he could take the castle, informing O'Sullivan on the same day, 'The cannon are not come up, if they do soon this castle may be taken…my best endeavours shall not be wanting. There are but 300 regular troops in the garrison'.[21]

The Jacobites then laid siege to the castle on 18 March; at between eight and nine, Murray placed his men to prevent the defenders from securing any provisions or from sallying out.[22] The men were eager for the offensive, 'The

15 Tayler and Tayler (eds), *1745*, p.143; Elcho, *Short Account*, p.403; Forbes, *Jacobite Memoirs*, p.107.
16 RA, CP13/145, Agnew to Cumberland, 4 April 1746.
17 Atholl (ed.), *Chronicles*, Vol.III, pp.239, 263-264.
18 Atholl (ed.), *Chronicles*, Vol.III, p.264.
19 RA, CP13/145, Agnew to Cumberland, 4 April 1746.
20 NLS, ADV 23.3.28, 152, Agnew to Cumberland, 17 March 1746.
21 RA, CP12/404, Murray to O'Sullivan, 17 March 1746.
22 Forbes, *Jacobite Memoirs*, p.108.

rebels were highly inraged against the King's troops, because some of their houses in Atholl had been plundered'.[23]

The attackers had achieved a fair degree of surprise by marching through the night towards Blair Castle. They were within two miles of the castle before anyone within had any inkling of the danger they were in. As soon as the Jacobite advance was known, the sick of the garrison were moved from the 'office houses' near the castle to within the walls. Horses, forage and fuel that was nearby was also brought in. Agnew called out his men and arrayed them outside the castle and offered the Jacobites battle, but the latter stood behind park dykes and so Agnew had his men return to the castle.[24]

The Jacobites then opened fire with the two cannon on 18 March. According to Maxwell: 'Lord George, having got up some field pieces from Inverness, endeavoured to set fire to Blair Castle, as his cannon was too light to make an impression on the walls, but that proved ineffectual'.[25] The small guns were ineffective because the walls were seven feet thick. Moreover, as Murray later wrote, 'The cannon were not only small, but bad. One of them seldom hit the castle, though not half-musket from it'.[26] However, according to Agnew, firing continued from the Jacobite guns for four days from 18 March and then recommenced at midnight of 25 March for a further five hours.[27]

The Jacobites, 'finding that it had not had the desired effect' had access to a furnace and here they heated cannon balls to make them red hot to set the castle roof on fire, 'a work I was by no means fond of' wrote Murray – after all, the castle was his brother's home. The defenders were able to extinguish the flames, helped by some carpenters amongst them, who cut out the hot bullets wherever they struck, throwing them out or cooling them in water. Apparently 207 heated shot of this type were fired. This may have been the last time that the Jacobite artillery fired.[28]

The attackers also fired their muskets against the defenders, but as Agnew stated, 'they were not wanting to play us from the beginning with their small arms but at such a distance that it did little harme'. The besieged could do little in return, as Agnew wrote, 'I was so ill provided with arms that I took care that our men should not fire till they came near as which they very seldom did'.[29] Apparently the garrison began the siege with only 24 musket balls per man, 'if they had had sufficient powder and ball at first they could have killed a great many of the rebels but were obliged to hold their shot a great deal' and towards the siege's end each man only had eight musket balls remaining. No one was to fire without an order from an officer.[30]

23 Douglas, *History*, p.168.
24 Douglas, *History*, p.170.
25 Maxwell, *Narrative*, p.132.
26 Forbes, *Jacobite Memoirs*, p.108.
27 RA, CP13/145, Agnew to Cumberland, 4 April 1746.
28 RA, CP13/145, Agnew to Cumberland, 4 April 1746; Douglas, *History*, p.170.
29 RA, CP13/145, Agnew to Cumberland, 4 April 1746.
30 NRS, GD126/30 State of Blair Castle, 1746.

The castle was situated on rocky ground so, unlike the case with Fort George, it could not be successfully mined.[31] Apparently this proposal had been made at Inverness before Murray had left, but he noted 'I had no positive orders to attempt that'. Contrary to Elcho's opinion, Murray thought that it was possible, a mine could have been laid by the old stabling under the cover of a wall, had he a number of workmen.[32]

Even so, the garrison were concerned about the possibility of Jacobite mining, with an officer later writing, 'But it suffered one alarm of danger, which, had it not proved to be false, must have been of the most decisive effect'. A week following the blockade, perhaps on 24 March, those within the walls heard knocking which seemed to emanate from beneath the ground floor of the castle, 'as if miners were hard at work forming a mine to blow it up…which indeed seemed to be very practicable'.[33]

This seemed possible for the Jacobites had complete possession of the bowling green and the offices on the north side and of the high wall to the west. It was thought that the back of the bowling house could have been where the beginning of a tunnel could have been made. A tunnel leading to a man-made cave could have been filled with gunpowder and set alight, enough to destroy the castle. Murray knew the castle and its environs well, as it was his family home, 'as well as [being] a man of known sagacity'. It might take a week to accomplish but there were 'no workmen capable of executing such work'. A Jacobite mine could not have been interrupted except by counter mining from the ground floor of the castle. However, the noise transpired to be 'nothing more than a soldier's cutting a block of wood, which lay on a floor in the uppermost room, with repeated strokes of the axe, which occasion'd a pretty general merriment in the garrison'.[34]

However, as Maxwell observed, there was another way. Murray 'had still a prospect of reducing the castle by famine till the approach of the Hessian troops obliged him to retire'.[35] According to Murray, 'We understood the garrison had not much provisions; and that in a fortnight or three weeks, they must be obliged to surrender: and this was what I thought best'. In the meantime 300 men, the MacPhersons under Cluny, were placed in the village of Blair and the same number by the Mains, at the new stables.[36] However, the Jacobite supply situation was no better and because there was no money to pay the troops, they took meal and sheep from the countryside.[37]

Supplies were indeed low. Agnew later reported that a quarter of the biscuits were mouldy and so he could not use them as food. Firewood was also low and so wainscoting from the castle was used. He later told Cumberland 'I was very ill provided during the siege'.[38] Strict rationing had to be introduced. A lieutenant recalled:

31 Elcho, *Short Account*, p.404.
32 Forbes, *Jacobite Memoirs*, p.108.
33 Atholl (ed.), *Chronicles*, Vol.III, p.266.
34 Atholl (ed.), *Chronicles*, Vol.III, p.266.
35 Maxwell, *Narrative*, p.132.
36 Forbes, *Jacobite Memoirs*, p.108.
37 Forbes, *Jacobite Memoirs*, p.110.
38 RA, CP13/145, Agnew to Cumberland, 4 April 1746.

> The provisions of the castle, excepting what was accidentally in it, for the use of the commandant and officers, consisted chiefly, if not wholly, of biscuits and cheese, of which the quantity was so small that the whole allowance fixed per diem for each man was only one pound of biscuit, and a quarter of a pound of cheese, and a bottle of water.[39]

He spelt out the consequences, 'the smallness of the present quantity; with the certainty of an approaching want of provisions for men and of horses provender, were circumstances constantly in view'.[40]

The surgeon had no medicines with him and the siege was to cost two men dead whilst 33 became sick. There were also the eight horses there, belonging to the officers, but there was no food for them, either. They were at risk, for 'Sir Andrew Agnew, his garrison, would certainly have preferred the eating of horseflesh'. Yet it was noted that 'they were reduced to great extremity, and if the blockade had lasted a few days longer, it seems probable that they would have been obliged to surrender'.[41]

Meanwhile, Jacobite numbers rose. About 400-500 men from the nearby countryside who had once been part of the Jacobite army rallied to their old standard. The fiery cross was sent throughout the country to summon all able-bodied men to the Jacobite army, by force if necessary. Murray sent a party of men to Dunkeld to gain intelligence of their enemy, where they later retreated to Pitlochry under pressure.[42]

There were a number of elements of black humour during the siege. A group of the garrison's officers found an old uniform of Agnew's, which they decided to stuff with straw and place at a prominent window, with a telescope as if he were reconnoitring the Jacobite positions. This attracted Jacobite musketry 'without any adequate effect'. Agnew wondered why there was so much fire directed against the window and when he saw what had happened was scandalised. He eventually found the principal culprit and 'let the loon who set it up just go up himself and take it down again'. This was a potentially dangerous activity but it was apparently done without any injury. Agnew provided additional humour with his caustic remarks on other occasions; once remarking, 'My Lord [George Murray] is playing ball against the walls of Blair castle' and 'Is the loon clear daft, knocking down his own brother's house?' The officers discussed Agnew at length, swapping stories about him and noting that he had never been wounded in battle, nor fallen sick on campaign, nor had he ever taken part in a battle in which his side lost. This helped give them confidence of final victory.[43]

Yet for most of the siege the Jacobites only had a covering force around the castle to prevent the garrison leaving. Most troops were needed elsewhere. Unlike the case with some of the sieges of the campaign, there were substantial relief forces in the neighbourhood of the besieged. These had

39 Atholl (ed.), *Chronicles*, Vol.III, p.263.
40 Atholl (ed.), *Chronicles*, Vol.III, p.267.
41 NRS, GD126/30 Heads for John Home, 1801.
42 Forbes, *Jacobite Memoirs*, pp.108-109; Douglas, *History*, p.168.
43 Atholl (ed.), *Chronicles*, Vol.III, p.270, 268.

been directed to the south of the castle by Cumberland on 24 February, who had instructed the Earl of Crauford to 'immediately march four battalions to Perth and two to Stirling…St George's dragoons will be cantoned at Eam Bridge & the remains of Naizon's and Hamilton's [dragoons] will be cantoned at Bannockburn near Stirling'. The infantry in question were the Hessian troops under Prince Frederick of Hesse. Initially seen as being unnecessary and merely a drain of the meagre food supplies of the army, Cumberland told Crauford to 'make them usefull whilst they are here' and deemed that their major role would be 'for the security of our corps'.[44]

Crauford noted that the majority of the troops were in place by 9 March and included artillery as well as infantry. He noted that there was no obvious danger. On the same day Cumberland wrote giving additional instructions, which were later to be either misinterpreted or seen as an excuse for inaction. Cumberland wrote:

> If there should be any Reason to think the Rebels would attempt to penetrate south, whilst we are north, then the Prince [Frederick] will immediately gather together his Troops & your Body of dragoons & march directly to attack them. But, as the Hessians are quite strangers in the Country, I don't think it advisable they should engage themselves in the mountains, either to seek the Rebels to attack them, or even after an Action if there should be one.[45]

On 16 March the bulk of Crauford's and Frederick's troops were stationed in and around Stirling. However, on that day, four companies were advanced to Dunkeld (about a day's march to the south of Killiecrankie), with a lieutenant and 20 hussars further north than Dunkeld and a corporal and ten men were to be stationed at an unnamed bridge.[46] They did not march towards Blair Atholl, however.

By 19 March, Cumberland had heard of the castle's plight and the inaction of Crauford and the Hessians and wrote thus to the former:

> I was very surprised at your Packet of the 17th which I have just now received, & with the Resolutions of the Council of War, that have been taken for evacuating Perth, & leaving our Magazines there, upon the news of two of our paltry posts on the Hills being surprised.
>
> I can easily excuse the Hessian General Officers, but I cant express my astonishment that you who should so well know the Country, & the people could put so much trust in our Highland posts, as to expect anything else from them.
>
> I imagined that I had sufficiently explaind that the only use of that Chain of Posts in the Hills was to prevent any little partys from them, from coming down to take meal. As you knew that the Rebels were besieging Fort William & that there was a considerable Body of them opposing us, in this country, I should be glad to know what Number of them you should imagine was coming sufficient to disturb the four battalions that were at Perth, & the Regiment of Dragoons, or

44 RA, CP11/62, Cumberland to Crauford, 24 February 1746.
45 RA, CP12/27, Cumberland to Crauford, 9 March 1746.
46 RA, CP12/122, Crauford to Fawkener, 16 March 1746.

whether you could suppose they would pass Tay Bridge leaving a regular force in Menzies Castle behind them, to march to Sterling, & let you be in the rear.

Whenever you shall have certain notice that the whole force of the Rebels is coming down to you, then it will be time to take the measures you have now taken & not before. I send Colonel Yorke with these Letters because he can better explain to you the meaning of these Posts as well, & to Prince Frederick, I would have you follow the opinion of Captain Campbell of the Perthshire Company in every thing relating to those posts.[47]

Crauford replied on 20 March:

[I]t was unanimously thought far from being safe to hazard a check in the mountains in attempting to relieve Sir Andrew Agnew and his detachment in Blair Castle they embarking themselves so far in the mountains, where they could not at present pretend to maintain themselves, and at the same time defend the Low Country seeming to be also intirley contrary to your Royal Highness Inclination signified to the Prince…To attack them in their strong grounds (as Your Royal Highness judges it very well in ordering us even after a victory to be cautious of embarking ourselves in the mountains.[48]

Cumberland replied on the next day:

I have this moment received yours of the 20th by which I see that Blair Castle is actually invested by the Rebels, & that there is no thought at Perth of relieving it, which much surprises me, but still more the reasons you seem to mention. Vizt. That I had orderd the Troops should not engage themselves too far in the Hills, even after a Victory, but I take this case to be entirely different, as they have but two marches up to Blair, wherefore I think it absolutely necessary for his Majesty's Service, that the Castle at Blair be immediately relieved & that for that purpose, Prince Frederick shall immediately on the receit of these Letters, march his whole Hessian Corps now at Perth, & St George's Dragoons, forward to Dunkeld the first day, & the next on to Blair. I am very sure that on the Hessians moving, the Rebels will quit their attempt, or should they not that the Prince will purchase a Victory at a very cheap rate.[49]

Meanwhile, knowledge of the castle's situation was virtually non-existent outside the Jacobite lines, which had closely invested it and this led to gloom. Glenorchy wrote on 22 March, 'I fear Sir Andrew must at last submit'.[50] Glenorchy wrote that Cumberland's orders to relieve the castle 'has put all here in a flurry, and great difficulties are started about crossing the river'.[51] Cumberland also informed his political masters of the situation, writing on 26 March to Newcastle:

---

47 TNA, SP54/29/19E, Cumberland to Crauford, 19 March 1746.
48 RA, CP12/201, Crauford to Cumberland, 20 March 1746.
49 RA, CP12/260, Cumberland to Crauford, 21 March 1746.
50 NLS, MS 3734. 114, Glenorchy to Unknown, 22 March 1746.
51 NLS, MS 3734, 213, Glenorchy to Unknown, 23 March 1746.

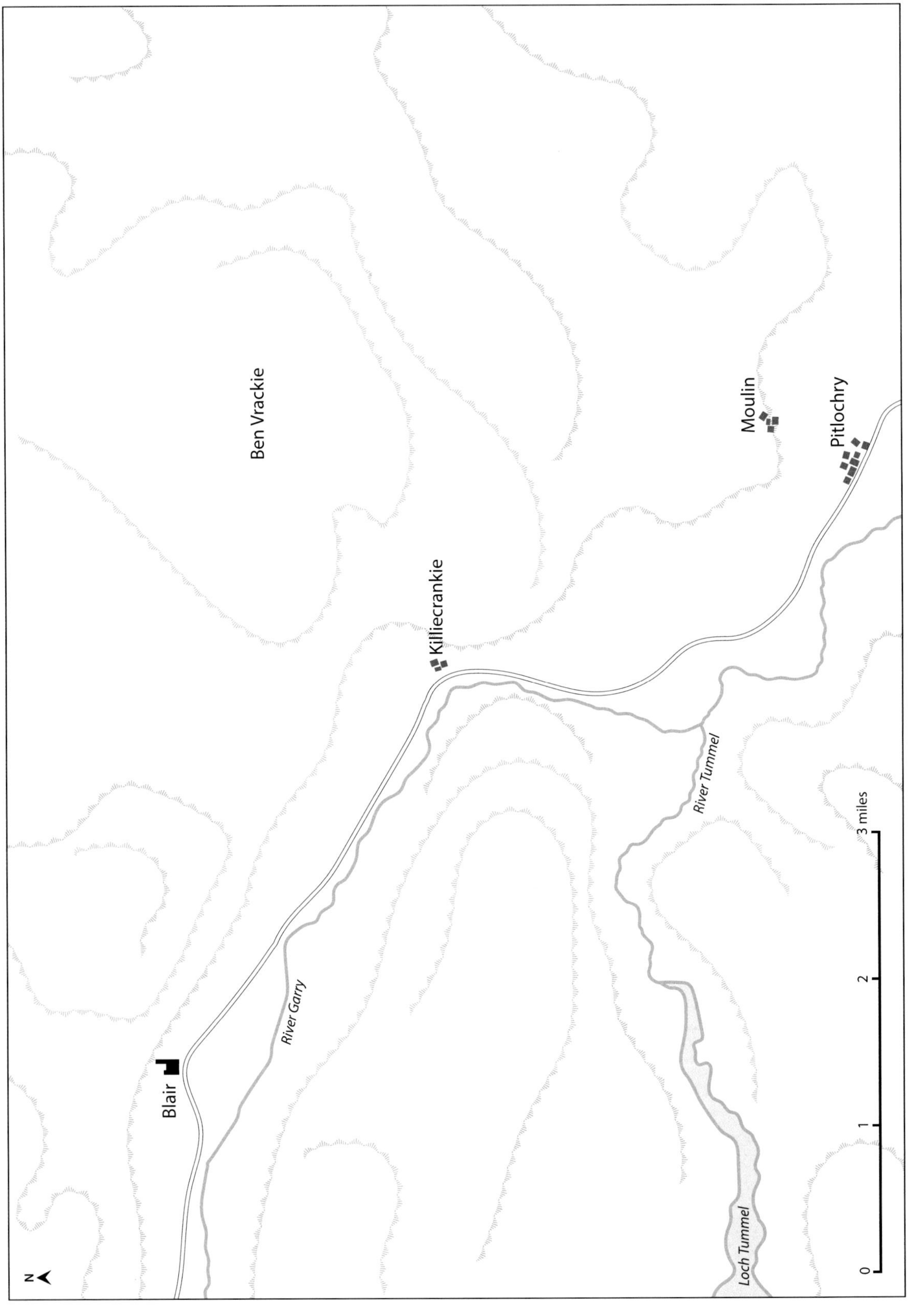

Plan of area surrounding Blair Castle and the Pass of Killiecrankie.

> In my last of the 19th I acquainted you by a Post script, of the alarm taken at Perth, & by the Answers to Prince Frederick, & Lord Crauford, copys of which I then sent you; you saw my opinion. Two Days after they wrote me word, that as Blair was taken, which proved false, they ought to retire to Crief, & form there. But, upon two Letters received at the same time, from Lord Glenorchy, copys of which I inclose, & the intelligence given to the Duke of Athole, I sent immediately positive orders to Prince Frederick & Lord Crauford to march the four Battalions, & what Dragoons they had directly to raise the Siege of Blair which orders were immediately complyed with as his Majesty will see by the inclosed copys of the Letters from Prince Frederick & Lord Crauford, & I doubt not but upon their first March the few Rebels who were there will have retired.
>
> His Majesty will also see by Lord Craufords answer to me, of the 21st how much he desires to be recalled from the Service he is now emploied in, & that he seems to be picqued at my reprimand, which might be warm, but which the event shews was not undeserved. If however, his head was but as good as is heart, his Majesty would not have a better officer in his whole army. I should therefore, for many considerations be glad if his Majesty would be pleased to allow me to send him by his Majestys orders to Flanders, I then might replace him by sending Lord Albermarle to Prince Frederick, as the Hessians themselves seem to desire an Englishman with them, in which they are extremely in the right, & no one will be more proper for that Service than Lord Albermarle. If his Majesty should approve of this, I should be glad if the Brigadiers Bligh & Douglas could be sent to the North.[52]

As soon as it was known that the Jacobites were menacing the castle, the Hessians had to march to its relief. On 19 March the two battalions at Stirling marched to Crieff. On 24 March the four Hessian battalions at Perth began their march towards Blair. They camped at Nairn House and on the next night at Dunkeld. On 26 March all six battalions gathered at Dunkeld. It was then that skirmishing between the two forces begun. On 27 March some of the Hessians, who had marched from Crieff, were at the Tay Bridge. At this point Lord George sent them a message to state that if 1,200 Hessians were advanced, he would fight them on an advantageous ground, but Frederick refused this because 'he Could not send him them in the way his army was then situated'.[53]

There were a number of skirmishes between the Jacobites on the one hand and the Hessian hussars and St George's Dragoons on the other. In one Johnstone claimed that five or six Hessians were killed, the Highlanders 'with rapidity and impetuosity' running as fast as the horses.[54] Elcho seems more dismissive of the success of these, however.[55] Another source stated that only one Hessian was wounded.[56]

52 RA, CP12/353, Cumberland to Newcastle, 26 March 1746.
53 Elcho, *Short Account*, pp.404-405.
54 Johnstone, *Memoir*, p.107.
55 Elcho, *Short Account*, p.405.
56 Douglas, *History*, p.169.

There was concern in the castle for relief. There had been no communication between the garrison and Crauford since the onset of the siege. One Mr Wilson, a gardener employed at the castle and deemed 'a loyal, stout and sensible man' was selected to take a message from Agnew to Crauford. If Wilson was in danger of capture, he was to destroy the note. He was given an officer's horse and would leave the castle at one in the morning of 29 March. Soldiers at the windows at the front of the castle would fire at any Jacobite sentries who tried to stop Wilson.[57]

When the time came, the castle's great doors were unbarricaded and opened. This was apparently done noiselessly. Wilson left the castle and mounted a horse belonging to Captain Wentworth. He then rode down the main road. It was then that the Jacobites opened fire and the castle's sentries replied. Apparently 'everyone hoping that Mr Wilson had made his escape'. However, on the following day, hopes were dashed when the horse used was seen ridden by a Jacobite in Blair, so it was feared that Wilson had been captured.[58]

Eventually there was action taken to relieve Blair, as Cumberland told Newcastle on 31 March:

> The Hessian Corps that marched from Perth, under Prince Frederick's command was to be as yesterday at Blair. So that I suppose that part of the Country is once more freed from the Rebels. This fresh attempt of the Rebells at Blair has fully proved the Duke of Atholl to be of no weight in this country when he is in his Majesty's service, for all the men that he raised for Lord Loudoun's Regiment, deserted with their officers to the Rebells on the first breaking out of this Rebellion, & upon my putting him into possession again of Dunkeld, Blair & the rest of his estate, he offered to recruit that company a fresh & to raise 500 men for his Majesty's service. As to his first proposal I utterly refused it, but consented to his trial of this latter, in which he has totally failed, as I fear he will do in every attempt in favour of the Government.
>
> The instant I have received the inclosed from Prince Frederick, & Lord Crawford, I own, I am not without fears for the Castle of Blair, for Sir Andrew Agnew, has but five days Provisions left, and I am afraid, in the manner the Hessians go on, they will loyter away the time. But I have sent them positive orders to go on, & not stay for the junction, which if they obey in time will immediately save Blair. You have also the copies of my orders. [59]

On 31 March, Crauford, with St George's Dragoons, 500 Hessian infantry and 50 Hessian hussars, marched four miles to the north of Dunkeld, camping that night at Dowally. On the next day they marched to Pitlochry, just south of Killiecrankie.[60] The cavalry advanced towards the Jacobites and the latter retreated to the foot of the pass 'where we made a disposition to contest it'.

57 Atholl (ed.), *Chronicles*, Vol.III, p.267.
58 Atholl (ed.), *Chronicles*, Vol.III, p.267.
59 TNA, SP54/29/32a, Cumberland to Newcastle, 31 March 1746.
60 Elcho, *Short Account*, p.405.

The stand-off lasted six hours, until Crauford began to retire. That night Crauford's forces retreated to Dunkeld, though some stayed near Pitlochry.[61]

A letter to the Duke of Atholl claimed, 'had the Earl of Crauford a sufficient number of troops he could have marched them safely without going through the Pass of Killiecrankie and might have been at Blair by three…but as he had no foot with him and too few dragoons he retired'.[62]

During this period, a lieutenant of the Hessian forces, a Swede, who 'spoke very good Latin – was a gentleman' was taken prisoner after his horse had been shot underneath him. He had 'ventured too near them'. Murray, without consulting Charles, sent the man back with a letter. Apparently 'yt was a Cartel for the prisoners he proposed to the Prince of Hesse, but he had no powers for so doing & no General officer can send a prisoner to the enemy without the General in Chefs orders'.[63] The hussar had not expected quarter 'for hussars seldom give it'.[64]

Murray found the siege and counter siege an exhausting experience as he recounted, 'I was, for the first seventy four hours, that I had not four hours sleep'. It was no better in the later stages of the siege; 'I was commonly back and forwards twice a day betwixt that [Killiecrankie] and Blair'. There was a lot he had to do; orders to give, dispositions to make, and unlike everyone else, he had no one who could relieve him. At least he had the co-operation of the men in his command, 'I was as well assisted by the officers and men as I could desire, particularly Cluny'.[65]

According to Maxwell, 'Lord George was by no means in a condition to fight the Hessians, he had not half of their number'.[66] Despite this, according to Elcho, on 1 April, Murray drew out his forces in battle order opposite Crauford's in front of Pitlochry, then retreated before him in order to draw him into the pass of Killiecrankie. Crauford refused the bait and sent for reinforcements from Frederick.[67]

There was certainly intelligence, provided by a woman, that 'the rebels left Dunkeld so precipitately was in hopes to draw the Hessians into an ambuscade some miles distant from Dunkeld…they had taken possession of all the woods, rocks on this side and in end about the pass of Killiecrankie'. Jacobite numbers were said to be as high as 6,000 men.[68]

Upon learning that the Hessian troops at Tay Bridge were marching to Blair via Kynachan and that Crauford was to receive reinforcements, Murray retreated. He marched his men to Strathspey and then to Speyside, before riding into Inverness itself.[69] Murray had called a council of war of his officers. They concluded that the pass could not be held because 'it could be

61 Forbes, *Jacobite Memoirs*, p.109.
62 EUL, Dc1. 37 (1), Atholl Papers, Unknown to Atholl, 2 April 1746.
63 Tayler and Tayler (eds), *1745*, p.143.
64 Forbes, *Jacobite Memoirs*, p.109.
65 Forbes, *Jacobite Memoirs*, pp.109-110.
66 Maxwell, *Narrative*, p.133.
67 Elcho, *Short Account*, p.405.
68 RA, CP13/19, Schaw to Fawkener, 25 March 1746.
69 Elcho, *Short Account*, p.406.

surrounded on all hands by such a vastly superior number'. They decided that they must therefore abandon the castle and the pass.[70]

However, Murray reported on 2 April that he had received both that day and the one before, messages for him to return to Inverness, for it was feared that Cumberland was about to march from Aberdeen to Inverness. Murray had already ordered that his cannon be moved back there, so as not to slow the march of the main body. At ten that night he withdrew his forces from the pass and arrived at Blair. He had left orders for the remainder of the men to be ready to march away, and ready they were. They left at two in the morning of 3 April.[71]

He found himself surrounded by other enemies there. Charles had been told by them that he could have taken the castle. Murray was also censured for his failure to take or destroy the castle, 'as being too tender of a family seat'. Maxwell was uncertain of the veracity of this accusation, writing 'As I do not know the situation of the castle, I cannot determine whether it was in his power to blow it up, or whether he had time to do it after he was informed of the march of the Hessians'. Maxwell stated that Murray of Broughton and his allies had so often blamed Lord George 'that nothing less than a direct proof ought to have any weight against him'. He continued:

> In this case it is absurd to suspect him, because the family seat could never be in danger. If it was in his power to blow it up, he had only to acquaint the governor when the mine was ready, and let him send one of his officers to view it; the governor would certainly have prevented the effect of it, and saved the castle.[72]

The question of the cartel proposition was also brought up as evidence against him, 'in Short they made the prince Believe that in that letter he had wrote to the Prince of Hesse he had engaged to betray him the first opportunity, and that by the Prince of Hesse and his brothers means he was entirely reconciled with the government'.[73]

Once the Jacobites had left, Molly, the popular maid, returned to the castle grounds to tell the garrison the news and that the officers were now welcome once more in the inn. When Agnew was told of the news, he disbelieved it, having not personally seen the Jacobites leaving, so had the garrison remain where it was. It was only when there was a rider from Crauford that his cavalry would be arriving in the hour that he believed the Jacobites had gone. He then drew his men up in formation outside the castle to receive his saviours. Typically, Agnew was not entirely tactful when they arrived, addressing Crauford thus, 'My Lord, I am very glad to see you, but, by all that's good, you have been very dilatory, and we can give you nothing to eat'. Crauford gave the following reply, 'I assure you, Sir Andrew, I made all the

70 Forbes, *Jacobite Memoirs*, p.135.
71 Forbes, *Jacobite Memoirs*, pp.109-110.
72 Maxwell, *Narrative*, p.133.
73 Elcho, *Short Account*, p.406.

haste I possibly could; and I hope that you and the officers will do me the honour to partake with me of such fare as I can give you'.[74]

Glenorchy was unimpressed with Crauford's behaviour, writing on 3 April, 'which had been executed a fortnight ago if they had been under the absolute command of Lord Crauford', alleging that Frederick had not submitted to Crauford's orders.[75]

It was only after Crauford learnt that the Jacobites had retreated that he would venture towards the castle. Despite receiving artillery, 'it was the opinion of his generals that this expedition could not be supported and therefore that he had ordered his troops back again to this place [Dowlie]'.[76]

Although casualties had been minimal, with one or two men dead and three slightly wounded, damage to the castle was not so, as Agnew wrote after the siege was lifted, 'The whole roof of the house of Blair Castle is much broke & damaged by the Rebles. It requires immediate Reparation, as also almost all the windows, for the warmth and comfort of the garrison'. Meanwhile Crauford left 30-40 dragoons there. They and the others were to send out patrols to burn and destroy any property of Jacobites within six miles of the castle, and to confiscate any arms held illegally. Crauford was also to provide a month's provisions to the garrison and have the Hessians ready to relieve the castle again if needed.[77] Wilson, incidentally, returned; he had been unhorsed but had reached Crauford on foot on 30 March and Agnew's letter apparently helped influence Frederick in his decision to advance against the Jacobites.[78] Meanwhile, once the Jacobite forces left Blair, Crauford marched with a party of dragoons to Blair Castle on 4 April. He was followed by Atholl and both were received by Agnew. Prince Frederick marched into Blair with his hussars, the remainder of the dragoons and 1,000 Hessian infantry on 5 April. They remained there of a day or two before returning to Dunkeld and then to Perth.[79] Agnew considered that there might be another attack, 'I do not know how soon I may have a second attack'.[80]

On 6 April, Newcastle was told by Cumberland:

> As I wrote fully in my last Despatch of the 4th and that nothing of consequence has happened since, but a confirmation of the Raising of the Siege of Blair, in a letter from Lord Glenorchy of the 3d to Colonel Yorke, of which I send an Extract, I only write this that his Majesty may be informed, that we are at last getting into Motion.
>
> I am extremely surprised, that neither Prince Frederick nor Lord Crauford should have sent me the least notice of the raising the siege of Blair. I can no way account for it, but by supposing and really believing they knew nothing of it. For, the Terror which seems to have been spread among them, was so great, that they

74 Atholl (ed.), *Chronicles*, Vol.III, p.268.
75 NLS, MS 3734, 248, Glenorchy to Unknown, 3 April 1746.
76 EUL, Dc1.37 (1), Atholl Papers, Unknown to Atholl, 2 April 1746.
77 RA, CP13/145, Agnew to Cumberland, 4 April 1746; Atholl (ed.), *Chronicles*, Vol.III, p.271.
78 Atholl (ed.), *Chronicles*, Vol.III, p.269.
79 Elcho, *Short Account*, p.407; Douglas, *History*, p.169.
80 RA, CP13/145, Agnew to Cumberland, 4 April 1746.

> would not allow one of their Partys to go further than the Entrance of the pass of Killiecrankie.
>
> I late last night also received Letters from Prince Frederick, & Lord Crauford acquainting me with the Raising the Siege of Blair; copies of which I inclose with my answers to them. His Majesty will be pleased to observe that by our stay here longer than we intended, the whole March Route will be one Day later.[81]

Agnew's behaviour 'was highly applauded' by a contemporary historian, yet an officer of the garrison wrote, 'It gives me some pain, to observe that your news writers have taken so little notice of the gallant defence made by the garrison at Blair'. Relief had not come too soon, for 'The garrison were so reduced, that they had nothing to live upon but horse flesh for some days before the rebels left the country'. Meanwhile, it was claimed that the Hessian 'hussars were guilty of some irregularities in Atholl'.[82]

Agnew wrote that he felt that he must tell Cumberland what had happened. He emphasised the lack of resources he had had. He hoped that he could be relieved from his present duty. However, he would stay 'to do my duty and behave myself like ane honest man'. He hoped 'if his Royal Highness approves of my conduct I should think myself very happy'.[83] Cumberland was certainly pleased with the exertions of the garrison, writing to Agnew on 7 April: 'I return you my hearty thanks for your defence of the castle of Blair, and I desire you should also acquaint the officers and soldiers, who have done their duty, that I am very much obliged to them for the same, not doubting but that they have all done it'.[84]

The Jacobites had succeeded entirely in the first part of the operation, in neutralising the militia posts and achieving a near complete surprise of the castle, thus preventing any gathering in of substantial supplies within the walls. This opened the possibility of starving the garrison into surrender and given time this would have been successful. However, they then faced several major difficulties. Starvation as a weapon required time. As ever, the Jacobite artillery, few in number and small in calibre, even by their standards, could not make any impact on the castle's walls. Mining seems to have been ruled out. Finally, the proximity of major relief forces of several thousand troops, outnumbering the Jacobite besiegers, meant that it would only be a matter of time before the castle was relieved. Even through Crauford and Frederick were reluctant to make the attempt, they were prodded into a more forceful attitude by Cumberland.

The episode was thus a setback for the Jacobite cause: its being held meant that the Jacobites were unable to threaten the Lowlands and thus endanger or at least delay Cumberland's main thrust from Aberdeen to Inverness. This was the last siege of a castle in Scotland.

The ending of the siege of Fort William and the raising of that of Blair Castle, ended the string of victories enjoyed by the Jacobite army. Troops

81 TNA, SP54/30, ff84r-86v, Cumberland to Newcastle, 6 April 1746.

82 Douglas, *History*, pp.169-170.

83 RA, CP13/145, Agnew to Cumberland, 4 April 1746.

84 Atholl (ed.), *Chronicles*, Vol.III, pp.270-271.

had to be pulled back to Inverness to meet the new offensive of the army led by the Duke of Cumberland and eventually take to the field of Culloden on 16 April. There the Jacobite army fought its last battle and suffered such a defeat that the campaign was effectually over. Ironically, the Jacobite army finally dispersed two days later after having marched to the ruins of Ruthven Barracks.

9

Aftermath

Despite the crushing victory of the British Army at Culloden, there was no reason to be certain that this would be the last of the Jacobite attempts to regain the British thrones. George II believed that fortresses in Scotland were still relevant to his dynasty's security and he had Newcastle relay this message to Cumberland on 12 May:

> His Majesty is every day more and more concerned of the Necessity there is that Fort George, Fort Augustus and Fort William should be enlarged, and that Fort Augustus which is in the centre, should be made capable to receive a Garrison of 2,000 men; and the two others (especially Fort George) more than 1,000 men each, as such a number of troops would effectually prevent any further disturbance in the Highlands. His majesty would have your Royal Highness consider, whether there may be some place, near Inverness, more proper for placing a fort, than where Fort George Stood and particularly, the place where a fort was formerly built, or begun, by Cromwell. [1]

Cumberland was busy and was no expert on fortifications, so, a week later, informed Newcastle thus, 'as His Majesty thinks proper to have the chain repaired, I will wait the arrival of Major Marcel, and then lay before His majesty a project for the whole'.[2]

Major Lewis Marcell drew up plans for a new fort on the site of Cromwell's and Major General William Skinner drew up another in 1747, but this scheme was opposed by Inverness Burgh Council. Skinner was told to find a new site, and this he did, about 10 miles from the town and five from Culloden. It was at Ardersier, the furthest point on the isthmus, and was designed to hold two battalions. William Adams was appointed as contractor in 1747 but he died and his three sons took over, estimating the fort would cost just under £100,000.[3] Fort George was a huge fortress; covering 42 acres and needing 1,000 workmen. It was a bastioned fortress and had a powder magazine which could hold 2,500 barrels. It was built so as to survive a direct hit. It was

1 TNA, SP54/31, 17, Newcastle to Cumberland, 12 May 1746.
2 TNA, SP54/31, 24A, Cumberland to Newcastle, 19 May 1746.
3 Tabraham and Groves, *Fortress Scotland*, pp.93-95.

Gateway to Fort George, 2007.
(Author's Photo)

Barracks at Fort George, 2007.
(Author's Photo)

finally completed in 1767 at double the estimate, after the deaths of George II, Cumberland, and James Stuart.

Dr Samuel Johnson, on seeing Fort George in 1773 was impressed, describing it as 'the most regular fortification in the Island…There was everywhere the appearance of the utmost neatness and regularity'.[4] He and James Boswell visited Fort Augustus and it led them to conclude that it was of lesser military use despite its being rebuilt, 'is much less than that of Fort George and is said to be commanded by the neighbouring hills. It was not long ago taken by the Highlanders. But its situation seems well chosen for pleasure, if not for strength'. They noted that it was supplied by boat from Inverness.[5]

Over the decades, the Jacobite threat receded. There was a brief moment in 1759 when the danger of a French invasion loomed again, but naval victories resulted in this risk being removed. Jacobitism as a political force which potentially could rock governments and dynasties became less and less. James Stuart died in 1766 and his sons were not granted the international status that his father had enjoyed as King *de jure*.

In the nineteenth century, questions were raised about the forts' usefulness. Fort George was retained as a military base for recruiting and training purposes. The others were disposed of. In 1864 Fort William was sold and by the end of the century most of it was destroyed. In 1867 Fort Augustus was sold and in 1876 it became a monastery, with only a little of the original structure remaining.[6]

It is also worth casting a brief gaze about those involved in these sieges. Molloy served as a lieutenant before selling his commission. The Carlisle magistrates were investigated for Jacobitism but were acquitted, as was Edinburgh's Provost; there was no investigation in the behaviour of Stirling's magistracy. Guest was feted by the King. Blakeney had to surrender Minorca in 1756 but was not disgraced; both he and Guest were buried at Westminster Abbey. Scott rose in the ranks but died relatively young in India. As for the Jacobites, Mirabelle surrendered after Culloden and was eventually repatriated to France, Grant escaped to France, Stapleton was killed at Culloden and Perth died en route to France. There was also the price for failure. Towneley was executed at Kensington Green and those surrendering Forts George and Augustus lost their commissions.

Some of these fortresses still exist today and can be visited. Ironically, of the purpose-built forts which saw service in 1745-1746, only one still exists and that is Ruthven Barracks, albeit in a ruined condition. There is an information board about its role in the campaign outside the main entrance. The four castles which took part are all major tourist attractions, none more so than Edinburgh Castle, which dominates the great little city and is rightly high on the agenda of any visitor. Both it and Stirling Castle, another major landmark, are managed by the National Trust for Scotland. Carlisle Castle

4 Ronald Black (ed.), *To the Hebrides, Samuel Johnson's Journey to Western Islands of Scotland and James Boswell's Tour to the Hebrides* (Edinburgh: Birlinn, 2007), p.77.

5 Black (ed.), *To the Hebrides*, p.84.

6 Tabraham and Grove, *Fortress Scotland*, pp.114-116.

includes an exhibition about the '45 and Carlisle's role in it, and is managed by English Heritage. Blair Castle remains the formal seat of the Dukes of Atholl and is also recommended to potential visitors.

The fort which never heard a shot fired in anger is Fort George and is also well worth a visit. It has remained intact because of its military role following 1746 and is the only eighteenth-century fortification remaining whole in Britain. Less well known are the city walls of Edinburgh, examples of which can be seen just off the south end of the Royal Mile and just to the north of the Grassmarket. The gates, though, have long ceased to exist. Much of Stirling's old walls are still visible, too.

10

Conclusion

During 1745-1746, three forts, four castles, three towns or cities and one barracks had been under siege; two of them twice. Of these thirteen sieges, eight had been successful whilst the other five had seen the besieged garrison hold out. Ironically two out of the three Medieval castles had held, along with the more modern Blair Castle, but only one out of the modern forts managed to do likewise. Most of these sieges, with the exception of Stirling Castle, Blair Castle and Fort William were fairly short lived, being over and done within a matter of days, and even these three lasted only a little over two weeks. Other than to a limited extent at Blair Castle, there were no lengthy attempts to starve a garrison into submission. No fortress, castle of city went to the extreme of suffering an assault or subsequent pillage.

Why had these results occurred? Often it was the case that the defences were relatively weak or became so, and thus the morale of the garrisons, in face of a potential assault by overwhelming numbers, surrendered. This was the case at Edinburgh city, Carlisle city and castle, Ruthven (in 1746), Forts George and Augustus, and at Stirling town. In other cases, the strongpoint was far stronger than the offensive capacity of the attackers, such as with Stirling and Edinburgh Castles, Fort William, and Blair Castle. The garrison commanders at these were also men with firm resolve, though in the first and last cases the arrival of relief forces were also crucial.

Could the results have been different? The siege of Edinburgh, had it lasted longer, could have been influential, for any prolonged resistance could have given Cope's army time to arrive in the city and then perhaps have held up the Jacobite army indefinitely, giving them the unpalatable choice of a formal siege, a risky assault, or ignoring the city. The same could perhaps have been said of the first siege of Carlisle. Some of the defenders at Fort George believed that the defence could have been carried on, and the master gunner at Fort Augustus was critical of the lieutenant governor's faulty defence and hasty surrender. In both of the Carlisle sieges, senior officers among the defenders believed that resistance could have been prolonged, though the final result would have been the same but with more men's lives lost.

Finally, the impact of the sieges on the campaign is worthy of consideration. These vary considerably. It seems unlikely that the result of either of the sieges of Ruthven Barracks had much wider impact for it was too small a place to have much significance. Edinburgh's significance was that it forced Cope to give battle and so resulted in the first Jacobite victory of the campaign, the first they had enjoyed since Killiecrankie in 1689, and the greatest that they were ever to achieve. The taking of Edinburgh and then Carlisle allowed the Jacobite army to continue an uninterrupted progress from the Highlands into England. Likewise, the time spent by the Government forces on retaking Carlisle enabled the Jacobite army to make good their retreat into Scotland and to join up with the reinforcements there, making their army the strongest ever. The siege of Stirling Castle led to the Battle of Falkirk, and the taking of Fort George allowed the Jacobite army to make Inverness their headquarters for the remainder of the campaign. The holding of Blair Castle allowed Cumberland's campaign to continue without interruption. The sieges of Forts Augustus and William had less of an obvious strategic impact, though both served to tie down Jacobite forces when they might have been better used elsewhere, and failure at the latter cannot have helped Jacobite morale at a crucial time in the campaign.

However, for all the importance invested in the fortifications as a deterrent against rebellion, they were, at a strategic level, a failure. After 1715 it was envisaged, it must be remembered, that they would deter a future insurrection, or at worst, quash it at the outset. Instead, the Jacobite army was to pose the greatest threat to the state in the eighteenth century and the forts and their garrisons sat on the sidelines. This was because the garrisons in the forts were at their minimum levels; they could only be used defensively and not proactively as had been the plan when the forts were designed. Instead, they played a more modest role, as has been explained.

That said, the sieges occupied the minds and actions of men on both sides of the struggle. They invested time, munitions, and men's lives in the various attempts to hold, take, or retake them throughout the campaign. The sieges were not as bloody as the battles; probably less men died in all the sieges put together than at any one of the three battles. Yet they remind us that siege warfare at this time was important and that with differing results the campaign would have taken a different turn of events, though whether the end outcome would have been different is another question. However, the forts' primary strategic role in preventing or at least containing another insurrection was a failure; the forts were bypassed and the garrisons too small to sally out for any decisive impact. They did, however, make life more difficult for the Jacobites in 1746 than would otherwise have been the case had they not existed.

Bibliography

Manuscripts

British Library
Additional Manuscripts of committee meetings, 33004
Cumbria Archives: Carlisle
Corporation Accounts, Ca2/6
Corporation Accounts, 4/41
Cumbria Archives: Whitehaven
YD/Da8
Edinburgh City Archives
Town Council Minutes, 1744-1745, SL1/1/65
Treasurers' Accounts, 1742-1752
Edinburgh University Library Special Collections
Atholl Papers, Dc 37 (1), 1-2
National Archives
Admiralty, ADM52/739, 8/25
State Papers Domestic SP36/67-70, 76, 78, 80
State Papers Scotland, SP54/15, 17, 25-31
State Papers: Entry Books, SP44/133
State Papers Scotland, Letter Books, SP55/13
War Office: Papers concerning establishment, WO24/246,
War Office: General Courts Martial, WO71/19
War Office: Royal Chelsea Hospital, Disability Out Pensions, Admission Books, Cavalry and Infantry, WO116/4
National Records of Scotland
E96/33
GD1/53, 1440
G26/9
GD122/3, 10
GD124/1, 519
GD126/30
GD248/48
GD406
RH4/213
National Library of Scotland
ADV 23.3.28
MS 3036, 3412, 3733, 3734, 7069, 7073, 16604, 16636, 17154, 17526, 70712
Royal Archives
Cumberland Papers, Main Series Vols. 5, 7-13
Stuart Papers Miscellany, Vol. 11
Stirling Council Archives
Town Council Minutes, 1745-1752, SBC11/15
Memorial of Prince Charles, B66/25/335

Printed Primary Sources

Allardyce, James (ed.), *Historical Papers relating to the Jacobite Period, 1699-1750* (Edinburgh: New Spalding Club, 1895).

Anon., *A True Account of the Defence and Conduct of Alastair Stewart* (London: Unknown Publisher, 1748),

Anon., *Memoirs of the Life and Actions of General Blakeney* (London: Unknown Publisher, 1756).

Anon., *The Miscellany of the Spalding Club* (Aberdeen: Spalding, 1841).

Anon., *Authentic Copies of the Letters and other Papers delivered at their execution by the nine rebels* (London: Unknown Publisher, 1746),

Anon., *Report on Commission of various Collections*, Vol. VIII (London: Historic Manuscripts Commission, 1913).

Atholl, James, Duke of (ed.), *Chronicles of the Atholl and Tullibardine Families* (Edinburgh, Privately Published, 1908).

Bell, Robert (ed.), 'Memorials of John Murray of Broughton, 1740-1747, *Scottish History Society*, 1st series, Vol. 27 (Edinburgh, 1897).

Black, Ronald (ed.), *To the Hebrides, Samuel Johnson's Journey to Western Islands of Scotland and James Boswell's Tour to the Hebrides* (Edinburgh: Birlinn, 2007)

Blaikie, Walter (ed.), 'Origins of the Forty Five', *Scottish History Society*, 2nd series, 2 (Edinburgh, 1916).

Burt, Edward, *Letters from a Gentleman in the north of Scotland to his friend in London* (London: R. Fenner,1818).

Carlyle, Alexander, *Autobiography of the Rev. Alexander Carlyle, Minister of Inverness* (Edinburgh: Unknown Publisher, 1860).

Brown, Iain Gordon and Cheape, Hugh (eds), *Witness to Rebellion* (East Linton: Tuckwell Press, 1995).

Dalton, J.P. (ed.), 'Cumberland and the Forty Five: Some Letters', *Transactions of the Cumberland and Westmorland Antiquarian and Archaeological Society*, 2nd series, Vol. XLV (1946).

Douglas, Francis, *History of the Rebellion* (Aberdeen: F. Douglas and W. Murray, 1755).

Elcho, Lord (ed. Ewan Charteris), *Short Account of the Affairs of Scotland, 1744-1746* (Edinburgh: John Donald, 1907).

Forbes, Robert, *Jacobite Memoirs of the Rebellion of 1745* (Edinburgh: William and Robert Chambers,1834).

Fraser, William, *The Earls of Cromartie: their kindred, country and correspondence* (Edinburgh: Unknown Publisher, 1876)

Hedman, B.A. (ed.), 'Colin MacLaurin's Journal of the Forty Five', *Scottish History Society* 5th series, Miscellany 13 (Edinburgh, 2004).

Henderson, Andrew, *History of the Rebellion* (Edinburgh: R. Griffiths, 1748).

Henderson, Andrew, *The Life of William Augustus, Duke of Cumberland* (London: J. Ridley), 1766).

Home, John, *History of the Rebellion* (London: T. Cadell jun. and W. Davies, 1802).

Jarvis, Rupert (ed.), *Jacobite Risings of 1715 and 1745* (Carlisle: Cumberland County Council, 1954).

Johnstone, James, A *Memoir of the Forty Five* (London: Folio Society, 1958).

Kinsley, James (ed.), *Autobiography of Dr Alexander Carlyle: Anecdotes and Characters of the Times* (Oxford: Oxford University Press, 1973).

Lewis, W.S. (ed.), *Correspondence of Horace Walpole* (New Haven: Yale University Press, 1955).

McCann, T.J. (ed.), *The Correspondence of the Dukes of Newcastle and Richmond, 1724-1750* (Lewes: Sussex Record Society, 1983).

Mackay, Hugh, *Memoirs of the War carried out in Scotland and Ireland, 1689-1691* (Edinburgh: Bannantyne Club, 1833).

Marchant, John, *History of the Present Rebellion* (London: R. Walker, 1746).

Maxwell, James, *Narrative of the Expedition in Scotland of Prince Charles Stuart* (Edinburgh: T. Constable, 1841)

Miller, James, 'Diary of James Miller, 1745-1750', *Journal of the Society of Army History Research*, Vol. III (1924), pp.208-226.

Morris, Christopher (ed.), *The Journeys of Celia Fiennes* (London: Cresset Press,1949).

Mounsey, George Gill, *Carlisle in 1745* (London: Unknown Publisher, 1846)

Nicholas, Donald (ed.), *Intercepted Post* (London: Bodley Head, 1956).

Oates, Jonathan and Navickas, Katharine (eds), *Jacobites and Jacobins: Two Eighteenth Century Perspectives* (Bristol: 4word for the Record Society of Lancashire and Cheshire, 2006).

Paton, Henry (ed.), 'Leaves from the Diary of John Campbell, an Edinburgh Banker in 1745', *Scottish History Society, Miscellany*, 1 (Edinburgh, 1895), pp.537-559.

Paton, Henry (ed.), 'Lyon in Mourning', I, *Scottish History Society*, 1st series (Edinburgh, 1895).
Patten, Robert, *History of the Rebellion* (London: J. Baker and T. Warner, 1745).
Ray, James, *A Compleat History of the Rebellion* (Bristol: S. Farley, 1754).
Rogers, Pat (ed.), Daniel Defoe's *Tour of the Whole Island* (Harmondworth: Penguin,1971).
Saville, A. (ed.), 'Secret Comment: The Diaries of Gertrude Saville, 1722-1757', *Thoroton Society* 42 (1997).
Seton, Bruce (ed.), 'Commentary on the Expedition to Scotland made by Prince Charles Edward Stuart', *Scottish History Society* 3rd series, Vol. IX, Miscellany, Vol. IV (Edinburgh, 1926).
Stewart, Francis (ed.), *Woodhouselee MS: A narrative of events in Edinburgh and district during the Jacobite occupation, September to October 1745* (Edinburgh: W.R. Chambers, 1908).
Tayler, Alastair and Henrietta (eds), *1745 and After* (London: Thomas Nelson and Sons, 1938).
Tayler, Henrietta (ed.), A *Jacobite Miscellany* (Oxford: Roxburghe Club,1948)
Tayler, Henrietta (ed.), 'Marchmont Correspondence', *Scottish History Society*, 3rd series, Miscellany Vol. V (1933).
Wade, George, *A Report of the Proceedings and Opinions of the Board of General Officers, on Their Examination of the Conduct, Proceedings and Behaviour of Lieutenant General Sir John Cope* (Dublin: George Faulkner, 1749).
Yorke, Philip (ed.), *The Life and Correspondence of Philip, Earl of Hardwicke and Lord Chancellor of Great Britain*, I (Cambridge: Cambridge University Press, 1913),

Newspapers

Caledonian Mercury, 1745
The Daily Post, 1745
The General Evening Post, 1745
St. James Evening Post, 1746.

Published Secondary Sources

Arnot, B.S. and Seton, J.G. (eds), 'Prisoners of the '45', *Scottish History Society*, 3rd series, 13, I (Edinburgh, 1928).
Bamford, Andrew, (ed.), *Rebellious Scots to Crush: The Military Response to the Jacobite '45,* (Solihull: Helion, 2020).
Black, Jeremy, *Culloden and the '45* (Stroud: Sutton, 1997),
Duffy, Christopher, *Fight for a Throne: the Jacobite '45 Reconsidered* (Solihull: Helion, 2015).
Duffy, Christopher, *The Fortress on the Age of Vauban and Frederick the Great, 1660-1789* (London: Routledge and Kegan Paul, 1985).
Duffy, Christopher, *The Best of Enemies: Germans against Jacobites, 1746* (London: Bitter Books, 2013).
Mair, Craig, *Stirling: The Royal Burgh* (Edinburgh: John Donald, 1993).
McLynn, Frank, *The Final Campaign: the Jacobite Army in England, 1745* (Edinburgh: J. Donald, 1998).
Riding, Jacqueline, *Jacobites: A New History of the '45 Rebellion* (London: Bloomsbury, 2016).
Speck, W.A., *The Butcher: the Duke of Cumberland and the suppression of the '45* (Oxford: Blackwell, 1981).
Tabraham, Chris, and Grove, Doreen, *Fortress Scotland and the Jacobites* (London: Batsford, 1995).

Journal Articles

Hepburn, D., and Richardson, C., 'Documents relating to the transportation of cannon from Whitehaven to Carlisle during the Jacobite Rising of 1745', *Transactions of the Cumberland and Westmorland Antiquarian and Archaeological Society,* series 2, LXXXIV (1984), pp.141-166.
Kingsford, C.L., 'The Highland Forts in the Forty Five', *English Historical Review*, XXXVII (1922), pp.361-397.
Oates, Jonathan, 'The Last siege on English Soil: Carlisle, 1745', *Transactions of the Cumberland and Westmorland Antiquarian and Archaeological Society,* series 3 (2003), pp.169-184.